Group Policy Administration:
The Personal Trainer

Windows Server 2008 &
Windows Server 2008 R2

William R. Stanek

PUBLISHED BY

Stanek & Associates
PO Box 362
East Olympia, WA 98540-0362

Cover Design: Creative Designs Ltd.
Editorial Development: Andover Publishing Solutions
Technical Review: L & L Technical Content Services

You can provide feedback related to this book by emailing the author at williamstanek@aol.com. Please use the name of the book as the subject line.

Contents at a Glance

Table of Contents

Introduction

Group Policy Administration: The Personal Trainer for Windows Server 2008 & Windows Server 2008 R2 is the authoritative quick reference guide to Group Policy and is designed to be a key resource you turn to whenever you have questions about Group Policy. To this end, the book zeroes in on the key aspects of Group Policy that you'll use the most.

Inside this book's pages, you'll find comprehensive overviews, step-by-step procedures, frequently used tasks, documented examples, and much more. One of the goals is to keep the content so concise that the book remains compact and easy to navigate while at the same time ensuring that the book is packed with as much information as possible—making it a valuable resource.

What's This Book About?

Group Policy Administration: The Personal Trainer for Windows Server 2008 & Windows Server 2008 R2 is designed to be used in the daily administration of Group Policy. In this book, I teach you how features work, why they work the way they do, and how to customize them to meet your needs. I also offer specific examples of how certain features can meet your needs, and how you can use other features to troubleshoot and resolve issues you might have. In addition, this book provides tips, best practices, and examples of how to fine-tune all major aspects of Group Policy.

What Do I Need to Know?

This book covers Group Policy for small, medium, and large organizations. To get practical and useful information into your hands without the clutter of a ton of background material, I had to assume several things. If you are reading this book, I hope that you have basic networking skills and a basic understanding of Windows Server operating systems, and that Windows Server is already installed on your systems. With this in mind, I don't devote entire chapters to understanding Windows Server architecture, installing Windows Server, or Windows networking. I do, however, provide complete details on the components of Group Policy and how you can use these components. I provide detailed guidance to help you quickly and easily perform common tasks, solve problems, and implement features such as filtering Group Policy processing, migrating the SYSVOL, implementing change control, restoring Group Policy objects (GPOs), and troubleshooting GPO replication.

How Is This Book Organized?

Making this book easy to follow and understand was my number one goal! I really want anyone, skill level or work schedule aside, to be able to learn how to effectively manage Group Policy.

To make the book easy to use, I've divided it into 8 chapters. In Chapters 1 and 2, you'll roll up your sleeves and dive right in to the good stuff while also learning how Group Policy works.

Chapter 1 provides an overview of tools, techniques, and concepts related to Group Policy. Chapter 2 examines important changes to Group Policy and how these changes affect the way you use Group Policy. The chapter also provides detailed advice on using both policy preferences and policy settings, including tips on which technology to use when.

Chapters 3, 4, and 5 discuss the core tools and techniques you'll use to manage Group Policy. Chapter 3 explores techniques for configuring both Local Group Policy objects (LGPOs) and Active Directory–based Group Policy objects (GPOs). Not only will you learn about essential implementation considerations, you'll also find tips and techniques for working across domains, sites, and -forests. Chapter 4 examines the change control features available when you implement Advanced Group Policy Management (AGPM). You'll learn how to manage workflow within the change control system and how to configure AGPM itself. In Chapter 5, you'll learn how to search and filter Group Policy. You can use the techniques discussed not only to find policy settings and search GPOs but also to control the security groups and computers to which policy is applied.

GPOs have two parts: a Group Policy container (GPC) stored in Active Directory, and a Group Policy template (GPT) stored in the SYSVOL. Chapter 6 shows you how to migrate the SYSVOL to Distributed File System (DFS) Replication and how to maintain SYSVOL storage. You'll also find tips and techniques for troubleshooting replication. Chapter 7 discusses essential Group Policy concepts and provides tips and techniques for managing the way Group Policy works. Chapter 8 examines how to maintain, restore, and troubleshoot Group Policy.

What Conventions Are Used in This Book?

I've used a variety of elements to help keep the text clear and easy to follow. You'll find code terms and listings in monospace type, except when I tell you to actually enter a command. In that case, the command appears in bold type. When I introduce and define a new term, I put it in italics.

This book also has notes, tips and other sidebar elements that provide additional details on points that need emphasis.

Other Resources

Although some books are offered as all-in-one guides, there's simply no way one book can do it all. This book is intended to be used as a concise and easy-to-use resource. It covers everything you need to perform core tasks for Active Directory, but it is by no means exhaustive.

As you encounter new topics, take the time to practice what you've learned and read about. Seek additional information as necessary to get the practical experience and knowledge that you need.

I truly hope you find that *Group Policy Administration: The Personal Trainer for Windows Server 2008 & Windows Server 2008 R2* helps you manage Group Policy successfully and effectively.

Thank you,

William R. Stanek

(williamstanek@aol.com)

Chapter 1. Introducing Group Policy

Whether you are a skilled administrator who has worked with Windows networks for years or a novice with a basic understanding, your long-term success in the ever-changing technology landscape increasingly depends on how well you understand Group Policy. *Group Policy* is a collection of preferences and settings that can be applied to user and computer configurations. It simplifies administration of common and repetitive tasks as well as unique tasks that are difficult to implement manually but can be automated (such as deploying new software or controlling which programs can be installed). Group Policy allows you to apply desired configuration preferences and settings in discrete sets. This means that you can configure user desktops to meet the specific preferences and requirements of your organization and control the configuration of every computer on your network.

Group Policy Preferences and Settings

One way to think of Group Policy is as a set of rules that you can apply throughout the enterprise. Although you can use Group Policy to manage Windows desktops and Windows servers, Group Policy has changed since it was first implemented. For Windows Vista with Service Pack 1 or later and Windows Server 2008 or later, Group Policy includes both managed settings, referred to as *policy settings*, and unmanaged settings, referred to as *policy preferences*.

Group Policy settings enable you to control the configuration of the operating system and its components. You can also use policy settings to configure computer and user scripts, folder redirection, computer security, software installation, and more.

Group Policy preferences enable you to configure, deploy, and manage operating system and application settings that you were not able to manage using earlier implementations of Group Policy, including data sources, mapped drives, environment variables, network shares, folder options, shortcuts, and more. In many cases, you'll find that using Group Policy preferences is a better approach than configuring these settings in Windows images or using logon scripts.

The key difference between preferences and policy settings is enforcement. Group Policy strictly enforces policy settings. You use policy settings to control the configuration of the operating system and its components. You also use policy settings to disable the user interface for settings that Group Policy is managing, which prevents users from changing those settings. Most policy settings are stored in policy-related branches of the registry. The operating system and compliant applications check the policy-related branches of the registry to determine whether and how various aspects of the operating system are controlled. Group Policy refreshes policy settings at a regular interval, which is every 90 to 120 minutes by default.

> **Note** When discussing whether applications support Group Policy, the terms *compliant application* and *Group Policy–aware application* are often used. A compliant or Group Policy–aware application is an application specifically written to support Group Policy. Whether an application is Group Policy–aware is extremely important. Group Policy–aware applications are programmed to check the policy-related branches of the registry to determine whether and how their features and various aspects of the operating system are controlled. Noncompliant, unaware applications are not programmed to perform these checks.

In contrast, Group Policy does not strictly enforce policy preferences. Group Policy does not store preferences in the policy-related branches of the registry. Instead, it writes preferences to the same locations in the registry that an application or operating system feature uses to store the setting. This allows Group Policy preferences to support applications and operating system features that aren't Group Policy–aware and also does not disable application or operating system features in the user interface to prevent their use. Because of this behavior, users can change settings that were configured using policy preferences. Finally, although Group Policy by default refreshes preferences using the same interval as Group Policy settings, you can prevent Group Policy from refreshing individual preferences by choosing to apply them only once.

When working with policy settings, keep the following in mind:

- Most policy settings are stored in policy-based areas of the registry.
- Settings are enforced.
- User interface options may be disabled.
- Settings are refreshed automatically.
- Settings require Group Policy–aware applications.
- Original settings are not changed.
- Removing the policy setting restores the original settings.

When working with policy preferences, keep the following in mind:

- Preferences are stored in the same registry locations as those used by the operating system and applications.
- Preferences are not enforced.
- User interface options are not disabled.
- Settings can be refreshed automatically or applied once.
- Supports non-Group Policy–aware applications.
- Original settings are overwritten.
- Removing the preference item does not restore the original setting.

> ***Real World***   The way you use policy settings or policy preferences depends on whether you want to enforce the item. To configure an item without enforcing it, use policy preferences and then disable automatic refresh. To configure an item and enforce the specified configuration, use policy settings or configure preferences and then enable automatic refresh.

Understanding Group Policy Objects

Group Policy is so important to a successful Active Directory implementation that most administrators think of it as a component of Active Directory. This is mostly true—and it is okay to think of it this way—but you don't necessarily need Active Directory to use Group Policy. You can use Group Policy in both enterprise (domain) and local (workgroup) environments.

Global Group Policy

For enterprise environments in which Active Directory is deployed, the complete set of policy settings and policy preferences is available. This policy set is referred to as *domain-based Group Policy*, *Active Directory–based Group Policy*, or simply *Group Policy*. On domain controllers, Group Policy is stored in the SYSVOL that Active Directory uses for replicating policies.

Group Policy is represented logically as an object called a Group Policy object (GPO). A GPO is simply a collection of policy settings and preferences. As discussed in detail in the section "Maintaining GPO Storage" in Chapter 8 "Maintaining and Restoring Group Policy," every GPO has a related Group Policy Container (GPC) and a related Group Policy Template (GPT).

The Group Policy Container for a GPO is stored in the Active Directory database and replicated through normal Active Directory replication. The GPC is used to store properties related to the GPO and is identified with a globally unique identifier (GUID).

The Group Policy Template (GPT) for a GPO is stored in the SYSVOL and replicated through SYSVOL replication. The GPT is used to store files related to the GPO on disk and is identified with the same GUID as the Group Policy Container.

Linking a GPO to components of the Active Directory structure is how you apply Group Policy. In your Active Directory structure, GPOs can be linked to:

- **Sites** A *site* is a combination of one or more IP subnets connected by highly reliable links. You use sites to create a directory structure that mirrors the physical structure of your organization. A site typically has the same boundaries as your local area networks (LANs). Because site mappings are separate and independent from logical components in the directory, there's no necessary relationship between your network's physical structures and the logical structures in the directory.

- **Domains** A *domain* is a logical grouping of objects that share a common directory database. In the directory, a domain is represented as a container object. Within a domain, you can create accounts for users, groups, and computers as well as for shared resources such as printers and folders. Access to domain objects is controlled by security permissions.

- **Organizational units** An *organizational unit (OU)* is a logical container used to organize objects within a domain. Because an OU is the smallest scope to which you can delegate authority, you can use an OU to help manage administration of accounts for users, groups, and computers and for administration of other resources, such as printers and shared folders. By adding an OU to another OU, you can create a hierarchy within a domain. Because each domain has its own OU hierarchy, the OU hierarchy of a domain is independent from that of other domains.

You can create multiple GPOs, and by linking them to different locations in your Active Directory structure, you can apply the related settings to the users and computers in those Active Directory containers.

Because of the object-based hierarchy in Active Directory, the settings of top-level GPOs are applied to lower-level GPOs automatically by default. For example, a setting for the imaginedlands.com domain is applied to the Sales OU within that domain, and the domain settings will be applied to users and computers in the Sales OU. If you don't want policy settings to be applied, you may be able to override or block settings to ensure that only the GPO settings for the low-level GPOs are applied.

> **Note**   With domain-based Group Policy, you might think that the forest or domain functional level would affect how Group Policy is used, but this is not the case. The forest and domain do not need to be in any particular functional mode to use Group Policy.

When you create a domain, two Active Directory GPOs are created automatically:

- **Default Domain Controllers Policy GPO**   A default GPO created for and linked to the Domain Controllers OU that is applicable to all domain controllers in a domain as long as they are members of this OU.
- **Default Domain Policy GPO**   A default GPO that is created for and linked to the domain within Active Directory.

You can create additional GPOs as necessary and link them to the sites, domains, and OUs you created. For example, you could create a GPO called Sales Policy and then link it to the Sales OU. The policy then applies to that OU.

Local Group Policy

For local environments, you can use a subset of Group Policy called *local Group Policy*. As the name implies, local Group Policy allows you to manage policy settings that affect everyone who logs on to the local machine. This means local Group Policy applies to any user or administrator who logs on to a computer that is a member of a workgroup, as well as to any user or administrator who logs on locally to a computer that is a member of a domain. Local Group Policy is stored locally on individual computers in the %SystemRoot%\System32\GroupPolicy folder.

Like Active Directory–based Group Policy, local Group Policy is managed through a GPO. This GPO is referred to as the Local Group Policy object (LGPO). On Windows Vista and later, which support multiple LGPOs, additional user-specific and group-specific LGPOs are stored in the %SystemRoot%\System32\GroupPolicyUsers folder.

Because local Group Policy is a subset of Group Policy, there are many things you can't do locally that you can do in a domain setting. First, you can't manage any policy preferences. Second, you can only manage a limited subset of policy settings. Generally speaking, the policy settings that you can't manage locally have to do with features that require Active Directory, such as software installation.

Beyond these fundamental differences between local Group Policy and Active Directory–based Group Policy, both types of policy are managed in much the same way. In fact, you use the same tools to manage both. The key difference is in the GPO you use. On a local machine, you work exclusively with the LGPOs. If you have deployed Active Directory, however, you can work with domain, site, and OU GPOs in addition to LGPOs.

All computers running Windows have LGPOs. The LGPOs are always processed. However, they have the least precedence, which means their settings can be superseded by site, domain, and OU settings. Although domain controllers have LGPOs, Group Policy for domain controllers is managed best through the Default Domain Controllers GPO.

> **Tip**   Keep in mind that Group Policy is set within the directory itself. Settings are applied in this basic order: local, site, domain, and then OU. In the default configuration (where enforcement and blocking are not used), the last setting applied is the one in effect.

Managing Group Policy

Now that you know how GPOs are used, let's look at how you manage Group Policy. I discuss basic tools and techniques in this section as well as how to install additional tools you might need. You'll find in-depth discussions for working with Group Policy throughout the rest of the book.

Working with Group Policy

When you install Active Directory to configure your infrastructure, Active Directory creates default user accounts and groups to help you manage the directory and configure security. The default users and groups available include:

- **Administrator** A default user account with domainwide access and privileges. By default, the Administrator account for a domain is a member of these groups: Administrators, Domain Admins, Domain Users, Enterprise Admins, Group Policy Creator Owners, and Schema Admins.
- **Administrators** A local group that provides full administrative access to an individual computer or a single domain, depending on its location. Because this group has complete access, you should be very careful about adding users to it. To make someone an administrator for a local computer or domain, all you need to do is make that person a member of this group. Only members of the Administrators group can modify this account. Default members of this group include Administrator, Domain Admins, and Enterprise Admins.
- **Domain Admins** A global group designed to help you administer all the computers in a domain. Members of this group have administrative control over all computers in a domain because they are members of the Administrators group by default. To make someone an administrator for a domain, make that person a member of this group.
- **Enterprise Admins** A global or universal group designed to help you administer all the computers in a domain tree or forest. Members of this group have administrative control over all computers in the enterprise because the group is a member of the Administrators group by default. To make someone an administrator for the enterprise, make that person a member of this group.
- **Group Policy Creator Owners** A global group designed to help you administer group policies. Members of this group have administrative control over Group Policy.

- **Schema Admins** A global group designed to help you administer Active Directory schema. Members of this group have administrative control over schema.

Whenever you work with Group Policy, be sure that you are using a user account that is a member of the appropriate group or groups.

Group Policy Administration Tools

You can manage Group Policy by using both graphical administration tools and command-line tools. The graphical tools are the easiest to work with, but if you master the command-line tools, you will often be able to accomplish tasks more quickly. When you use the command-line tools with the Task Scheduler, you might even be able to automate routine tasks.

> **Note** Appendix A, "Installing Group Policy Extensions and Tools," provides detailed instructions on installing additions and extensions for Group Policy. The appendix discusses:
>
> 1. Installing the Remote Server Administration Tools.
>
> 2. Installing Group Policy client-side extensions.
>
> 3. Installing the client and server components for Advanced Group Policy Management (AGPM).

Graphical Administration Tools

The graphical administration tools for working with Group Policy are provided as custom consoles as well as individual snap-ins for the Microsoft Management Console (MMC). You can access these tools directly on the Administrative Tools menu or add them to any updatable MMC. If you're using another computer with access to a Windows Server 2008 domain, the tools won't be available until you install them. One technique for installing these tools is to use the Add Feature Wizard.

You manage Active Directory–based Group Policy by using the Group Policy Management Console (GPMC), shown in Figure 1-1. You can add the GPMC to any installation of Windows Server 2008 by using the Add Features Wizard.

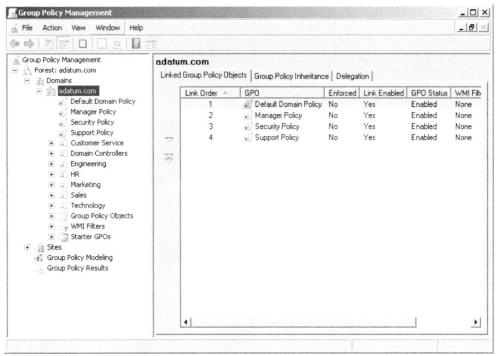

FIGURE 1-1 Group Policy Management Console.

Windows Server 2008 includes an updated version of the Group Policy Management Console (GPMC). In this updated version, the Group Policy preferences are built in. Additionally, you can configure preferences by installing the Remote Server Administration Tools (RSAT) on a computer running Windows Vista SP1 or later. For Windows Vista SP1 or later, the version of GPMC included with RSAT is the updated version of GPMC. After you add the GPMC to a computer running Windows Vista, it is available on the Administrative Tools menu.

You use GPMC to perform these tasks:

- Create, edit, and delete GPOs
- Copy, import, and export GPOs
- Back up and restore GPOs

- Model GPOs prior to deployment to determine how their settings would affect users and computers
- Model existing GPOs to determine how their settings are affecting users and computers

When you want to edit a GPO in the GPMC, the GPMC opens the Group Policy Management Editor, shown in Figure 1-2. You use the editor to manage policy settings and preferences.

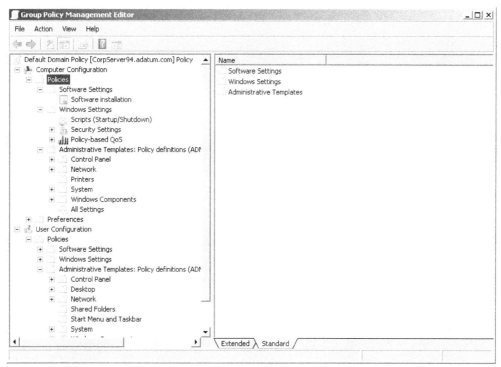

FIGURE 1-2 Group Policy Management Editor.

Also available are the Group Policy Starter GPO Editor and the Local Group Policy Editor. You use the Group Policy Starter GPO Editor to create and manage Starter Group Policy objects, which are meant to provide a starting point for new policy objects that you want to use throughout your organization. When you create a policy object, you can specify a starter GPO as the source or basis of the new object. You use the Local Group Policy Editor, shown in Figure 1-3, to create and manage policy objects for the local computer—as opposed to settings for an entire site, domain, or organizational unit.

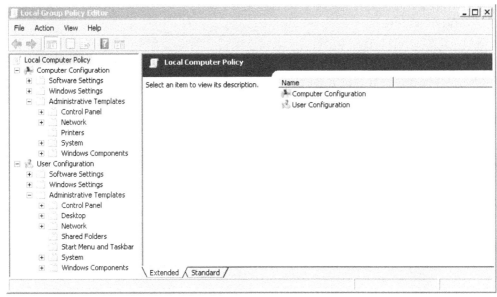

FIGURE 1-3 Local Group Policy Editor.

Command-Line Tools

GPMC provides a comprehensive set of Component Object Model (COM) interfaces that you can use to script many of the operations supported by the console. Samples scripts are available at the Microsoft Download Center Web site (*http://www.microsoft.com/downloads*). For the most recent version of the scripts, search the download site for "Group Policy Management Console Sample Scripts." Other command-line tools for working with Group Policy include:

- **ADPREP** Used to prepare a forest or domain for installation of domain controllers. To prepare a domain prior to installing Windows Server 2008 for the first time, you run *adprep /domainprep /gpprep* on the server that holds the infrastructure operations master role.
- **GPFIXUP** Used to resolve domain name dependencies in Group Policy objects and Group Policy links after a domain rename operation.

- **GPRESULT**   Used to see what policy is in effect and to troubleshoot policy problems.
- **GPUPDATE**   Used to refresh Group Policy manually. If you enter **gpupdate** at a command prompt, both the Computer Configuration settings and the User Configuration settings in Group Policy are refreshed on the local computer.
- **LDIFDE**   Used to import and export directory information. You'll use this tool to help you perform advanced backup and recovery of policy settings that are stored outside GPOs. Specifically, you can use this tool to back up and restore a large number of Windows Management Instrumentation (WMI) filters at one time (as discussed on the Group Policy team blog at *http://go.microsoft.com/fwlink/?linkid=109519*).
- **NETSH IPSEC**   Used to view and manage a computer IP Security (IPSec) configuration. Use *netsh ipsec static show all* to display the static settings and policies for IPSec. Use *netsh ipsec dynamic show all* to display dynamic settings and policies for IPSec.

> *Real World*   I include NETSH IPSEC in the list of important Group Policy tools because Group Policy backups created in the GPMC do not contain IPSec settings. These settings are backed up with system state backups. Because of this, you may want to track any IPSec settings and policies used, and NETSH IPSEC allows you to do this.

The Group Policy management tools provide access to Group Policy objects. While I'll discuss techniques for working with these tools in detail in Chapter 2, "Deploying Group Policy," there are several quick and easy ways to work with GPOs directly. At an elevated, administrator command line, you can open the computer's LGPO for editing in the Local Group Policy Editor by entering **gpedit**. To open another computer's LGPO, use the following syntax:

```
gpedit.msc /gpcomputer:"ComputerName"
```

where *ComputerName* is the host name or fully qualified domain name of the computer. The remote computer name must be enclosed in double quotation marks such as:

```
gpedit.msc /gpcomputer:"CorpServer82"
```

or

```
gpedit.msc /gpcomputer:"CorpServer82.imaginedlands.com"
```

At an elevated, administrator command line, you can open a GPO for editing in the Group Policy Management Editor. The basic syntax is:

```
gpedit.msc /gpobject:"LDAP://CN=GPOID,
CN=Policies,CN=System,DC=DomainName,DC=com"
```

where *GPOID* is the unique identifier for the GPO as listed on the Details tab when a GPO is selected in the Group Policy Management Console, and *Domain Name* is the single part name of the domain in which you created the GPO. The entire object path must be enclosed in double quotation marks, such as:

```
gpedit.msc /gpobject:"LDAP://CN={6AC1786C-145d-21E3-956D-
00C04FB123D4},CN=Policies,CN=System,DC=imaginedlands,DC=com"
```

In this example, the GPO being opened for editing is the GPO with the unique identifier {6AC1786C-145d-21E3-956D-00C04FB123D4} in the imaginedlands.com domain.

You can use an editor command that targets a specific GPO to quickly open a GPO that you commonly view or modify. If you save the command in a Shortcut on the desktop or the Start menu, you'll have a fast and easy way to access the GPO. In a Command Prompt window, you can copy an editor command you've entered by right-clicking within the Command Prompt window, and then clicking Mark. If you drag the mouse pointer over the command and then press Enter, you'll copy the command to the Windows clipboard. You can then create a desktop shortcut by right-clicking an open area of the desktop, pointing to New and then clicking Shortcut.

When the Create Shortcut wizard starts, press Ctrl+V to paste the copied command into the Type The Location Of The Item box, and then click Next. When prompted, enter a Name for the shortcut, such as Enhanced Security

GPO, and then click Finish. Now, when you double-click the shortcut, you'll start the Group Policy Management Editor with your target GPO opened for viewing and editing.

Chapter 2. Deploying Group Policy

Group Policy provides a convenient and effective way to manage both preferences and settings for computers and users. With Group Policy, you can manage preferences and settings for thousands of users or computers in the same way that you manage preferences and settings for one computer or user—and without ever leaving your desk. To do this, you use one of several management tools to change a preference or setting to the value you want, and this change is applied throughout the network to the subset of computers and users you target.

Previously, making many of the administrative changes that Group Policy enables was possible only by hacking the Windows registry, and each change had to be made individually on each target computer. With Group Policy, you can simply enable or disable a policy to tweak a registry value or other preference or setting, and the change will apply automatically the next time Group Policy is refreshed. Because changes can be modeled through the Group Policy Management Console before the modifications are applied, you can be certain of the effect of each desired change. Prior to deploying a change, you can save the state of Group Policy. If something goes wrong, you can restore Group Policy to its original state. When you restore the state of Group Policy, you can be certain that all changes are undone the next time Group Policy is refreshed.

Before you deploy Group Policy for the first time or make changes to existing policy, you should ensure you have a thorough understanding of:

- How Group Policy has changed with the introduction of each new version of the Windows operating system.
- How you can update Group Policy to include the preferences and settings available in a new Windows operating system.
- How Group Policy is applied to a local computer as well as throughout an Active Directory environment.
- How default policy sets are used and when default policy applies.

- When to use policy preferences and when to use policy settings.

I discuss each of these subjects in this chapter.

Keeping Group Policy Up to Date

Group Policy applies only to Windows desktops and Windows servers. Each new version of the Windows operating system has brought with it changes to the way Group Policy works, and I'll explore important changes in this section.

Core Process Changes

Unlike earlier releases of Windows and Windows Server, Windows Vista, Windows Server 2008 and later use the Group Policy Client service to isolate Group Policy notification and processing from the Windows logon process. Separating Group Policy from the Windows logon process reduces the resources used for background processing of policy while increasing overall performance and allowing delivery and application of new Group Policy files as part of the update process without requiring a restart.

Windows Vista, Windows Server 2008 and later don't use the trace logging functionality in Userenv.dll and don't write to the Application log. Instead, they write Group Policy event messages to the System log. Additionally, the Group Policy operational log replaces Group Policy trace logging events that previously were logged to %SystemRoot%\Debug\Usermode\Userenv.log. Thus, when you are troubleshooting Group Policy issues, you'll use the detailed event messages in the operational log rather than the Userenv log. In Event Viewer, you can access the operational log under Applications And Services Logs\Microsoft\Windows\GroupPolicy.

Unlike earlier releases of Windows and Windows Server, Windows Vista, Windows Server 2008 and later use Network Location Awareness instead of ICMP protocol (ping). With Network Location Awareness, a computer is aware of the type of network to which it is currently connected and can also be responsive to changes in the system status or network configuration. By using Network Location Awareness, the Group Policy client can determine the computer state, the network state, and the available network bandwidth. This change also allows Group Policy to be refreshed over Virtual Private Network (VPN) connections.

Policy Changes

Each new version of the Windows operating system introduces policy changes. Sometimes these changes have made older policies obsolete on newer versions of Windows. In this case the policy works only on specific versions of the Windows operating system, such as only on Windows 7 and Windows Server 2008 R2. Generally speaking, however, most policies are forward compatible. This means that policies introduced in Windows 7 and Windows Server 2008 R2 can, in most cases, be used on Windows 8, Windows 8.1, Windows Server 2012 and later. It also means that Windows 7 and Windows Server 2008 R2 policies usually aren't applicable to Windows Vista, Windows Server 2008 or earlier releases of Windows and Windows Server.

If a policy isn't applicable to a particular version of the Windows operating system, you can't apply it to computers running those versions of the Windows operating system. You will know if a policy is supported on a particular version of Windows because this is stated explicitly whenever you are working with a preference or setting.

Like Group Policy, the Group Policy Management Console (GPMC) has changed with new versions of Windows. When you install the Remote Server Administration Tools (as discussed in Chapter 1, "Overview of Group Policy") and select GPMC as a tool you want to use, you install the version of GPMC for the operating system you are using. For example, GPMC version 2.0 is the version included with the original release of Windows Vista and Windows Server 2008.

When you start using GPMC 2.0 or later in your domain environment, you should stop using previous versions of GPMC because GPMC 2.0 and later have been updated to work with new features and file formats that can only be managed using GPMC 2.0 or later. Because of this, you can only manage Windows Vista, Windows 7, Windows Server 2008, Windows Server 2008 R2 and later policies from computers running these current versions of Windows and Windows Server.

On a computer running Windows Vista, Windows Server 2008, or later versions, you'll automatically see the new features and policies as well as standard features and policies when you use GPMC 2.0 or later to work with Group Policy. However, the new features and policies aren't automatically added to Group Policy objects (GPOs). Don't worry—there's an easy way to fix this, and afterward you'll be able to work with new features and policies as appropriate throughout your enterprise.

To push new features and policies into your Active Directory domains, you need to update the appropriate GPOs. Once you make the update, compatible clients are able to take advantage of the enhanced policy set, and incompatible clients simply ignore the settings they don't support.

You update a GPO for new features and policies by following these steps:

1. Log on to a computer running Windows Vista or a later release of Windows using an account with domain administrator privileges.
2. Open the Group Policy Management Console (GPMC) by clicking Start, pointing to Administrator Tools, and then selecting Group Policy Management.
3. In the GPMC, you'll see a Forest node representing the current forest to which you are connected (see Figure 2-1). When you expand the Forest node, you'll then see the Domains and Sites nodes. Use these nodes to work your way to the Group Policy object (GPO) you want to work with.

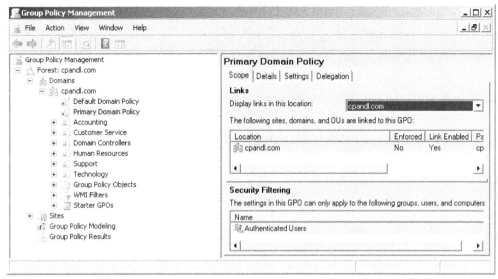

FIGURE 2-1 Group Policy Management Console connects to the local forest by default.

4. When you find the GPO you want to work with, right-click it and then select edit to open the Group Policy Management Editor, as shown in Figure 2-2.

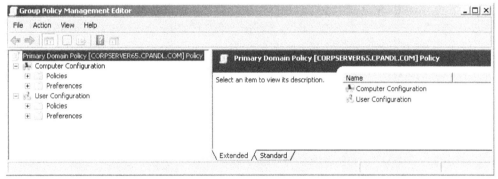

FIGURE 2-2 Editing a GPO in Group Policy Management Editor.

5. In the Group Policy Management Editor, click the Computer Configuration node and then click the User Configuration node. When you select these nodes, the current administrative templates are read in and applied to the GPO you've selected. After Group Policy is refreshed, you can modify policy settings as necessary, and the

changes will be updated as appropriate in the selected site, domain, or organizational unit.

6. Repeat this procedure to update the GPOs for other sites, domains, or organizational units.

Normally, nothing else about how Group Policy is used would change when you make this update. However, computers running Windows Vista, Windows Server 2008 and later support a new file format called ADMX. ADMX uses XML to format policies and changes the way data is stored in the SYSVOL.

SYSVOL Changes

With the original file format used with policies, called ADM, policy definition files are stored in the GPO to which they relate. As a result, each GPO stores copies of all applicable policy definition files and can grow to be multiple megabytes in size. In contrast, with the ADMX format, policy definition files are not stored with the GPOs with which they are associated by default. Instead, the policy definition files can be stored centrally on a domain controller and only the applicable settings are stored within each GPO. As a result, GPOs that use ADMX are substantially smaller than their counterparts that use ADM. For example, while a GPO that uses ADM may be 4 megabytes (MB) in size, a GPO that uses ADMX may be only 4 kilobytes (KB) in size.

The ADMX file format is entirely different from the ADM format previously used. ADMX files are divided into language-neutral files ending with the .admx file extension and language-specific files ending with the .adml extension. The language-neutral files ensure that a GPO has identical core policies. The language-specific files allow policies to be viewed and edited in multiple languages. Because the language-neutral files store the core settings, policies can be edited in any language for which a computer is configured, thus allowing one user to view and edit policies in English and another to view and edit policies in Spanish, for example. The mechanism that determines the language used is the language pack installed on the computer.

Language-neutral ADMX files are installed on computers running Windows Vista, Windows Server 2008 or later in the %SystemRoot%\PolicyDefinitions folder. Language-specific ADMX files are installed on computers running Windows Vista, Windows Server 2008 or later in the %SystemRoot%\PolicyDefinitions*LanguageCulture* folder. Each subfolder is named after the appropriate International Standards Organization (ISO) language/culture name, such as en-US for U.S. English.

Only policy editors that are compatible with the ADMX file format can read the policies that have been updated to use ADMX. When you start a compatible policy editor, it automatically reads in the ADMX files from the policy definitions folders. Because of this, you can copy ADMX files that you want to use to the appropriate policy definitions folder to make them available when you are editing GPOs. If the policy editor is running when you copy the file or files, you must restart the policy editor to force it to read in the file or files.

In domains, ADMX files can be stored in a central store rather than in the Policy-Definitions folder on each computer you use for GPO editing. Using a central store makes management of ADMX files easier and more efficient by allowing administrators to manage GPOs from any compliant computer on the network, simplifying version management of policy files and making it easier to add new policy files.

To create a central store for ADMX files, you must access a domain controller using an account that is a member of the Domain Admins group and then create a folder called PolicyDefinitions within the SYSVOL. This folder is where you'll place the language-neutral ADMX files. You'll also need to create subfolders within the PolicyDefinitions folder for each language that is supported in your ADMX files. These subfolders will store the language-specific resource files, which have the extension .adml. After you create the required folders, you need to copy the language-neutral ADMX definition files and the language-specific ADMX resource files to the appropriate folders in the central store.

Because the default location for the SYSVOL is %SystemRoot%\Sysvol, you would do the following to create and establish the central store in the default SYSVOL location:

1. Access a domain controller running Windows Server 2008 or later in the target domain using an account that is a member of Domain Admins, and then create a PolicyDefinitions folder under %SystemRoot%\Sysvol*DomainName*\Policies, where *DomainName* is the name of the domain in which the domain controller is located and for which you want to establish a central store. Within the PolicyDefinitions folder, create subfolders for each language that is supported in your ADMX files.

> ***Real World***   As discussed in "Replication Changes" later in the chapter, domain controllers can replicate the SYSVOL using either File Replication Service (FRS) replication or Distributed File System (DFS) replication. The default SYSVOL location is %SystemRoot%\Sysvol when domain controllers replicate the SYSVOL using FRS replication. When domain controllers replicate the SYSVOL using DFS replication, the default SYSVOL location is %SystemRoot%\Sysvol_dfsr. If your domain controllers use DFS replication, you create the PolicyDefinitions folder under %SystemRoot%\Sysvol_dfsr*DomainName*\Policies and copy files to this location.

2. Copy all the ADMX and ADML files from their original location on a target computer to the appropriate SYSVOL folders. Windows and Windows Server have many default ADMX files. Each ADMX file has an associated ADML file located under one or more language-specific folders, such as en-US for U.S. English. These files are stored by default under %SystemRoot%\PolicyDefinitions and %SystemRoot%\PolicyDefinitions\LanguageCulture, respectively. If you've created custom ADMX files, these files are stored on the workstation on which they were created. Some additional ADMX files may be available only on computers with the current Windows or Windows Server operating system and service pack installed.

If you want to create a central store for all languages supported by the computer on which you are currently logged on, you could copy all the required policy files from your computer to a target domain controller in a single step. Simply run the following commands at an elevated, administrator command prompt:

```
xcopy /s /y %SystemRoot%\PolicyDefinitions
\\DC\Sysvol\DomainName\policies\PolicyDefinitions\
```

where *DC* is the host name of the target domain controller, and *DomainName* is the fully qualified DNS name of the domain in which the domain controller is located. In the following example, you copy the ADMX and ADML files from your computer to CorpServer56 in the Imaginedlands.com domain:

```
xcopy /s /y %SystemRoot%\PolicyDefinitions
\\CorpServer56\Sysvol\imaginedlands.com\
policies\PolicyDefinitions\
```

Two helpful environment variables when you are working with policy files are %UserDNSDomain% and %LogonServer%. %UserDNSDomain% represents the current log on domain, and %LogonServer% represents the domain controller that authenticated you during logon. Therefore, you could also copy all required policy files by entering the following command at an elevated, administrator command prompt:

```
xcopy /s /y %SystemRoot%\PolicyDefinitions \\%LogonServer%\Sysvol\
%UserDNSDomain%\policies\PolicyDefinitions\
```

As a recommended best practice, you should create the central store on the domain controller that holds the PDC (primary domain controller) Emulator role in the target domain. Why? By default, the PDC emulator is the domain controller that Group Policy relies on when you access GPOs for editing. Therefore, when you create the central store on the PDC emulator, you ensure that anyone who edits Group Policy objects sees the central store immediately rather than having to wait for SYSVOL replication. As part of normal SYSVOL replication, the PDC emulator will then replicate the central store to other domain controllers in the domain.

You can determine which domain controller in your logon domain has the PDC Emulator role by entering the following command at a command prompt:

```
dsquery server -o rdn -hasfsmo pdc
```

The resulting output is the host name of the PDC emulator in your logon domain. If you want the name for the PDC emulator in another domain, you must use the *–Domain* parameter. Consider the following example:

```
dsquery server -o rdn -hasfsmo pdc -domain tech.imaginedlands.com
```

Here you obtain the host name for the PDC emulator in the tech.imaginedlands.com domain. If there are multiple domains in the forest, you might also want a list of all the domain controllers that have the PDC emulator role on a per-domain basis. To do this, use the *-Forest* parameter, such as:

```
dsquery server -hasfsmo pdc -forest
```

For more information on why Group Policy relies on the PDC emulator by default, see "Connecting to and Working with GPOs" later in this chapter.

Replication Changes

A key change between earlier implementations of Active Directory and implementations for Windows Server 2008 and later has to do with how policies and related data are replicated. The Active Directory system volume (SYSVOL) contains domain policy; scripts used for log on, log off, shutdown, and startup; other related files; and files stored within Active Directory. While I'll provide an in-depth discussion of the SYSVOL in Chapter 7, "Managing and Maintaining the SYSVOL," let's take a quick look at the way SYSVOL replication works.

The way domain controllers replicate the SYSVOL depends on the domain functional level. When a domain is running at Windows Server 2003 functional level, domain controllers replicate the SYSVOL using File

Replication Service (FRS). When a domain is running at Windows Server 2008 functional level, domain controllers replicate the SYSVOL using Distributed File System (DFS).

FRS and DFS are replication services that use the Active Directory replication topology to replicate files and folders in the SYSVOL shared folders on domain controllers. The way this works is that the replication service checks with the Knowledge Consistency Checker (KCC) running on each domain controller to determine the replication topology that has been generated for Active Directory replication. Then the replication service uses this replication topology to replicate SYSVOL files to other domain controllers in the domain.

The storage techniques and replication architectures for DFS and FRS are decidedly different. File Replication Service (Ntfrs.exe) stores FRS topology and schedule information in Active Directory and periodically polls Active Directory to retrieve updated information using Lightweight Directory Access Protocol (LDAP). Internally, FRS makes direct calls to the file system using standard input and output. When communicating with remote servers, FRS uses the remote procedure call (RPC) protocol.

FRS stores configuration data in the registry and also stores various types of data in the NTFS file system. For example, FRS stores transactions in the FRS Jet database (Ntfrs.jdb), events and error messages in the FRS Event log (NtFrs.evt), and debug logs in the debug log folder (%SystemRoot%\Debug). The contents of the Replica tree determines what FRS replicates. The Replica tree for Active Directory is the SYSVOL. The SYSVOL contains domain, staging, and SYSVOL folders.

NTFS uses the update sequence number (USN) journal to track information about added, deleted, and modified files. FRS in turn uses the USN journal to determine when changes are made to the contents of the Replica tree and then replicates those changes according to the schedule in Active Directory.

Distributed File Service (Dfssvc.exe) stores information about stand-alone namespaces in the registry and information about domain-based namespaces in Active Directory. The stand-alone DFS metadata contains information about the configuration of each stand-alone namespace and is maintained in the registry of the root server at HKLM\SOFTWARE\Microsoft\Dfs\Roots\Standalone. Domain-based root servers have a registry entry for each root under HKLM\SOFTWARE\Microsoft\Dfs\Roots\Domain, but these entries do not contain the domain-based DFS metadata.

When the DFS service starts on a domain controller using Active Directory with DFS, DFS checks this path for registry entries that correspond to domain-based roots. If these entries exist, the root server polls the PDC emulator master to obtain the DFS metadata for each domain-based namespace and stores the metadata in memory.

In Active Directory, the DFS object stores the DFS metadata for a domain-based namespace. The DFS object is created in Active Directory when you establish a domain at or promote a domain to the Windows Server 2008 domain functional level. Active Directory replicates the entire DFS object to all domain controllers in a domain.

DFS uses a client-server architecture. A domain controller hosting a DFS namespace has both the client and the server components, allowing the domain controller to perform local lookups in its own data store and remote lookups in data stores on other domain controllers. DFS uses the Common Internet File System (CIFS) for communication between DFS clients, root servers, and domain controllers. CIFS is an extension of the Server Message Block (SMB) file sharing protocol.

It is an easy choice whether to use FRS or DFS. FRS enables interoperability with Windows Server 2003 but does not support the latest replication enhancements. DFS offers incremental improvements in Active Directory performance and features but is only available when all domain controllers are running Windows Server 2008 and the domain is running in the Windows Server 2008 functional level.

DFS supports the latest replication enhancements, including replication of changes only within files, bandwidth throttling, and improved replication topology. When you make a change to a GPO and FRS is being used, FRS replicates the entire GPO. When you make a change to a GPO and DFS is being used, only the changes in GPOs are replicated, thereby eliminating the need to replicate an entire GPO after a change.

FRS uses an older, less efficient technology for replication, called Rsync. DFS uses Remote Differential Compression (RDC) instead of Rsync to provide replication that is up to 300 percent faster and compression that is 200 to 300 percent faster. With DFS, operational overhead for managing content and replication is also reduced by approximately 40 percent. Additionally, DFS supports automated recovery from database loss or corruption as well as replication scheduling. Together these features make DFS significantly more scalable than FRS.

Applying and Linking Group Policy Objects

You store Group Policy preferences and settings in Group Policy objects (GPOs). While I'll cover the nitty-gritty details in later chapters, I'll examine the basic concepts related to Group Policy application (initial processing) and refresh (subsequent processing) in this section.

Policy Sets Within GPOs

Within Group Policy, two distinct sets of policies are defined:

- **Computer policies**   These apply to computers and are stored under Computer Configuration in a Group Policy object.
- **User policies**   These apply to users and are stored under User Configuration in a Group Policy object.

Both Computer Configuration and User Configuration have Policies and Preferences nodes. You use:

- Computer Configuration\Policies to configure policy settings targeted to specific computers.
- Computer Configuration\Preferences to configure policy preferences targeted to specific computers.
- User Configuration\Policies to configure policy settings targeted to specific users.
- User Configuration\Preferences to configure policy preferences targeted to specific users.

Initial processing of the related policies is triggered by two unique events:

- **Processing of computer policies is triggered when a computer is started.** When a computer is started and the network connection is initialized, computer policies are applied.
- **Processing of user policies is triggered when a user logs on to a computer.** When a user logs on to a computer, user policies are applied.

Once applied, policies are automatically refreshed to keep settings current and to reflect any changes that might have been made. By default, Group Policy on domain controllers is refreshed every 5 minutes. For workstations and other types of servers, Group Policy is refreshed every 90 to 120 minutes by default. In addition, most security settings are refreshed every 16 hours regardless of whether any policy settings have changed in the intervening time. Other factors can affect Group Policy refreshes, including how slow-link detection is defined (per the Group Policy Slow Link Detection Policy under Computer Configuration\Policies\Administrative Templates\System\Group Policy) and policy processing settings for policies under Computer Configuration\Policies\Administrative Templates\System\Group Policy. As discussed in "Determining Policy Settings and Last Refresh" in Chapter 7, you can check the last refresh of Group Policy using the Group Policy Management Console.

GPO Types

As discussed in Chapter 1, there are two types of policy objects: Active Directory--based Group Policy objects (GPOs) and Local Group Policy objects (LGPOs).

Active Directory supports three levels of Group Policy objects:

- **Site GPOs**   Group Policy objects applied at the site level to a particular Active Directory site.
- **Domain GPOs**   Group Policy objects applied at the domain level to a particular Active Directory domain.
- **Organizational Unit (OU) GPOs**   Group Policy objects applied at the OU level to a particular Active Directory OU.

Through inheritance, a GPO applied to a parent container is inherited by a child container. This means that a policy preference or setting applied to a parent object is passed down to a child object. For example, if you apply a policy setting in a domain, the setting is inherited by organizational units within the domain. In this case, the GPO for the domain is the parent object and the GPOs for the organizational units are the child objects.

In an Active Directory environment, the basic order of inheritance goes from the site level to the domain level to the organizational unit level. This means that the Group Policy preferences and settings for a site are passed down to the domains within that site, and the preferences and settings for a domain are passed down to the organizational units within that domain.

> **Tip**   As you might expect, you can override inheritance. To do this, you specifically assign a policy preference or setting for a child container that contradicts the policy preference or setting for the parent. As long as overriding the policy is allowed (that is, overriding isn't blocked), the child's policy preference or setting will be applied appropriately. To learn more about overriding and blocking GPOs, see the section "Managing Group Policy Inheritance" in Chapter 7.

Windows Vista, Windows Server 2008, and later versions allow the use of multiple LGPOs on a single computer (as long as the computer is not a domain controller). On compliant computers, there are three layers of LGPOs:

- **Local Group Policy object**   The Local Group Policy object is at the top of the policy hierarchy for the local computer. The LGPO is the only local computer policy object that allows both computer configuration and user configuration settings to be applied to all users of the computer.
- **Administrators Local Group Policy object / Non-Administrators Local Group Policy object**   Whether the Administrators Local Group Policy object or the Non-Administrators Local Group Policy object applies depends on the account being used. If the account is a member of the local computer's Administrator's group, the Administrators Group Policy object is applied. Otherwise, the Non-Administrators Group Policy object is applied. This object contains only user configuration settings.
- **User-specific Local Group Policy object**   A user-specific Local Group Policy object applies only to an individual user or to members of a particular group. This object contains only user configuration settings.

These layers of LGPOs are processed in the following order: Local Group Policy object, Administrators or Non-Administrators Local Group Policy object, and then user-specific Local Group Policy object.

> ***Real World***   When computers are being used in a stand-alone configuration rather than a domain configuration, you may find that multiple LGPOs are useful because you no longer have to explicitly disable or remove settings that interfere with your ability to manage a computer before performing administrator tasks. Instead, you can implement one local policy object for administrators and another local policy object for nonadministrators. In a domain configuration, however, you might not want to use multiple LGPOs. In domains, most computers and users already have multiple Group Policy objects applied to them—adding multiple LGPOs to this already varied mix can make managing Group Policy confusing. Therefore, you might want to disable processing of LGPOs, and you can do this through Group Policy. To disable processing of Local Group Policy objects on

computers running Windows Vista, Windows Server 2008 or later, you must enable the Turn Off Local Group Policy Objects Processing setting in an Active Directory–based Group Policy object that the computer processes. When you are editing a GPO in the Group Policy Management Editor, this setting is located under Computer Configuration\Policies. Expand Administrative Templates\System\Group Policy, and then double-click the Turn Off Local Group Policy Objects Processing entry.

Putting this all together when both Active Directory and local policies are in place, policies are applied in the following order:

1. Local GPOs
2. Site GPOs
3. Domain GPOs
4. Organizational unit GPOs
5. Child organizational unit GPOs

Because the available preferences and settings are the same for all policy objects, a preference or setting in one policy object can possibly conflict with a preference or setting in another policy object. Compliant operating systems resolve conflicts by overwriting any previous preference or setting with the last read and most current preference or setting. Therefore, the final preference or setting written is the one that Windows uses. For example, by default, organizational unit policies have precedence over domain policies. As you might expect, there are exceptions to the precedence rule. These exceptions are discussed in the section "Managing Group Policy Inheritance" in Chapter 7.

GPO Links

In Active Directory, each site, domain, or OU can have one or more GPOs associated with it. The association between a GPO and a site, domain, or OU is referred to as a *link*. For example, if a GPO is associated with a domain, the GPO is said to be linked to that domain.

GPOs are stored in a container called Group Policy Objects. This container is replicated to all domain controllers in a domain, so by default all GPOs are also replicated to all domain controllers in a domain. The link (association) between a domain, site, or OU is what makes a GPO active and applicable to that domain, site, or OU.

Linking can be applied in two ways:

- You can link a GPO to a specific site, domain, or OU. For example, if a GPO is linked to a domain, the GPO applies to users and computers in that domain. The main reason for linking a GPO to a specific site, domain, or OU is to keep with the normal rules of inheritance.
- You can link a GPO to multiple levels in Active Directory. For example, a single GPO could be linked to a site, a domain, and multiple OUs. In this case, the GPO applies to each of these levels within Active Directory. The main reason for linking a GPO to multiple levels within Active Directory is to create direct associations between a GPO and multiple sites, domains, and OUs irrespective of how inheritance would normally apply.

You can also unlink a GPO from a site, domain, or OU. This removes the direct association between the GPO and the level within Active Directory from which you've removed the link. For example, if a GPO is linked to a site called First Seattle Site and also to the imaginedlands.com domain, you can remove the link from the imaginedlands.com domain, removing the association between the GPO and the domain. The GPO is then linked only to the site. If you later remove the link between the site and the GPO, the GPO is completely unlinked. A GPO that has been unlinked from all levels within Active Directory still exists within the Group Policy Objects container, but it is inactive.

Connecting to and Working with GPOs

When you use the GPMC to work with GPOs, by default the corresponding changes are made on the domain controller that is acting as the PDC emulator. In this way, the PDC emulator is the central point of contact for

GPO creation, modification, and deletion. Active Directory manages policy in this way to ensure that changes to the GPO structure can be implemented only on a single authoritative domain controller and that only one administrator at a time is granted access to a particular GPO. Because the PDC emulator role is specified at the domain level, there is only one PDC emulator in a domain, and therefore only one place where policy settings are changed by default. If the PDC emulator is unavailable when you are trying to work with policy settings, you get a prompt that enables you to work with policy settings on the domain controller to which you are connected or on any available domain controller.

Any user who is a member of the Domain Admins or Enterprise Admins group can view and work with Active Directory–based Group Policy. Unlike local Group Policy, GPO creation and linking are separate operations with Active Directory–based Group Policy. First you create a GPO and define a group of policy settings to achieve desired results. Then you apply your GPO and make it "live" by linking it to the container or containers within Active Directory where it will be applied.

Although creating and linking GPOs are two distinct operations, the GPMC does allow you to create GPOs and simultaneously link them to a domain or OU within the directory. This means you have two options for creating and linking GPOs. You can:

- Create a GPO and then later link it to a domain or OU within the directory.
- Create a GPO and simultaneously link it to a domain or OU within the directory.

To link a GPO to a site, the GPO must already exist.

The link is what tells Active Directory to apply the preferences and settings specified in the GPO. For example, you can create a GPO called Main Imaginedlands.com Domain Policy and then link it to the Domain container for imaginedlands.com. According to the default (standard) inheritance and policy processing rules, once you link a GPO to a container, the related policy preferences and settings are applied to that container, and lower-level containers within the directory can also inherit the preferences settings. This means a linked GPO can affect every user and computer throughout the enterprise—or some subset of users and computers throughout the enterprise.

Using Default Policies

With Windows Server, you create a domain by establishing the first domain controller for that domain. This typically means logging on to a stand-alone server as a local administrator, running the Domain Controller Installation Wizard (DCPROMO), and then specifying that you want to establish a new forest or domain. When you establish the domain and the domain controller, two GPOs are created by default:

- **Default Domain Policy GPO**   A GPO created for and linked to the domain within Active Directory. This GPO is used to establish baselines for a selection of policy settings that apply to all users and computers in a domain.
- **Default Domain Controllers Policy GPO**   A GPO created for and linked to the Domain Controllers OU that is applicable to all domain controllers in a domain (as long as they aren't moved from this OU). This GPO is used to manage security settings for domain controllers in a domain.

These default GPOs are essential to the proper operation and processing of Group Policy. By default, the Default Domain Controllers Policy GPO has the highest precedence among GPOs linked to the Domain Controllers OU, and the Default Domain Policy GPO has the highest precedence among GPOs linked to the domain. As you'll learn in the sections that follow, the purpose and use of each default GPO is a bit different.

> **Note**   The default GPOs are used to establish defaults for a limited subset of policy settings. Neither default GPO is used to establish default preferences.

Working with the Default Domain Policy GPO

The Default Domain Policy GPO is a complete policy set that includes settings for managing any area of policy, but it isn't meant for general management of Group Policy. As a best practice, you should edit the Default Domain Policy GPO only to manage the default Account policies settings and three specific areas of Account policies:

- **Password policy**   Determines default password policies for domain controllers, such as password history and minimum password length settings.
- **Account lockout policy**   Determines default account lockout policies for domain controllers, such as account lockout duration and account lockout threshold.
- **Kerberos policy**   Determines default Kerberos policies for domain controllers, such as maximum tolerance for computer clock synchronization.

To manage other areas of policy, you should create a new GPO and link it to the domain or an appropriate OU within the domain. That said, several policy settings are exceptions to the rule that the Default Domain Policy GPO (or the highest precedence GPO linked to the domain) is used only to manage Account policies. These policies (located in the Group Policy Management Editor under Computer Configuration\Policies\Windows Settings\Security Settings\Local Policies\Security Options) are as follows:

- **Accounts: Rename Administrator Account**   Renames the built-in Administrator account on all computers throughout the domain, setting a new name for the account so that it is better protected from malicious users. Note that this policy affects the logon name of the account, not the display name. The display name remains Administrator or whatever you set it to. If an administrator changes the logon name for this account through Active Directory Users And Computers, it automatically reverts to what is specified in this policy setting the next time Group Policy is refreshed.

- **Accounts: Administrator Account Status**   Forcibly disables the built-in Administrator account on all computers throughout the domain. If you disable the Administrator account, keep in mind that this account is always available when you boot a computer in safe mode.
- **Accounts: Guest Account Status**   Forcibly disables the built-in Guest account on all computers throughout the domain. If you disable the Guest account, keep in mind that network logons will fail if you set the security option Network Access: Sharing And Security Model For Local Accounts to Guest Only.
- **Accounts: Rename Guest Account**   Renames the built-in Guest account on all computers throughout the domain, setting a new name for the built-in Guest account so that it is better protected from malicious users. Note that this policy affects the logon name of the account, not the display name. The display name remains Guest or whatever else you set it to. If an administrator changes the logon name for this account through Active Directory Users And Computers, it automatically reverts to what is specified in this policy setting the next time Group Policy is refreshed.
- **Network Security: Force Logoff When Logon Hours Expire**   Forces users to log off from the domain when logon hours expire. For example, if you set the logon hours as 8 A.M. to 6 P.M. for the user, the user is forced to log off at 6 P.M.
- **Network Security: Do Not Store LAN Manager Hash Value On Next Password Change**   Determines whether at the next password change the LAN Manager hash value for the new password is stored. Because this value is stored locally in the security database, a password could be compromised if the security database was attacked. On Windows Vista, Windows Server 2008 and later, this setting is typically enabled by default.

- **Network Access: Allow Anonymous SID/Name Translation**
  Determines whether an anonymous user can request security identifier
  (SID) attributes for another user. If this setting is enabled, a malicious
  user could use the well-known Administrators SID to obtain the real
  name of the built-in Administrator account, even if the account has been
  renamed. If this setting is disabled, computers and applications running
  in legacy Windows domains may not be able to communicate with
  Windows Server 2003 and later domains.

Additionally, certificates stored as policy settings for data recovery agents in
the domain are also exceptions. These policies are stored under Computer
Configuration\Policies\Windows Settings\Security Settings\Public Key
Policies\Encrypting File System). You typically manage these policy settings
through the GPO that is linked to the domain level and has the highest
precedence. As with Account policies, this is the Default Domain Policy GPO
by default.

Wondering why configuring policy in this way is a recommended best
practice? Well, if Group Policy becomes corrupted and stops working, you
can use the Dcgpofix tool to restore the Default Domain Policy GPO to its
original state (which would mean that you would lose all the customized
settings you've applied to this GPO). Further, some policy settings can only
be configured at the domain level, and configuring them in the Default
Domain Policy GPO (or the highest precedence GPO linked to the domain)
makes the most sense.

> **Note**   Bottom line, if you define Account policies in multiple GPOs
> linked to a domain, the settings will be merged according to the link
> order of these GPOs. The GPO with a link order of 1 will always have
> the highest precedence. I discuss link order in "Changing Link Order
> and Precedence" in Chapter 7. For more information on working with
> Dcgpofix, see "Recovering the Default GPOs" in Chapter 8 "Maintaining
> and Restoring Group Policy."

You can access the Default Domain Policy GPO in several ways. If you are using the GPMC, you'll see the Default Domain Policy GPO when you click the domain name in the console tree, as shown in Figure 2-3. Right-click the Default Domain Policy node and select Edit to get full access to the Default Domain Policy GPO.

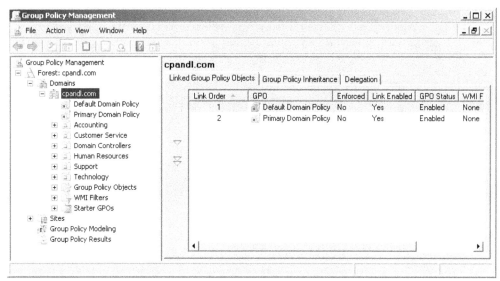

FIGURE 2-3 Accessing the Default Domain Policy GPO in GPMC.

In the Group Policy Management Editor, under Computer Configuration, expand Policies\Windows Settings\Security Settings\Local Policies as shown in Figure 2-4. You can then work with Audit Policy, User Rights Assignment, and Security Options as necessary.

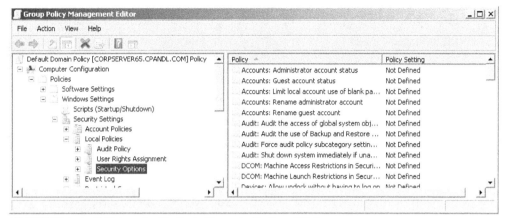

FIGURE 2-4 Editing the Default Domain Policy GPO.

Working with the Default Domain Controllers Policy GPO

The Default Domain Controllers Policy GPO is designed to ensure that all domain controllers in a domain have the same security settings. This is important because all domain controllers in an Active Directory domain are equal. If they were to have different security settings, they might behave differently, and this would be counter to the way Active Directory is designed to work. If one domain controller has a specific policy setting, this policy setting should be applied to all domain controllers to ensure consistent behavior across a domain.

The Default Domain Controllers Policy GPO is linked to the Domain Controllers OU. This ensures that it is applicable to all domain controllers in a domain as long as they aren't moved from this OU. Because all domain controllers are placed in the Domain Controllers OU by default, any security setting changes you make will apply to all domain controllers by default. The key security areas that you should manage consistently include:

- **Audit policy**   Determines default auditing policies for domain controllers.
- **User rights assignment**   Determines default user rights assignment for domain controllers.

- **Security options** Determines default security options for domain controllers.

Microsoft recommends that you not make any other changes to the Default Domain Controllers Policy GPO. Keep in mind that this GPO applies only to domain controllers because it is linked to the Domain Controllers OU and all domain controllers are members of this OU by default.

Moving a domain controller out of the Domain Controllers OU can adversely affect domain management and can also lead to inconsistent behavior during logon and authentication. Why? When you move a domain controller out of the Domain Controllers OU, the Default Domain Controllers Policy GPO no longer applies unless you've linked this GPO to the destination OU. Further, any GPO linked to the destination OU is applied to the domain controller.

Therefore, if you move a domain controller out of the Domain Controllers OU, you should carefully manage its security settings thereafter. For example, if you make security changes to the Default Domain Controllers Policy GPO, you should ensure that those security changes are applied to domain controllers stored in OUs other than the Domain Controllers OU.

You can access the Default Domain Controllers Policy GPO in several ways. If you are using the GPMC, you'll see the Default Domain Controllers Policy GPO when you click the Domain Controllers node in the console tree. Then right-click the Default Domain Controllers Policy and select Edit to get full access to the Default Domain Controllers Policy GPO.

Real World Microsoft product support does not support moving a domain controller out of the Domain Controllers OU. If you've done so and are having problems with your domain controllers that could be related to this action, Microsoft product support will ask you to move the domain controller back to the Domain Controllers OU.

Other components and products rely on the Default Domain Controllers Policy GPO being present and linked in the domain. For

---

example, Exchange Server may generate error events stating it cannot find a global catalog. Often, this occurs because you do not have the Default Domain Controllers Policy linked to the Domain Controllers OU or because you have moved domain controllers out of the Domain Controllers OU.

Using Policy Preferences and Settings

So far we've discussed how Group Policy has changed, how you can update policy, and how policy is applied, but I haven't discussed the specific ways in which you can use preferences and settings to help you better manage your network. I'll remedy that now by detailing uses for both preferences and settings. Because some overlap occurs in management areas for preferences and settings, I'll also discuss whether using settings or preferences is better suited to a particular task.

Using Policy Settings for Administration

A policy setting is a managed setting that you apply to control configuration, such as to restrict access to the Run dialog box. Most policy settings have three basic states:

- **Enabled**   The policy setting is turned on, and its settings are active. You typically enable a policy setting to ensure that it is enforced. Once enabled, some policy settings allow you to configure additional options that fine-tune how the policy setting is applied.
- **Disabled**   The policy setting is turned off, and its settings are not applied. Typically, you disable a policy setting to ensure that it is not enforced.
- **Not Configured**   The policy setting is not being used. No settings for the policy are either active or inactive and no changes are made to the configuration settings targeted by the policy.

By themselves, these states are fairly straightforward. However, these basic states can be affected by inheritance and blocking (which I touched on briefly and will discuss in detail in Chapter 5, "Searching and Filtering Group Policy"). That said, with the following two rules about inheritance and blocking in mind, you'll be well on your way to success with Group Policy:

- If inherited policy settings are strictly enforced, you cannot override them. This means the inherited policy setting is applied regardless of the policy state set in the current GPO.
- If inherited policy settings are blocked in the current GPO and not strictly enforced, the inherited policy setting is overridden. This means the inherited policy setting does not apply, and only the policy setting from the current GPO is applied.

Now that you know exactly how to apply individual policy settings, let's look at the administrative areas to which you can apply Group Policy. Through a special set of policies called Administrative Templates, you can manage just about every aspect of the Windows graphical user interface (GUI), from menus to the desktop, the taskbar, and more. The Administrative Template policy settings affect actual registry settings, so the available policies are nearly identical whether you are working with local Group Policy or domain-based Group Policy. You can use administrative templates to manage:

- **Control Panel** Controls access to and the options of Control Panel. You can also configure settings for Add Or Remove Programs, Display, Printers, and Regional And Language Options.
- **Desktop** Configures the Windows desktop, the availability and configuration of Active Desktop, and Active Directory search options from the desktop.
- **Network** Configures networking and network client options, including offline files, DNS clients, and network connections.
- **Printers** Configures printer publishing, browsing, spooling, and directory options.
- **Shared folders** Allows publishing of shared folders and Distributed File System (DFS) roots.
- **Start menu and taskbar** Configures the Start menu and taskbar, primarily by removing or hiding items and options.

- **System** Configures policies related to general system settings, disk quotas, user profiles, logon, power management, system restore, error reporting, and more.
- **Windows components** Configures whether and how to use various Windows components, such as Event Viewer, Task Scheduler, and Windows Updates.

Real World You can obtain additional administrative templates for Microsoft Office at the Microsoft Download Center (*http://download.microsoft.com*). At the Download Center, click Home & Office under Download Categories. Search the Home & Office category for "Office customization tool," and then click the link for the most recent release. Next, download and run the self-extracting executable. When prompted, accept the license terms and then click Continue. You will then be able to select a destination folder for the related files. Review the files you've just extracted.

To use the administrative templates in GPMC on your computer, copy the ADMX files to the %SystemRoot%\PolicyDefinitions folder and the ADML files to the appropriate language-specific subfolder of the PolicyDefinitions folder. Otherwise, to make the administrative templates available throughout the domain, copy the ADMX and ADML files to the appropriate folders within the SYSVOL on a domain controller.

Table 2-1 provides a comprehensive list of administrative areas you can manage using Group Policy. Whether you are working with local Group Policy or Active Directory–based Group Policy, the areas of administration are similar. However, you can do much more with Active Directory–based Group Policy primarily because you cannot use local Group Policy to manage any features that require Active Directory.

TABLE 2-1 Key Administrative Areas That Can Be Managed with Policy Settings

Device/Drive installation	Controls the way device and driver installation works.
	Computer Configuration\Policies\Administrative Templates\System\Device Installation
	Computer Configuration\Policies\Administrative Templates\System\Drive Installation
	User Configuration\Policies\Administrative Templates\System\Drive Installation
Device Installation restriction	Restricts the devices that can be deployed and used.
	Computer Configuration\Policies\Administrative Templates\System\Device Installation\Device Installation Restrictions
Disk quotas	Configures the way disk quotas are used and whether quotas are enforced, logged, or both.
	Computer Configuration\Policies\Software Settings
Encrypted data recovery agents	Configures data recovery agents and their related certificates for use with the Encrypting File System (EFS).
	Computer | User Configuration\Policies\Windows Settings\Security Settings\Public Key Policies\Encrypting File System
File and folder security	Configures security permissions for files and folders.
	Computer Configuration\Policies\Windows Settings\Security Settings\File System
Folder redirection	Moves critical data folders for users to network shares where they can be better managed and backed up regularly (domain-based Group Policy only).
	User Configuration\Policies\Windows Settings\Folder Redirection

General computer security	Establishes security settings for accounts, event logs, restricted groups, system services, the registry, and file systems. (With local Group Policy, you can only manage general computer security for account policies.)
	Computer Configuration\Policies\Windows Settings\Security Settings
Internet settings	Controls the ways Windows Internet Explorer can be used and establishes lockdown settings.
	Computer Configuration\Policies\Administrative Templates\Windows Components\Internet Explorer
Internet Explorer maintenance	Configures the browser interface, security, important URLs, default programs, proxies, and more.
	User Configuration\Policies\Windows Settings\Internet Explorer Maintenance
IP security	Configures IP security policy for clients, servers, and secure servers.
	Computer Configuration\Policies\Windows Settings\Security Settings\IP Security Policies
Local security policies	Configures policy for auditing, user rights assignment, and user privileges.
	Computer Configuration\Policies\Windows Settings\Security Settings\Local Policies
Offline files	Determines whether and how offline files are used.
	Computer	User Configuration\Policies\Administrative Templates\Network\Offline Files
Policy-based Quality of Service (QoS)	Manages network traffic to help improve quality of service for critical applications.
	Computer	User Configuration\Policies\Windows Settings\Policy-based QoS
Power options	Configure power management plans and settings for devices. (Windows Vista or later)

	Computer | User Configuration\Policies\Administrative Templates\System\Power Management
Printer deployment	Configures printers for use. (Windows Vista or later)
	User Configuration\Policies\Windows Settings\Deployed Printers
Public key security	Configures public key policies for autoenrollment, EFS, enterprise trusts, and more.
	Computer | User Configuration\Policies\Windows Settings\Security Settings\Public Key Policies
Registry security	Configures security permissions for registry keys.
	Computer Configuration\Policies\Windows Settings\Security Settings\Registry
Restricted groups	Controls the membership of both Active Directory–based groups and local computer groups.
	Computer | User Configuration\Policies\Windows Settings\Security Settings\Restricted Groups
Scripts	Configures logon/logoff scripts for users and startup/shutdown scripts for computers.
	Computer | User Configuration\Policies\Windows Settings\Security Settings\Scripts
Software installation	Configures automated deployment of new software and software upgrades (domain-based Group Policy only).
	Computer | User Configuration\Policies\Software Settings\Software Installation
Software restriction	Restricts the software that can be deployed and used. Local Group Policy does not support user-based software restriction policies, only computer-based software restriction policies.
	Computer | User Configuration\Policies\Windows Settings\Security Settings\Software Restriction Policies
Start menu	Defines the available options on and the behavior of the Start menu.

	User Configuration\Policies\Administrative Templates\Start Menu And Taskbar
System services	Configures startup state and security permissions for system services.
	Computer Configuration\Policies\Windows Settings\Security Settings\System Services
Wired networking (IEEE 802.3)	Configures wired network policies for authentication methods and modes that apply to wired clients (domain-based Group Policy only). Can also be used to validate server certificates, enable quarantine checks, enforce advanced 802.1X settings, and enable single sign on.
	Computer Configuration\Policies\Windows Settings\Security Settings\Wired Network Policies
Wireless networking (IEEE 802.11)	Configures wireless network policies for access points, wireless clients, and preferred networks (domain-based Group Policy only). Can also be used to define permitted types of connections and block disallowed types of connections.
	Computer Configuration\Policies\Windows Settings\Security Settings\Wireless Network Policies

Using Policy Preference for Administration

A policy preference is an unmanaged setting that you apply to preconfigure an option for a user, such as to map a network share to a drive. Most policy preferences can be established using one of four different actions:

- **Create** Creates the preference only if a preference does not already exist.
- **Replace** Deletes the preference if it exists and then creates it, or creates the preference if it doesn't yet exist.
- **Update** Modifies the preference if it exists. Otherwise, creates the preference.
- **Delete** Deletes the preference if it exists.

As with states for policy settings, these actions are fairly straightforward. However, these basic actions also can be affected by inheritance and blocking. To help you navigate inheritance and blocking, keep these basic rules in mind:

- If inherited policy preferences are strictly enforced, you cannot override them. This means the inherited policy preference is applied regardless of the action defined in the current GPO.
- If inherited policy preferences are blocked in the current GPO and not strictly enforced, the inherited policy preference is overridden. This means the inherited policy preference does not apply, and only the policy preference from the current GPO is applied.

Unlike policy settings, policy preferences apply only to Active Directory–based Group Policy. When you are working with Active Directory–based Group Policy, you can use policy preferences to configure the items discussed in Table 2-2.

TABLE 2-2 Key Elements That Can Be Configured with Policy Preferences

Applications	Application settings. Available when you install preference settings for an application.
	User Configuration\Preferences\Windows Settings\Applications
Data Sources	Open Database Connectivity (ODBC) data sources
	Computer | User Configuration\Preferences\Control Panel Settings\Data Sources
Devices	System devices, including USB ports, floppy drives, and removable media
	Computer | User Configuration\Preferences\Control Panel Settings\Devices
Drive Maps	Network shares mapped to drive letters.
	User Configuration\Preferences\Windows Settings\Drive Maps
Environment	System and user environment variables

	Computer	User Configuration\Preferences\Windows Settings\Environment
Files	Files that can be copied from a source location to a destination location.
	Computer	User Configuration\Preferences\Windows Settings\Files
Ini Files	Property values within .ini files.
	Computer	User Configuration\Preferences\Windows Settings\Ini Files
Folders	Folders in a particular location on the file system.
	Computer	User Configuration\Preferences\Windows Settings\Folders
Local Users And Groups	User and group accounts for the local computer.
	Computer	User Configuration\Preferences\Control Panel Settings\Local Users And Groups
Network Options	Virtual Private Networking and Dial-up Networking connections
	Computer	User Configuration\Preferences\Control Panel Settings\Network Options
Network shares	Shares, hidden shares, and administrative shares.
	Computer or User Configuration\Preferences\Windows Settings\
Printers	Printer configuration and mapping
	Computer	User Configuration\Preferences\Control Panel Settings\Printers
Registry	Registry keys and values.
	Computer	User Configuration\Preferences\Windows Settings\Registry
Scheduled Tasks	Scheduled tasks for automation
	Computer	User Configuration\Preferences\Control Panel Settings\Scheduled Tasks

Services	System services
	Computer Configuration\Preferences\Control Panel Settings\Services
Shortcuts	Shortcuts for file system objects, URLs, or shell objects.
	Computer | User Configuration\Preferences\Windows Settings\Shortcuts

Through special preferences for Control Panel, you can also manage various aspects of the Windows graphical user interface (GUI). You can use these special preferences to manage:

- Folder settings as if you were using the options available in the Folder Options utility in Control Panel. Located in Computer | User Configuration\Preferences\Control Panel Settings\Folder Options.
- Internet settings as if you are using the options available in the Internet Options utility in Control Panel. Located in User Configuration\Preferences\Control Panel Settings\Internet Settings.
- Power schemes and power management options as if you were using the related utilities in Control Panel. Located in Computer | User Configuration\Preferences\Control Panel Settings\Power Options. (Windows XP only.)
- Regional and language settings as if you were using the options available in the Regional And Languages utility in Control Panel. Located in User Configuration\Preferences\Control Panel Settings\Regional Options.
- Start menu as if you were using the Start Menu Properties dialog box. Located in User Configuration\Preferences\Control Panel Settings\Start Menu.

Choosing Between Preferences and Settings

Because some management areas overlap between policy preferences and policy settings, you can sometimes perform a particular task in more than one way. For example, using policy settings, you can identify logon scripts that should be used. Within these scripts, you can map network drives, configure printers, create shortcuts, copy files and folders, and perform other tasks. Using policy preferences however, you could perform these same tasks without the need of using logon scripts. So which one should you use? Well, the truth is that there really isn't one right answer. It depends on what you want to do. In the following sections, I describe some general guidelines for specific areas of overlap.

> **Real World**   When a conflict occurs between a policy setting and a policy preference defined in a particular GPO, a registry-based policy setting will normally win. For conflicts between non-registry-based policy settings and preferences, the last value written wins (as determined by the order in which the client-side extensions for policy settings and preferences are processed). Determining whether a policy setting is registry-based or not is easy. All registry-based policy settings are defined in administrative templates.

Controlling Device Installation

Through policy settings, you can control device installation and enforce specific restrictions. The goal is to prevent users from installing specific types of hardware devices. You can specify that certain approved devices can be installed (according to the hardware ID of the device). You can also prevent installation of specific disapproved devices (again according to the hardware ID of the device). These policy settings only apply to Windows Vista, Windows Server 2008 or later and are found under Computer Configuration\Policies\Administrative Templates\System\Device Installation\Device Installation Restrictions.

While restrictions block the installation of a new device or prevent a device from being plugged back in after it has been unplugged, it doesn't prevent existing devices from being used. Why? The device drivers are already installed and the devices are already available, and because the device or drive isn't rechecked, it continues to work.

Using policy preferences, you can disable device classes, individual devices, port classes, and individual ports, but you cannot prevent a driver from loading. You disable devices by selecting a device class or device already installed on your management computer. You disable ports by selecting a port class or specific port already in use on your management computer. The related preferences are found under Computer | User Configuration\Preferences\Control Panel Settings\Devices.

While you can disable devices and ports using preferences, this doesn't prevent device drivers from installing. It also doesn't prevent a user with appropriate rights from enabling ports or devices in Device Manager. However, as Group Policy by default refreshes policy preferences using the same refresh interval as for policy settings, the preference would be reapplied during the next refresh interval. Therefore, unless you specifically elect to apply the preference once and not reapply it, the preference would be reapplied every 90 to 120 minutes.

Given how these technologies work, the best solution for your environment may depend on your goal. If you want to completely lock things down and prevent specific devices from being installed and used, you may want to use both policy settings and policy preferences to do the job. Policy settings could prevent specific devices from being installed, providing they weren't already installed. Policy preferences could disable devices already installed, providing that you've already installed the device on your management computer so it can be selected.

As a final thought, it is important to point out that the related policy settings apply only to Windows Vista, Windows Server 2008 or later, while the related policy preferences apply to any computer on which the client-side extensions for Group Policy Preferences are installed.

Controlling Files and Folders

Through policy settings, you can specify security permissions for files and folders. The goal is to establish specific access control lists (ACLs) for important files and folders. However, the files and folders must already exist on the target computers so that the ACLs can be applied. These policy settings apply to any computer that supports Group Policy and are found under Computer Configuration\Policies\Windows Settings\Security Settings\File System.

Using policy preferences, you can manage files and folders. Preferences for files work differently than preferences for folders. With files, you can create, update, or replace a file on a target computer by copying it from a source computer. You can also delete a file on a target computer. With folders, you can create, update, replace, or delete a folder in a specific location on a target computer. You can also specify whether to delete existing files and subfolders during the create, update, replace, or delete operation.

File and folder preferences apply to any computer on which the client-side extensions for Group Policy Preferences are installed. For files, the related preferences are found under Computer | User Configuration\Preferences\Windows Settings\Files. For folders, the related preferences are found under Computer | User Configuration\Preferences\Windows Settings\Folders.

> **Tip**   Group Policy also provides preferences for working with .ini files and shortcuts. Preferences for .ini files are limited to modifying values for designated properties within a specific section of the .ini file. Shortcut preferences are used to create shortcuts to files, folders, URLs, and shell objects in a specific location, such as the desktop.

Here, using policy settings and preferences together gives you the best of both worlds. Through preferences you have an easy way to copy files from a source computer to target computers and to manage folders. Through settings you have an easy way to apply desired security settings. Additionally, with files and folders, you might want to apply preferences only once and not reapply them. Otherwise, the create, update, replace, or delete operations will be reapplied during Group Policy refresh.

Controlling Internet Explorer

Group Policy offers a wide array of settings and preferences for Internet Explorer. There are so many options that even a few experts are confused as to what does what. The key things to focus on are the following:

- Policy settings under Computer Configuration\Policies\Administrative Templates\Windows Components\Internet Explorer are primarily meant to control Internet Explorer behavior. These settings configure browser security enhancements and help to lockdown Internet security zones.
- Policy settings under User Configuration\Policies\Windows Settings\Internet Explorer Maintenance are used to specify important URLs, such as those for home pages, search, support, favorites, and links. These settings are also used to customize the browser interface by adding custom logos, titles, and buttons to Internet Explorer and to establish default programs, proxies, and more.
- Preference settings under User Configuration\Preferences\Control Panel Settings\Internet Settings allow you to configure any of the options available in the Internet Options utility in Control Panel (which essentially includes every user-configurable option).

Because policy settings are managed and policy preferences are unmanaged, you can use policy settings when you want to enforce specific settings for Internet Explorer. Although you can configure Internet Explorer with preferences, the preferences are not enforced and users can change settings. That said, if you apply the preferences so that they are refreshed automatically as part of normal Group Policy refreshes, settings users change may be overwritten by your preferences.

When you want to customize the interface, the settings under Internet Explorer Maintenance are the ones you'll use. These settings allow you to configure home page URLs, search URLs, support URLs, favorites, and links. They also allow you to add custom logos, titles, and buttons.

Controlling Power Options

When you want to control power management settings, the choice between policy settings and policy preferences is easy. You use policy settings for Windows Vista, Windows Server 2008 or later.

Policy settings for Windows Vista, Windows Server 2008 or later are found under Computer | User Configuration\Policies\Administrative Templates\System\Power Management.

Controlling Printers

With policy settings, you can deploy printers to computers running any version of Windows that supports Group Policy. This technology establishes a connection to an existing shared printer.

To deploy printers to computers running Windows Vista, Windows Server 2008 or later, you can use policy settings under User Configuration\Policies\Windows Settings\Deployed Printers. To deploy printers to computers running earlier versions of Windows, you can push a printer connection to the computer using PushPrinterConnection.exe as a logon or startup script.

With policy preferences, you can map and configure printers. These preferences include options for configuring local printers as well as for mapping both TCP/IP and shared network printers. These policy preferences apply to any computer on which the client-side extensions for Group Policy Preferences are installed.

As printer preferences are much more versatile than printer settings, you'll probably want to use preferences to deploy printers. That said, if you've already configured printers to be deployed using policy settings, you don't need to switch to policy preferences and redeploy the printers.

Controlling Registry Keys and Values

Through policy settings, you can specify security permissions for registry keys. The goal is to establish specific access control lists (ACLs) for important registry keys. However, the registry keys must already exist on the target computers so that the ACLs can be applied. These policy settings apply to any computer that supports Group Policy and are found under Computer Configuration\Policies\Windows Settings\Security Settings\Registry.

Using policy preferences, you can create, update, replace, or delete registry keys. The related preferences are found under Computer | User Configuration\Preferences\Windows Settings\Registry. Although you can modify just about any registry key, it is contradictory to widely manage registry values through preferences. Why? Policy settings defined within the administrative templates set registry values for you so that you don't have to modify the registry directly. You can install additional administrative templates to manage the registry settings of other applications. If administrative templates aren't available for a particular application, you can create your own custom administrative template to manage the registry settings for the application.

Because of the conflicting goals, I recommend using policy preferences to manage individual registry keys and only in a limited number of situations. When you need to work with multiple or many registry keys, you should use preexisting administrative templates or consider creating your own custom administrative templates. Additionally, with registry keys, you might want to apply preferences only once and not reapply them. Otherwise, the create, update, replace, or delete operation will be reapplied during Group Policy refresh.

Controlling the Start Menu

When it comes to the Start menu, there is a lot of overlap between what you can configure with policy settings and what you can configure with policy preferences. With this in mind, you use policy settings and policy preferences to work with the Start menu in very different ways.

Through policy settings, you can control the options available on the Start menu and define the behavior of various Start menu options. With over 70 settings to choose from under User Configuration\Policies\Administrative Templates\Start Menu And Taskbar, there are many possibilities. You can specify that you want to clear the history of recently opened documents when a user logs off or that drag and drop is disabled on the Start menu. You can lock the taskbar, remove system tray icons, and turn off notifications.

Policy preferences for working with the Start menu are located in User Configuration\Preferences\Control Panel Settings\Start Menu. With policy preferences, you manage the options and behavior of the Start menu as if you were using the Start Menu Properties dialog box. You can configure both the standard Start menu and the classic Start menu. There are, however, no options for configuring the taskbar.

Controlling System Services

When you want to control system services, the choice between policy settings and policy preferences is easy. You can use policy settings to:

- Configure the service startup mode
- Specify the access permissions for services (which control who can start, stop, and pause the service)

Policy settings for services are locatd under Computer Configuration\Policies\Windows Settings\Security Settings\System Services.

You can use policy preferences to:

- Configure the service startup mode
- Configure a service action that can be used to start a stopped service, stop a started service, or stop and restart a service

- Specify the account under which the service runs and set the password for this account
- Specify recovery actions that determine how the service responds to failure

Policy preferences for services are located under Computer Configuration\Preferences\Control Panel Settings\Services.

Because policy settings are managed and policy preferences are unmanaged, you can use policy settings when you want to enforce specific startup modes and access permissions. Although you can configure services with preferences, the preferences are not enforced and users can change settings. If you apply the preferences so that they are refreshed, settings users change may be overwritten by your preferences.

Controlling Users and Groups

When you want to control users and groups, the choice between policy settings and policy preferences is easy. You use policy settings when you want to restrict the membership of either a group defined in Active Directory or a group on the local computer. You do this by specifying the members of the group and the groups of which the group is a member. The related policy settings are found in Computer | User Configuration\Policies\Windows Settings\Security Settings\Restricted Groups.

You use policy preferences to create, replace, update, or delete users and groups on the local computer. With local user accounts, you can also:

- Rename existing user accounts
- Set user account passwords
- Set status flags for user accounts

Status flags can be used to require users to change passwords at next log on, disable the account, or set an expiration date.

With local groups, you can also:

- Rename existing groups
- Add or remove the current user as a member
- Delete member users, member groups, or both

Policy preferences for local users and groups are located under Computer | User Configuration\Preferences\Control Panel Settings\Local Users And Groups.

Chapter 3. Group Policy Management

The Group Policy Management Console (GPMC) is the primary tool you use to work with Group Policy. As discussed in Chapter 1, "Introducing Group Policy," and detailed step by step in Appendix A, you need to install the GPMC before you can use it, and the installation technique you use depends on the operating system running on your computer. As also detailed step by step in Appendix A, you can extend Group Policy in a variety of ways. If a computer doesn't already have Group Policy client-side extensions, you may be able to install the extensions so that you can configure the computer using policy preferences as well as policy settings.

If you want to manage other applications through Group Policy, such as applications in the Microsoft Office system, you may be able to install Group Policy templates and add-ons for the applications. If you want additional control over how Group Policy is used, you may want to install the client and server components for Advanced Group Policy Management (AGPM). Advanced Group Policy Management is a set of extensions for the Group Policy Management Console that adds change control and other features.

In this chapter, you'll learn techniques you can use to work with the GPMC. In Chapter 4, "Advanced Group Policy Management," you'll learn techniques you can use to take advantage of the additional features provided by AGPM.

Understanding Resultant Set of Policy

Group Policy applies only to users and computers. Group Policy settings are divided into two categories: Computer Configuration, which contains settings that apply to computers, and User Configuration, which contains settings that apply to user accounts. Each category can be divided further into two general types: policy settings and policy preferences.

Each general type can be divided further into several major classes of settings, each of which contains several subclasses of settings. For policy settings, the three major classes are:

- **Software Settings**   For automated deployment of new software and software upgrades. Also used for uninstalling software.
- **Windows Settings**   For managing key Windows settings for both computers and users, including scripts and security. For users, you can also manage remote installation services, folder redirection, and Windows Internet Explorer maintenance.
- **Administrative Templates**   For managing registry settings that configure the operating system, Windows components, and applications. Administrative templates are implemented for specific versions of the operating system.
- For policy preferences, the two major classes are:
- **Windows Settings**   For configuring key Windows settings for both computers and users, including environment variables, files, folders, registry values, and shortcuts. For computers, you can also manage network shares. For users, you can also manage applications and mapped drives.
- **Control Panel Settings**   For configuring various options and utilities in the Control Panel, including data sources, devices, folder options, network options, power options, and printers. For computers, you can also manage services. For users, you can also manage Internet settings and Start menu options.

When the Group Policy client running on a computer applies Group Policy objects (GPOs) to users and computers, their effects (the end result of inheritance and processing) are cumulative. These cumulative effects on an individual computer or user are referred to as the Resultant Set of Policy (RSoP). You'll need to determine the RSoP for a particular user or group to learn exactly how policy is being applied.

In the Group Policy Management Console, you can determine the RSoP for a user or group by using the Group Policy Results Wizard, and you can model policy changes that you'd like to make by using the Group Policy Modeling Wizard. These wizards are discussed in the section "Planning Group Policy Changes" in Chapter 7, "Managing Group Policy Processing."

Within Active Directory, objects are organized using a hierarchical tree structure called a *directory tree*. The structure of the tree is derived from the schema and is used to define the parent-child relationships of objects stored in the directory. Figure 3-1 shows a representation of a directory tree for a domain. The domain object is the parent object of all objects in a domain; as such, it is at the root of the directory tree. The domain object in turn contains other objects, including other container objects, such as subdomains or organizational units (OUs), and standard objects, such as users, computers, and printers. In the figure, na.imaginedlands.com is a subdomain of imaginedlands.com, and this subdomain has two top-level OUs: Sales and Services.

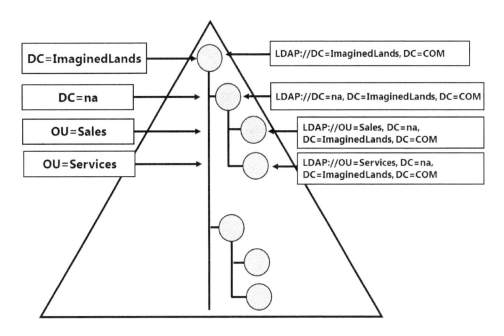

FIGURE 3-1 The imaginedlands.com domain and its related directory tree.

Active Directory uses Lightweight Directory Access Protocol (LDAP) for querying and managing objects in the directory. You can locate any object in the directory according to its LDAP path. The LDAP path to the Sales OU in the na.imaginedlands.com domain is LDAP://OU=Sales,DC=na,DC=Imaginedlands,DC=COM. Here *LDAP://* specifies that you are using the Lightweight Directory Access Protocol, and *OU=Sales,DC=na,DC=Imaginedlands,DC=COM* is the exact location of the Sales OU in the directory. Each component of the object's name is shown in the path. (OU stands for organizational unit, and DC stands for domain component.) The exact path to an object, excluding the protocol designator, is the object's distinguished name (DN).

Objects in the directory also have a relative name, referred to as the relative distinguished name (RDN). The RDN includes only the name component of the object. For example, the RDN of the Sales OU is OU=Sales. Within the Sales OU, you might have a user, Joe, and a computer, JoesPC. The RDN of these objects would be CN=Joe and CN=JoesPC, respectively. CN stands for common name. The DNs of these objects would be CN=Joe,OU=Sales,DC=na,DC=Imaginedlands,DC=COM and CN=JoesPC,OU=Sales,DC=na,DC=Imaginedlands,DC=COM, respectively.

The DN identifies an object's place within the directory. Not only does the DN tell you the exact containers in which the object is stored, but it also tells you the relationship of those containers to each other. The relationship of container objects is extremely important when it comes to applying Group Policy. When you know where an object is in the directory tree and in which container object it resides, you can determine the GPOs that would typically be applied to the object. That said, it is important to keep in mind that Group Policy is not inherited from parent to child domains and that an object's DN does not indicate the site in which the object is located.

> **Real World**   Inheritance works differently within and between domains. Within a domain, top-level GPOs are inherited automatically by lower-level GPOs, which means the domain GPO is automatically inherited by OUs. The domain GPO and the GPO of a top-level OU are

inherited by a second-level OU, and so on. Between parent and child domains, inheritance is not automatic. A child domain does not automatically inherit the GPO of the parent domain. Microsoft recommends that you avoid assigning GPOs across domains because if Group Policy is obtained from another domain, the processing of Group Policy objects could slow the startup and logon processes. Therefore, inheritance of child domains is rarely enforced.

Although the directory path tells you about most of the containers that might have GPOs that affect a user or computer, it doesn't tell you about all the GPOs that could possibly apply. One important piece is missing, and it has to do with sites.

You use sites to map your network's physical structure. Because site mappings are separate and independent from logical components in the directory, there's no necessary relationship between your network's sites and the domains in the directory. A domain can span one or more sites. A single site also can span multiple domains.

Figure 3-2 shows a deeper view of the na.imaginedlands.com domain and the objects within it. As you can see, this domain has two sites associated with it:

- **Toronto Site** This site has two OUs—Sales and Support—and has several resources that are physically located within it. Sales, a top-level OU, has two computer objects and one user object associated with it. Support, a child OU of Sales, has one computer object and one user object associated with it. CorpSvr01 is a domain controller. JoesPC and TimsPC are workstations.
- **NY Site** This site has one OU, Services, and has several resources physically located within it. Services, a top-level OU with no child OUs, has three computer objects and two user objects associated with it. CorpSvr02 is a domain controller. SallysPC and RonsPC are workstations.

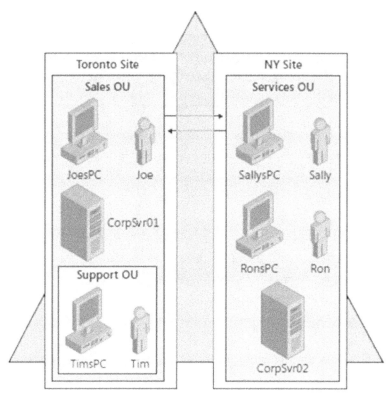

na.imaginedlands.com

FIGURE 3-2 A sampling of objects within the na.imaginedlands.com domain.

Based on this diagram, you know exactly which objects are stored in the directory and in which containers. You also know which sites are associated with which objects, and this gives you the complete picture of which GPOs will be applied to which objects. Since you know that computers and users are also affected by a local machine GPO (the LGPO), you now know that JoesPC would be affected by the following GPOs and in the following order:

1. The local machine GPO for the computer
2. The GPO for the Toronto site
3. The GPO for the na.imaginedlands.com subdomain
4. The GPO for the Sales OU

The user, Joe, would be affected by the same GPOs, which would be applied in the same order to set permitted actions and limitations on his account.

Continuing the example and excluding LGPOs, you can determine how GPOs affect computers and users.

- At the site level, any GPOs linked to the Toronto site affect JoesPC, Joe, CorpSvr01, TimsPC, and Tim. Any GPOs linked to the NY site affect SallysPC, Sally, RonsPC, Ron, and CorpSvr02.
- At the domain level, any GPOs linked to the na.imaginedlands.com domain affect JoesPC, Joe, CorpSvr01, TimsPC, Tim, SallysPC, Sally, RonsPC, Ron, and CorpSvr02.
- At the OU level, any GPOs linked to the Sales OU affect JoesPC, Joe, and CorpSvr01. Any GPOs linked to the Support OU affect TimsPC and Tim. Any GPOs linked to the Services OU affect SallysPC, Sally, RonsPC, Ron, and CorpSvr02.

Again, excluding LGPOs, you could also say that the RSoP for these objects is as follows:

- **Joe** The RSoP for Joe flows from the Toronto site to na.imaginedlands.com and then the Sales OU.
- **JoesPC** The RSoP for JoesPC flows from the Toronto site to na.imaginedlands.com and then the Sales OU.
- **CorpSvr01** The RSoP for CorpSvr01 flows from the Toronto site to na.imaginedlands.com and then the Sales OU.
- **Sally** The RSoP for Sally flows from the NY site to na.imaginedlands.com and then the Services OU.
- **SallysPC** The RSoP for SallysPC flows from NY site to na.imaginedlands.com and then the Services OU.

- **Ron**   The RSoP for Ron flows from the NY site to na.imaginedlands.com and then the Services OU.
- **RonsPC**   The RSoP for RonsPC flows from the NY site to na.imaginedlands.com and then the Services OU.
- **CorpSvr02**   The RSoP for CorpSvr02 flows from the NY site to na.imaginedlands.com and then the Services OU.
- **Tim**   The RSoP for Tim flows from the Toronto site to na.imaginedlands.com, Sales OU, and then the Support OU.
- **TimsPC**   The RSoP for TimsPC flows from the Toronto site to na.imaginedlands.com, Sales OU, and then the Support OU.

When you look at RSoP, it's also important to consider what will happen when changes are made: for example, if Sally visits the Toronto office and logs on to JoesPC, or if Tim from Support goes to New York and logs on to RonsPC. Here is what happens with regard to Group Policy:

- **Sally in Toronto logging on to JoesPC**   JoesPC is subject to the Computer Configuration settings in the GPOs for the Toronto site, na.imaginedlands.com, and the Sales OU. Sally (logging on to JoesPC while in Toronto) is subject to the User Configuration settings in the GPOs for the NY Site, na.imaginedlands.com, and the Services OU. By default, the User Configuration settings in the GPOs that apply to Sally have precedence.
- **Tim in New York logging on to RonsPC**   RonsPC is subject to the Computer Configuration settings in the GPOs for the NY site, na.imaginedlands.com, and the Services OU. Tim (logging on to RonsPC while in New York) is subject to the User Configuration settings in the GPOs for the Toronto site, na.imaginedlands.com, the Sales OU, and the Support OU. By default, the User Configuration settings in the GPOs that apply to Tim have precedence.
- **Moving CorpSvr01 into the Support OU**   CorpSvr01 (when it is moved into the Support OU) is subject to the GPOs for the Toronto site, na.imaginedlands.com, the Sales OU, and the Support OU. By default, the policy settings for the Support OU have precedence.

> **Tip** In this section I've focused on policy processing across sites and domains. While policy is processed in this way within a single forest, policy processing does not work this way across forests. To learn how policy is processed across forests, see "Policy Processing Across Forests" in Chapter 8 "Maintaining and Restoring Group Policy."

Managing Local Group Policies

As discussed in the section "GPO Types" in Chapter 2, "Deploying Group Policy," Windows Vista, Windows Server 2008, and later versions of Windows allow the use of multiple Local Group Policy objects (LGPOs) on a single computer (as long as the computer is not a domain controller). Previously, computers had only one LGPO.

When computers are being used in a stand-alone configuration rather than a domain configuration, you may find that multiple LGPOs are useful because you no longer have to explicitly disable or remove settings that interfere with your ability to manage a computer before performing administrator tasks. Instead, you can implement one LGPO for administrators and another LGPO for nonadministrators.

When computers are being used in a domain configuration, however, you might not want to use multiple LGPOs. In domains, most computers and users already have multiple GPOs applied to them. Adding multiple LGPOs to this already varied mix can make managing Group Policy confusing. For this reason, you might want to disable processing of LGPOs. As discussed in "GPO Types" in Chapter 2, you can use the Turn Off Local Group Policy Objects Processing setting under Computer Configuration\Policies\Administrative Templates\System\Group Policy to disable or enable processing of LGPOs.

To work with LGPOs, you must use an administrator account. In a domain, you can use an account that is a member of the Enterprise Admins, Domain Admins, or the Administrators domain local group. In a workgroup, you must use an account that is a member of the local Administrators group.

Working with Top-Level LGPOs

With the exception of domain controllers, all computers running Windows have an editable LGPO. The quickest way to access the LGPO on a local computer is to enter the following command at a command prompt:

```
gpedit.msc /gpcomputer: "%ComputerName%"
```

This command starts the Group Policy Management Editor in a Microsoft Management Console (MMC) with its target set to the local computer. Here, %ComputerName% is an environment variable that sets the name of the local computer and must be enclosed in double quotation marks as shown. To access the top-level LGPO on a remote computer, enter the following command at a command prompt:

```
gpedit.msc /gpcomputer: "RemoteComputer"
```

where *RemoteComputer* is the host name or fully qualified domain name (FQDN) of the remote computer. Again, the double quotation marks are required, as shown in the following example:

```
gpedit.msc /gpcomputer: "corpsvr24"
```

You can also manage the top-level LGPO on a computer by following these steps:

1. Click Start, type **mmc** into the Search box, and then press Enter.
2. In the Microsoft Management Console, click File and then click Add/Remove Snap-In.
3. In the Add Or Remove Snap-Ins dialog box, click Group Policy Object Editor and then click Add.
4. In the Select Group Policy Object dialog box, click Finish (because the local computer is the default object). Click OK.

You can now manage the local Group Policy settings using the options provided. Because local policy does not have policy preferences, you will not find separate Policies and Preferences nodes under Computer Configuration and User Configuration. (See Figure 3-3.)

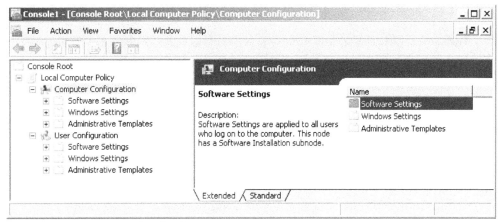

FIGURE 3-3 Manage local policy settings.

> **Tip**   You can use the same MMC to manage more than one LGPO. In the Add Or Remove Snap-Ins dialog box, you simply add one instance of the Local Group Policy Object Editor for each object you want to work with.

Because LGPOs have only policy settings, you cannot manage policy preferences using LGPOs. The policy settings you can manage locally depend on whether the computer is a member of a domain or a workgroup, and they include the following:

- Account policies for passwords, account lockout, and Kerberos
- Local policies for auditing, user rights assignment, and security options
- Event logging options for configuring log size, access, and retention options for the Application, System, and Security logs
- Security restriction settings for groups, system services, registry keys, and the file system
- Security settings for wireless networking, public keys, and Internet Protocol Security (IPSec)
- Software restrictions that specify applications that aren't allowed to run on the computer

Default LGPOs are stored in the %SystemRoot%\System32\GroupPolicy folder on each Windows Vista, Windows Server 2008 or later computer. In this folder you'll find the following subfolders:

- **Machine** Stores computer scripts in the Script folder and registry-based policy information for HKEY_LOCAL_MACHINE (HKLM) in the Registry.pol file.
- **User** Stores user scripts in the Script folder and registry-based policy information for HKEY_CURRENT_USER (HKCU) in the Registry.pol file.

You shouldn't edit these folders and files directly. Instead, you should use the appropriate features of one of the Group Policy management tools. Using the Group Policy Object Editor, you can configure local Group Policy in the same way that you configure Active Directory–based group policy. To apply a policy, you enable it and then configure any additional or optional values as necessary. An enabled policy setting is turned on and active. If don't want a policy to apply, you must disable it. A disabled policy setting is turned off and inactive. The enforcement or blocking of inheritance can change this behavior, as detailed in "Managing Group Policy Inheritance" in Chapter 7.

> ***Tip*** By default, policy files and folders are hidden. If you want to view hidden files and folders in Windows Explorer, select Folder Options from the Tools menu, click the View tab, choose Show Hidden Files And Folders, clear Hide Protected Operating System Files (Recommended), click Yes in the Warning dialog box, and then click OK.

Working with Other LGPOs

By default, the only local policy object that exists on a computer is the Local Group Policy object. You can create and manage other local objects as necessary. You can create or access the Administrator Local Group Policy object or the Non-Administrator Local Policy Group object by following these steps:

1. Click Start, type mmc in the Search box, and then press Enter. In the Microsoft Management Console, click File and then click Add/Remove Snap-In.

2. In the Add Or Remove Snap-Ins dialog box, click Group Policy Object Editor, and then click Add.

3. In the Select Group Policy Object dialog box, click Browse. In the Browse For A Group Policy Object dialog box, click the Users tab.

4. On the Users tab, shown in Figure 3-4, the entries in the Group Policy Exists column specify whether a particular local policy object has been created. Do one of the following:

-   Select Administrators to create or access the Administrator Local Group Policy object.
-   Select Non-Administrators to create or access the Non-Administrator Local Group Policy object.
-   Select the local user whose User-Specific Local Group Policy object you want to create or access.

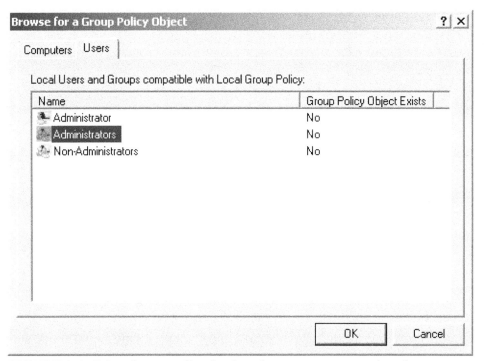

FIGURE 3-4 Select the type of local policy object to create or work with.

5. Click OK. If the selected object doesn't already exist, it will be created. Otherwise, you'll open the existing object for review and editing.

Policy settings for administrators, nonadministrators, and users are stored in the %SystemRoot%\System32\GroupPolicyUsers folder on each Windows Vista, Windows Server 2008 or later computer. Because these LGPOs only apply to user configuration settings, user-specific policy settings under %SystemRoot%\System32\GroupPolicyUsers have only a User subfolder, and this subfolder stores user scripts in the Script folder and registry-based policy information for HKEY_CURRENT_USER (HKCU) in the Registry.pol file.

Managing Active Directory–Based Group Policy

Active Directory–based Group Policy is available when Active Directory Domain Services (AD DS) is installed. Each site, domain, and organizational unit can have one or more group policies. Group policies listed higher in the Group Policy list have greater precedence than policies listed lower in the list. This ensures that policies are applied appropriately throughout the related sites, domains, and organizational units.

Working with GPOs in Sites, Domains, and OUs

When you want to work with Active Directory–based Group Policy, you'll find that each domain in your organization has two default GPOs: Default Domain Controllers Policy GPO and Default Domain Policy GPO. The default GPOs are essential to the proper operation and processing of Group Policy. By default, the Default Domain Controllers Policy GPO has the highest precedence among GPOs linked to the Domain Controllers organizational unit, and the Default Domain Policy GPO has the highest precedence among GPOs linked to the domain.

Site, domain, and organizational unit group policies are stored in the %SystemRoot%\Sysvol\Domain\Policies folder on domain controllers. In this folder you'll find one subfolder for each policy you've defined on the domain controller. The policy folder name is the policy's globally unique identifier

(GUID). You can find the policy's GUID on the policy's Properties page on the General tab in the Summary frame. Within these individual policy folders, the subfolders you'll find include:

- **Machine**   Stores computer scripts in the Script folder and registry-based policy information for HKEY_LOCAL_MACHINE (HKLM) in the Registry.pol file.
- **User**   Stores user scripts in the Script folder and registry-based policy information for HKEY_CURRENT_USER (HKCU) in the Registry.pol file.

As with files for local policies, do not edit these folders and files directly. Instead, use the appropriate features of one of the Group Policy management tools. The best way to manage Active Directory–based Group Policy is with the Group Policy Management Console. You can use the GPMC to manage policy settings in accordance with your administrative privileges. The account you use must be a member of the Enterprise Admins or Domain Admins group or have been delegated permissions to work with specific aspects of Group Policy.

Members of Enterprise Admins can manage policy settings for the specific forest of which they are a member. For example, if the user account WilliamS is a member of the Enterprise Admins group in the imaginedlands.com forest, WilliamS can manage the policy settings for any child domain in the imaginedlands.com domain as well as the parent domain (imaginedlands.com). This means he can manage the policy settings for tech.imaginedlands.com, cs.imaginedlands.com, and imaginedlands.com.

Members of Domain Admins can manage policy settings for the specific domain of which they are a member. For example, if the user account WilliamS is a member of the Domain Admins group in the tech.imaginedlands.com domain, WilliamS can manage the policy settings for the tech.imaginedlands.com domain, but he cannot manage policy settings for cs.imaginedlands.com or imaginedlands.com. He can manage the policy settings for other domains only if he has Domain Admins privileges in those domains (or Enterprise Admins privileges for the forest).

When you work with delegated administrative permissions, keep in mind that the account has only the specific permissions that were delegated. Delegated permissions for Group Policy include:

- Permission to manage Group Policy links
- Permission to generate RSoP for the purposes of logging
- Permission to generate RSoP for planning purposes

These delegated permissions are separate from AGPM roles, which I'll discuss in "Delegating Change Control Privileges" in Chapter 4. AGPM roles delegate privileges within the change control framework.

You manage Active Directory–based Group Policy by using the Group Policy Management Console. Once you install the GPMC, you can run it from the Administrative Tools menu. Click Start, click All Programs, Administrative Tools, and then click Group Policy Management Console.

As shown in Figure 3-5, the left pane of the GPMC has two top-level nodes by default: Group Policy Management (the console root) and Forest (a node representing the forest to which you are currently connected, which is named after the forest root domain for that forest). When you expand the Forest node, you see the following nodes:

- **Domains**   Provides access to the policy settings for domains in the forest being administered. You are connected to your logon domain by default; you can add connections to other domains. If you expand a domain, you can access the Default Domain Policy GPO, the Domain Controllers OU (and the related Default Domain Controllers Policy GPO), and GPOs defined in the domain.
- **Sites**   Provides access to the policy settings for sites in the related forest. Sites are hidden by default.
- **Group Policy Modeling**   Provides access to the Group Policy Modeling Wizard, which helps you plan policy deployment and simulate settings for testing purposes. Any saved policy models are also available.

- **Group Policy Results** Provides access to the Group Policy Results Wizard. For each domain to which you are connected, all the related GPOs and OUs are available to work with in one location.

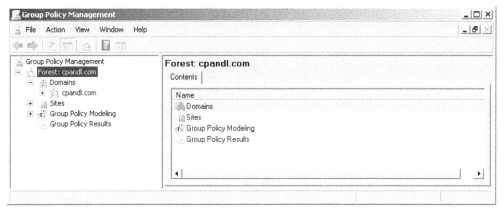

FIGURE 3-5 Access GPOs for domains, sites, and OUs.

GPOs found in domain, site, and OU containers in the GPMC are actually GPO links and not the GPOs themselves. The actual GPOs are found in the Group Policy Objects container of the selected domain. It is also helpful to note that the icons for GPO links have a small arrow at the bottom left, similar to shortcut icons.

Accessing Additional Forests

The GPMC is designed to work with multiple forests, domains, and sites. When you start the GPMC for the first time, you are connected to your logon domain and forest. You can connect to additional forests by taking the following steps:

1. Open the GPMC by clicking Start, All Programs, Administrative Tools, and then Group Policy Management Console. Or enter **gpmc.msc** at a command prompt.

2. Right-click the Group Policy Management node in the console tree, and then select Add Forest.

3. In the Add Forest dialog box, enter the name of a domain in the forest to which you want to connect, and then click OK.

As long as there is an external trust to the domain, you can establish the connection and obtain forest information—even if you don't have a forest trust with the entire forest. From now on, when you start the Group Policy Management Console, the additional forest should be listed.

Showing Sites in Connected Forests

The GPMC doesn't show available sites by default. If you want to work with the sites in a particular forest, follow these steps:

1. Open the GPMC by clicking Start, All Programs, Administrative Tools, and then Group Policy Management Console. Or enter **gpmc.msc** at a command prompt.

2. Expand the entry for the forest you want to work with by clicking the related node. Right-click the related Sites node, and then click Show Sites.

3. In the Show Sites dialog box, shown in Figure 3-6, select the check boxes for the sites you want to work with and clear the check boxes for the sites you don't want to work with. Click OK.

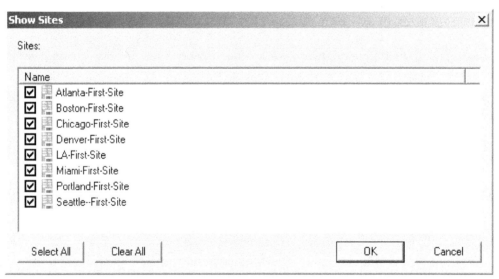

FIGURE 3-6   Select the sites to display in the GPMC.

From now on, when you start the GPMC, the additional site or sites should be listed under the Sites node, as shown in Figure 3-7.

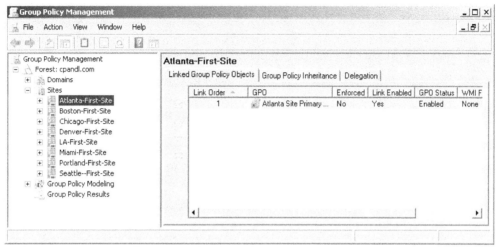

FIGURE 3-7 Access the sites in the GPMC.

Accessing Additional Domains

In the GPMC, you can view the domains to which you are connected on a per-forest basis. You are connected to your logon domain and forest by default. To work with other domains in a particular forest, follow these steps:

1. Open the GPMC by clicking Start, All Programs, Administrative Tools, and then Group Policy Management Console. Or enter **gpmc.msc** at a command prompt.

2. Expand the entry for the forest you want to work with, and then expand the related Domains node by double-clicking the node.

3. If the domain you want to work with isn't listed, right-click the Domains node in the designated forest, and then click Show Domains.

4. In the Show Domains dialog box, select the check boxes for the domains you want to work with and clear the check boxes for the domains you don't want to work with. Click OK.

From now on, when you start the GPMC, the additional domain or domains should be listed under the Domains node in the currently selected forest.

Setting Domain Controller Focus Options

When you start the GPMC, the console connects to Active Directory running on the domain controller that is acting as the PDC emulator for your logon domain and obtains a list of all GPOs and OUs in that domain. It does this by using LDAP to access the directory store and the Server Message Block (SMB) protocol to access the SYSVOL. If the PDC emulator isn't available for some reason, such as when the server is down or otherwise offline, the GPMC displays a prompt that lets you choose to work with policy settings on the domain controller to which you are currently connected or on any available domain controller. If you want to force the GPMC to work with a domain controller other than the PDC, you can configure this manually as well. This process is referred to as setting the *domain controller focus*.

You can choose the domain controller to work with on a per-domain basis:

1. Open the GPMC by clicking Start, All Programs, Administrative Tools, and then Group Policy Management Console. Or enter **gpmc.msc** at a command prompt.

2. Expand the entry for the forest you want to work with, and then expand the related Domains node by double-clicking the related node.

3. Right-click the domain for which you want to set the domain controller focus, and then click Change Domain Controller to open the Change Domain Controller dialog box, shown in Figure 3-8.

4. The domain controller to which you are currently connected is listed under Current Domain Controller. Use the following Change To options to set the domain controller focus, and then click OK.

   ▪ **The Domain Controller With The Operations Master Token For The PDC Emulator**   Choose this option if you aren't connected to the PDC emulator for some reason and want to try to establish a connection to this server at this time. For example, if the PDC emulator was offline for maintenance and is now online, you might want to try to reconnect to it.

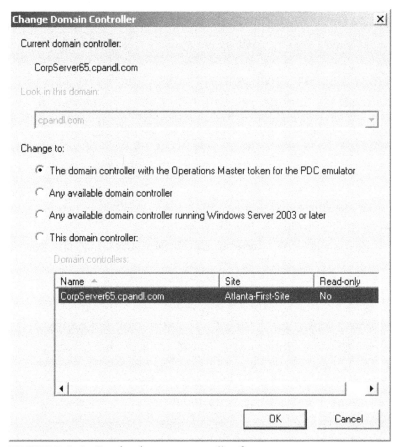

FIGURE 3-8 Set the domain controller focus.

- **Any Available Domain Controller** Choose this option to connect to any available domain controller. Use this option if you don't need to work with a domain controller running a specific version of the Windows server operating system.
- **Any Available Domain Controller Running Windows Server 2003 Or Later** Choose this option if you need to work with a domain controller that is running Windows Server 2003 or later.
- **This Domain Controller** Choose this option and then make a selection in the Domain Controllers area if you want to work with a specific domain controller. The site where each domain controller resides is listed as well, so you can work with a domain controller in a particular site if necessary.

Delegating Privileges for Group Policy Management

In Active Directory, administrators are automatically granted permissions for performing different Group Policy management tasks. Other individuals can be granted such permissions through delegation. In Active Directory, you delegate Group Policy management permissions for very specific reasons. You delegate permissions to allow a user who is not a member of Enterprise Admins or Domain Admins to perform any or all of the following tasks:

- View settings, change settings, delete a GPO, and modify security
- Manage links to existing GPOs or generate RSoP
- Create GPOs (and therefore also be able to manage any GPOs she has created)

Any privileges you delegate in this way are outside the change controls provided by AGPM and discussed in "Using Change Control" in Chapter 4. If you plan to use AGPM change controls, you'll want to limit and carefully monitor privileges delegated for Group Policy management.

Determining and Assigning GPO Creation Rights

In Active Directory, administrators have the ability to create GPOs in domains, and anyone who has created a GPO in a domain has the right to manage that GPO. To determine who can create GPOs in a domain, follow these steps:

1. In the GPMC, expand the entry for the forest you want to work with and then expand the related Domains node.

2. Expand the node for the domain you want to work with. If you don't see the domain you want to work with, right-click Domains and then click Show Domains. You can then select the domains you want to display.

3. Select the Group Policy Objects node. As shown in Figure 3-9, the users and groups who can create GPOs in the selected domain are listed on the Delegation tab.

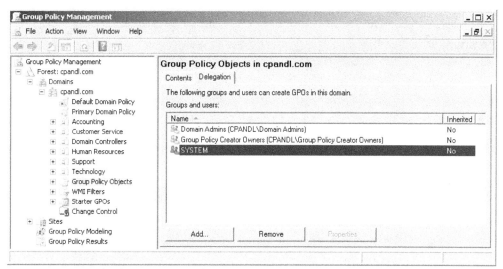

FIGURE 3-9 Check permissions for GPO creation.

You can allow a nonadministrative user or a group (including users and groups from other domains) to create GPOs (and thus implicitly grant them the ability to manage the GPOs they've created). To grant GPO creation permission to a user or group, follow these steps:

1. In the GPMC, expand the entry for the forest you want to work with and then expand the related Domains node.

2. Expand the node for the domain you want to work with. If you don't see the domain you want to work with, right-click Domains and then click Show Domains. You can then select the domains you want to display.

3. Select the Group Policy Objects node. In the right pane, select the Delegation tab. The current GPO creation permissions for individual users and groups are listed. To grant the GPO creation permission to another user or group, click Add.

4. In the Select User, Computer, Or Group dialog box, select the user or group you want to grant permissions to and then click OK.

The list of users and groups on the Delegation tab are updated as appropriate. If you want to remove the GPO creation permission in the future, access the Delegation tab, click the user or group, and then click Remove.

Determining Group Policy Management Privileges

The GPMC provides several ways to determine who has access permissions for Group Policy management. To determine Group Policy permissions for a specific site, domain, or OU, follow these steps:

1. In the GPMC, expand the entry for the forest you want to work with, and then expand the related Domains or Sites node as appropriate.

2. When you select the domain, site, or OU you want to work with, the right pane is updated with several tabs. Select the Delegation tab, as shown in Figure 3-10.

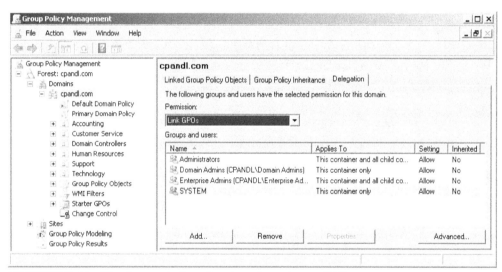

FIGURE 3-10 Check permissions for sites, domains, or OUs.

3. In the Permission list, select the permission you want to check. The options are:

   ▪ **Link GPOs** The user or group can create and manage links to GPOs in the selected site, domain, or OU.

   ▪ **Perform Group Policy Modeling Analyses** The user or group can determine the RSoP for the purposes of planning.

- **Read Group Policy Results Data** The user or group can determine the RSoP that is currently being applied for the purposes of verification or logging.

The individual users or groups with the selected permissions are listed under Groups And Users.

To determine which users or groups have access to a particular GPO and what permissions have been granted to them, follow these steps:

1. In the GPMC, expand the entry for the forest you want to work with and then expand the related Domains node.

2. Expand the node for the domain you want to work with. If you don't see the domain you want to work with, right-click Domains and then click Show Domains. You can then select the domains you want to display.

3. Expand the Group Policy Objects node. When you select the GPO whose permissions you want to check, the right pane is updated with several tabs. Select the Delegation tab, as shown in Figure 3-11.

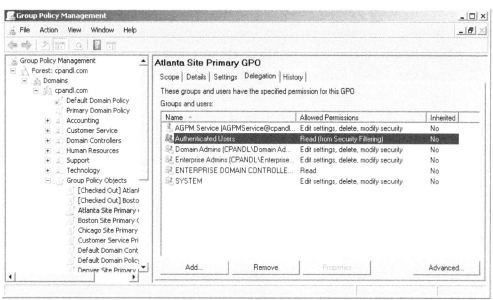

FIGURE 3-11 Check permissions for specific GPOs.

The permissions for individual users and groups are listed. You'll see three general types of allowed permissions:

- **Read** The user or group can view the GPO and its settings.
- **Edit Settings** The user or group can view the GPO and its settings and can also change settings. The user or group cannot delete the GPO or modify security.
- **Edit Settings, Delete, Modify Security** The user or group can view the GPO and its settings and can also change settings, delete the GPO, and modify security.

When you select a group on the Delegation tab, you can click the Properties button to display a Properties dialog box and get more information about the group. The tabs in the Properties dialog box provide the following information:

- **General** Shows the group name, description, and e-mail address (if applicable). Also shows the group type and scope.
- **Members** Shows the users and groups that are members of the selected group. Allows you to add and remove group members (providing you have appropriate permissions in the domain).
- **Member Of** Shows the groups that the selected group is a member of. Allows you to add and remove group memberships (providing you have appropriate permissions in the domain).
- **Managed By** Shows information about a user who has been designated as the manager of the selected group. Clicking Change allows you to designate or change the manager assignment. If a manager is assigned, you can click Properties to view the properties of the manager's account or click Clear to remove the manager.

Delegating Control for Working with GPOs

You can allow a nonadministrative user or a group (including users and groups from other domains) to work with a domain, site, or OU GPO by granting one of three specific permissions:

- **Read**   Allows the user or group to view the GPO and its settings.
- **Edit Settings**   Allows the user or group to view the GPO and its settings and also change settings. The user or group cannot delete the GPO or modify security.
- **Edit Settings, Delete, Modify Security**   Allows the user or group to view the GPO and its settings and also change settings, delete the GPO, and modify security.

To grant these permissions to a user or group, follow these steps:

1. In the GPMC, expand the entry for the forest you want to work with and then expand the related Domains node.

2. Expand the node for the domain you want to work with. If you don't see the domain you want to work with, right-click Domains and then click Show Domains. You can then select the domains you want to display.

3. Select the Group Policy Objects node, and then select the GPO you want to work with in the left pane. In the right pane, select the Delegation tab.

4. The current permissions for individual users and groups are listed. To grant permissions to another user or group, click Add.

5. In the Select User, Computer, Or Group dialog box, select the user or group and then click OK.

6. In the Add Group Or User dialog box, shown in Figure 3-12, select the permission to grant: Read; Edit Settings; or Edit Settings, Delete, Modify Security. Click OK.

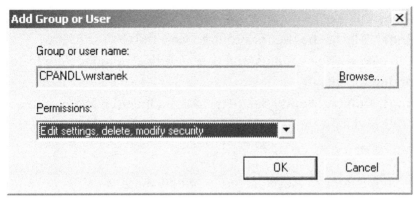

FIGURE 3-12 Grant permission to the user or group.

The list of users and groups on the Delegation tab is updated to reflect the permissions granted. If you want to remove this permission in the future, display the Delegation tab, click the user or group, and then click Remove.

> **Note** The best way to delegate authority is to use the Add and Remove options on the Delegation tab. That said, you can click the Advanced button to view and manage advanced security settings directly. Clicking the Advanced button displays the Security Settings dialog box for the GPO. In this dialog box, you can select users or groups that currently have permissions to view or change their advanced security permissions. You also can add or remove users and groups.

Delegating Authority for Managing Links and RSoP

You can allow a nonadministrative user or a group (including users and groups from other domains) to manage GPO links and RSoP. The related permissions can be granted in any combination and are defined as follows:

- **Link GPOs**   Allows the user or group to create and manage links to GPOs in the selected site, domain, or OU.
- **Perform Group Policy Modeling Analyses**   Allows the user or group to determine RSoP for the purposes of planning.

- **Read Group Policy Results Data**   Allows the user or group to determine the RSoP that is currently being applied for the purposes of verification or logging.

To grant these permissions to a user or group, follow these steps:

1. In GPMC, expand the entry for the forest you want to work with, and then expand the related Domains or Sites node as appropriate.

2. In the left pane, select the domain, site, or OU you want to work with. In the right pane, select the Delegation tab.

3. In the Permission list, select the permission you want to grant (see Figure 3-13). The options are Link GPOs, Perform Group Policy Modeling Analyses, and Read Group Policy Results Data.

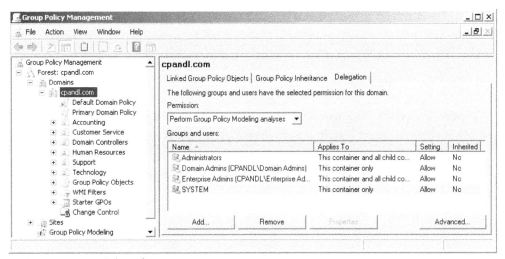

FIGURE 3-13 Select the permission to view or grant.

4. The current permissions for individual users and groups are listed. To grant the selected permission to another user or group, click Add.

5. In the Select User, Computer, Or Group dialog box, select the user or group and then click OK.

6. In the Add Group Or User dialog box, shown in Figure 3-14, specify how the permission should be applied. To apply the permission to the current container and all child containers, select This Container And All

Child Containers. To apply the permission only to the current container, select This Container Only. Click OK.

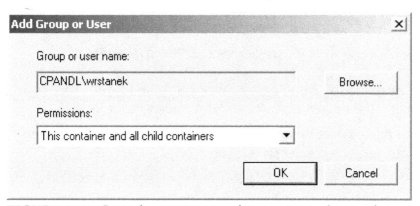

FIGURE 3-14 Grant the permission to this container only or to the container and its child containers.

The list of users and groups on the Delegation tab are updated to reflect the permissions granted. If you want to remove this permission in the future, display the Delegation tab, click the user or group, and then click Remove.

> **Note** As when you are working with the Delegation tab for individual GPOs, you have Properties and Advanced options. Clicking Properties allows you to view and manage the properties of a selected group. Clicking Advanced allows you to view and manage advanced security settings for the domain.

Managing Your GPOs in Production

When you've deployed AGPM in a domain, your GPOs are either controlled or uncontrolled. With controlled GPOs, you have offline copies of GPOs as well as live GPOs in production, and you also have additional management options, as discussed in "Managing Controlled GPOs" in Chapter 4.

Regardless of whether you've deployed AGPM, there are certain tasks that you'll use to manage your GPOs in the live production environment. These tasks include:

- Using starter GPOs
- Creating and linking GPOs
- Determining where GPOs are linked
- Enabling, disabling, and removing GPOs
- Enabling, disabling, and removing GPO links

This section discusses these tasks as they relate to production GPOs.

Using Starter GPOs

When you create a GPO in the Group Policy Management Console, you can base the new GPO on a starter GPO (except when working with the Change Control node). This allows you to use a starter GPO to define baseline settings for the new GPO. However, starter GPOs only store policy settings within the administrative templates. They do not store other types of policy settings, and they do not store any policy preferences.

Real World   In the enterprise, you can create different categories of starter GPOs, basing them on the users and computers they will be used with or on required security configurations. Although starter GPOs are limited to settings in administrative templates, you can modify the settings you've defined at any time. In contrast, AGPM provides GPO templates. A template is a predefined GPO that you use to create a baseline for new GPOs. Unlike starter GPOs, GPO templates store both policy preferences and policy settings. While this makes GPO templates more versatile than starter GPOs, you cannot edit a GPO template after you create it. For more information, see "Creating GPO Templates" in Chapter 4.

Starter GPOs are stored in a separate folder in the SYSVOL. Because this folder is not created by default, you must create the folder if you want to use starter GPOs. Because each domain has a separate starter GPO folder, you must create the starter folder in each domain where you will use starter GPOs.

To create the starter GPO folder in a domain, follow these steps:

1. In the GPMC, expand the entry for the forest you want to work with and then expand the related Domains node.

2. Expand the node for the domain you want to work with. If you don't see the domain you want to work with, right-click Domains and then click Show Domains. You can then select the domains you want to display.

3. Select the Starter GPOs node. If the starter GPO folder has not been created, the details pane will state this, as shown in Figure 3-15.

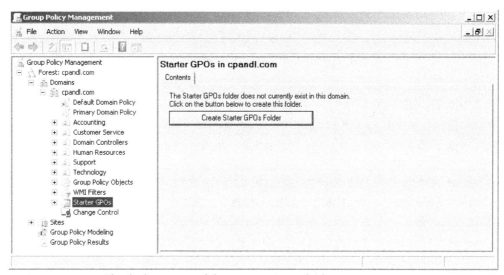

FIGURE 3-15 Check the status of the starter GPO folder.

4. If the starter folder hasn't been created yet, click Create Starter GPOs Folder.

To create a starter GPO, follow these steps:

1. In the GPMC, right-click the Starter GPOs node, and then select New.

2. In the New Starter GPO dialog box, shown in Figure 3-16, enter a descriptive name for the new starter GPO, such as Standard User GPO. If desired, enter comments describing the GPO's purpose. Click OK.

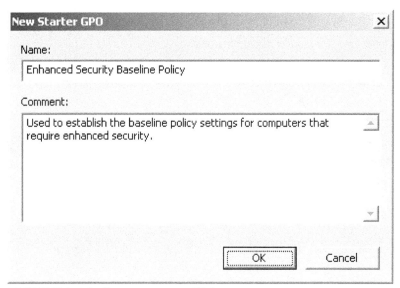

FIGURE 3-16 Create a starter GPO.

You can work with starter GPOs in much the same way that you work with standard GPOs. You can:

- **Edit starter GPOs** With the Starter GPOs node selected, right-click the starter GPO, and then choose Edit. In the Group Policy Management Editor, configure policy settings as necessary, and then close the Group Policy Management Editor.
- **Create a new GPO from a starter GPO** While you are working with the Starter GPOs node, you can create a new GPO from a starter GPO by right-clicking the starter GPO and selecting New GPO From Starter GPO.
- **Delete starter GPOs** With the Starter GPOs node selected, right-click the starter GPO, and then choose Delete. When prompted to confirm, click OK.
- **Rename starter GPOs** With the Starter GPOs node selected, right-click the starter GPO, and then choose Rename. Type the new name for the starter GPO and then press Tab or Enter.

To move starter GPOs between Active Directory domains or forests, you can store a starter GPO in a cabinet (.CAB) file. A CAB file stores all the information related to a starter GPO, including the preferences and settings you've configured for both users and computers.

To store a starter GPO in a cabinet file, complete the following steps:

1. In the GPMC, select the Starter GPOs node.
2. With the Contents tab selected in the details pane, you should see a list of available starter GPOs.
3. Select the starter GPOs that you want to place in a CAB file.
4. Click Save As Cabinet. Use the Save Starter GPO As Cabinet dialog box to select the save location and file name for the cabinet file. To more easily browse for a save location, click the Browse Folders button.
5. Click Save.

To load a starter GPO from a cabinet file, complete the following steps:

1. In the GPMC, select the Starter GPOs node.
2. With the Contents tab selected in the details pane, you should see a list of available starter GPOs.
3. Click Load Cabinet. In the Load Starter GPO dialog box, click Browse For CAB.
4. Select the location where you saved the cabinet file.
5. Select the cabinet file to load, and then click Open.
6. In the Load Starter GPO dialog box, use the details provided to confirm that you've selected the right starter GPO. Click OK to load the starter GPO.
7. If there's an existing starter GPO in the domain with the same name, you'll see a warning that you are about to overwrite the settings of that starter GPO. If you want to continue and overwrite the settings, click OK. Otherwise, click Cancel.

Creating and Linking GPOs

When you create and link a GPO to a site, domain, or OU, the GPO is applied to the user and computer objects in that site, domain, or OU according to the Active Directory options governing inheritance, the precedence order of GPOs, and other settings.

You can create and link GPOs as separate operations or as a single operation on a selected domain, site, or OU. You can, for example, create a GPO without linking it to any domain, site, or OU. You can also create a GPO for a selected domain or OU and have the GPO linked automatically to that domain or OU. With sites, you can only create and link a GPO in separate operations.

How you create and link GPOs is a matter of preference. There is no right or wrong way. Some administrators prefer to create a GPO first and then link it to a domain, site, or OU. Other administrators prefer to create a GPO and have it linked automatically to a specific domain or OU. However, you should remember that a GPO can be linked to multiple containers (domains, sites, and OUs) and at multiple levels.

Creating and Linking GPOs for Sites

In an Active Directory forest, only Enterprise Admins and forest root Domain Admins can create and modify sites and site links. Similarly, only Enterprise Admins and forest root Domain Admins can create and manage GPOs for sites.

Sites aren't listed automatically in the GPMC. If you don't see the site you want to work with, right-click Sites and then click Show Sites. You can then select the sites you want to display.

> ***Real World***   Site-level GPOs aren't used that often, and when they are implemented, they are used primarily for managing network-specific policy settings—which is in keeping with the purpose of sites to help you better manage the physical structure of the network (your subnets). For example, you might want to use site-level GPOs to manage IP security, Internet Explorer configurations for proxies, wireless networking, or public key security on a per-subnet basis.

In the GPMC, you can create and link a new site GPO by completing the following steps:

1. In the GPMC, access the domain in which you want to create the GPO. Under the domain node, right-click the Group Policy Objects node, and then click New.

2. In the New GPO dialog box, shown in Figure 3-17, enter a descriptive name for the GPO, such as Enhanced Security Policy. If you want to use a starter GPO as the source for the initial settings, select the starter GPO to use from the Source Starter GPO drop-down list. Click OK. You'll see the new GPO listed in the Group Policy Objects container.

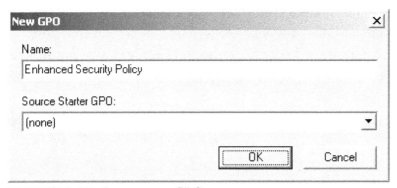

FIGURE 3-17 Create a new GPO.

3. Right-click the new GPO, and choose Edit. This opens the Group Policy Management Editor.

4. Configure the necessary policy settings, and then close the Group Policy Management Editor.

5. In the GPMC, expand the Sites node and select the site you want to work with. In the right pane, the Linked Group Policy Objects tab shows the GPOs that are currently linked to the selected site (if any).

6. Right-click the site to which you want to link the GPO, and then click Link An Existing GPO.

7. In the Select GPO dialog box, shown in Figure 3-18, use the Look In This Domain list to choose the domain where the GPO is stored.

8. In the Group Policy Objects list, select the GPO you want to link to the site, and then click OK.

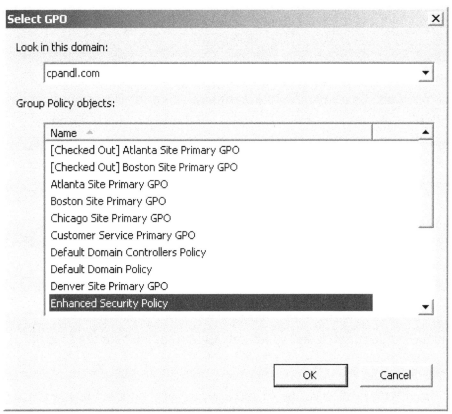

FIGURE 3-18 Select the GPO to which you want to link.

The GPO is now linked to the site. In the right pane, the Linked Group Policy Objects tab should show the linked GPO. After Group Policy is refreshed for computers and users in the site, the policy settings in the GPO will be applied. To learn how to manually refresh Group Policy, see "Refreshing Group Policy Manually" in Chapter 7.

Computer policy is refreshed during startup when the computer connects to the network. User policy is refreshed during logon when the user logs on to the network. Thus you can verify that computer policy settings have been applied as expected by restarting a workstation or server in the site and then checking the computer. To verify user policy settings, have a user who is logged on to a computer in the site log off and then log back on. You can then verify that user policy settings have been applied as expected.

Creating and Linking GPOs for Domains

In an Active Directory forest, only Enterprise Admins, Domain Admins, and those who have been delegated permissions can manage objects in domains. You must be a member of Enterprise Admins or Domain Admins or be specifically delegated permissions to be able to work with GPOs in a domain. With regard to Group Policy, delegated permissions are primarily limited to the management of Group Policy links and RSoP for the purposes of logging and planning.

Unlike site GPOs, which aren't frequently used, GPOs are used widely in domains. In the GPMC, you can create and link a new GPO for a domain in two separate operations or as a single operation.

Creating and Then Linking a GPO for a Domain

To create a GPO and then link it separately for a domain, take the following steps:

1. In the GPMC, right-click the Group Policy Objects node and then click New.

2. In the New GPO dialog box, enter a descriptive name for the GPO, such as Support Policy. If you want to use a starter GPO as the source for the initial settings, select the starter GPO to use from the Source Starter GPO drop-down list. Click OK.

3. The new GPO is now listed in the Group Policy Objects container. Right-click the GPO, and then choose Edit.

4. In the Group Policy Management Editor, configure the necessary policy settings and then close the Group Policy Management Editor.

5. In the GPMC, expand the Domains node and then select the domain you want to work with. In the right pane, the Linked Group Policy Objects tab shows the GPOs that are currently linked to the selected domain (if any).

6. Right-click the domain to which you want to link the GPO, and then select Link An Existing GPO. Use the Select GPO dialog box to select the GPO you want to link, and then click OK.

    The GPO is now linked to the domain. In the right pane, the Linked Group Policy Objects tab should show the linked GPO as well.

When Group Policy is refreshed for computers and users in the domain, the policy settings in the GPO are applied. To verify that computer policy settings have been applied as expected, restart a workstation or server in the domain and then check the computer. To verify user policy settings, have a user who is logged on to a computer in the domain log off and then log back on. You can then verify that user policy settings have been applied as expected.

Creating and Linking a Domain GPO as a Single Operation

In the GPMC, you can create and link a domain GPO as a single operation by taking the following steps:

1. In the GPMC, right-click the domain you want to work with, and then click Create And Link A GPO Here.

Tip If you don't see the domain you want to work with, right-click Domains and then click Show Domains. You can then select the available domains that you want to display.

---

2. In the New GPO dialog box, enter a descriptive name for the GPO, such as Support Policy. If you want to use a starter GPO as the source for the initial settings, select the starter GPO to use from the Source Starter GPO drop-down list. Click OK.

3. The GPO is created and linked to the domain. Right-click the GPO, and then choose Edit.

4. In the Group Policy Management Editor, configure the necessary policy settings and then close the Group Policy Management Editor.

When Group Policy is refreshed for computers and users in the domain, the policy settings in the GPO are applied. To verify that computer policy settings have been applied as expected, restart a workstation or server in the domain and then check the computer. To verify user policy settings, have a user who is logged on to a computer in the domain log off and then log back on. You can then verify that user policy settings have been applied as expected.

Creating and Linking GPOs for OUs

In an Active Directory forest, only Enterprise Admins, Domain Admins, and those who have been delegated permissions can manage objects in OUs. You must be a member of Enterprise Admins or Domain Admins or be specifically delegated permissions to be able to work with GPOs in OUs. With regard to Group Policy, delegated permissions are primarily limited to the management of Group Policy links and RSoP for the purposes of logging and planning.

Unlike site GPOs, which aren't frequently used, GPOs are used widely in OUs. The GPMC is fairly versatile when it comes to OUs. Not only can you use it to create and link a new GPO for an OU, but you can also create any necessary OUs without having to work with Active Directory Users And Computers.

Creating OUs in the GPMC

To create an OU in the GPMC, follow these steps:

1. In the GPMC, right-click the domain in which you want to create the OU, and then click New Organizational Unit.
2. In the New Organizational Unit dialog box, enter a descriptive name for the OU and then click OK.

Creating and Then Linking a GPO for an OU

To create a GPO for an OU and then link it separately, complete the following steps:

1. In the GPMC, right-click the Group Policy Objects node, and then click New.
2. In the New GPO dialog box, enter a descriptive name for the GPO, such as Support Policy. If you want to use a starter GPO as the source for

the initial settings, select the starter GPO to use from the Source Starter GPO drop-down list. Click OK.

3. The new GPO is now listed in the Group Policy Objects container. Right-click the GPO, and then choose Edit.

4. In the Group Policy Management Editor, configure the necessary policy settings and then close the Group Policy Management Editor.

5. In the GPMC, expand the Domains node and select the OU you want to work with. In the right pane, the Linked Group Policy Objects tab shows the GPOs that are currently linked to the selected OU (if any).

6. Right-click the OU to which you want to link the GPO, and then select Link An Existing GPO. Use the Select GPO dialog box to select the GPO you want to link, and then click OK.

7. The GPO is now linked to the OU. In the right pane, the Linked Group Policy Objects tab should show the linked GPO as well.

When Group Policy is refreshed for computers and users in the OU, the policy settings in the GPO are applied. To verify that computer policy settings have been applied as expected, restart a workstation or server in the OU and then check the computer. To verify user policy settings, have a user who is logged on to a computer in the OU log off and then log back on. You can then verify that user policy settings have been applied as expected.

Creating and Linking an OU GPO as a Single Operation

In the GPMC, you can create and link an OU GPO as a single operation by taking the following steps:

1. In GPMC, right-click the OU you want to work with, and then click Create And Link A GPO Here.

2. In the New GPO dialog box, enter a descriptive name for the GPO, such as Support Policy. If you want to use a starter GPO as the source for the initial settings, select the starter GPO to use from the Source Starter GPO drop-down list. Click OK.

3. The GPO is created and linked to the OU. Right-click the GPO, and then choose Edit.

4. In the Group Policy Management Editor, configure the necessary policy settings and then close the Group Policy Management Editor.

When Group Policy is refreshed for computers and users in the OU, the policy settings in the GPO are applied. To verify that computer policy settings have been applied as expected, restart a workstation or server in the OU and then check the computer. To verify user policy settings, have a user who is logged on to a computer in the OU log off and then log back on. You can then verify that user policy settings have been applied as expected.

Determining Where a GPO Is Linked

You can link a GPO to multiple sites, domains, and OUs. Linking a GPO ensures that the objects under the scope of a site, domain, or OU are affected by the policy preferences and settings in the GPO (according to the Active Directory options governing inheritance, the precedence order of GPOs, etc).

Because a link establishes a relationship between the GPO and the container to which it is linked, one way to view GPO links is to view the Active Directory node to which a GPO is linked. As discussed in "Enabling and Disabling GPO Links" later in the chapter, GPO links can be either active or inactive. When you access the container to which a GPO is linked, a GPO with an active link is displayed with an icon showing a black arrow, while a GPO with an inactive link is displayed with a dimmed icon.

To see which GPOs are linked to a particular Active Directory node as well as the state of each GPO, complete the following steps:

1. In the GPMC, select the container for the site, domain, or OU with which you want to work.
2. In the details pane, select the Linked Group Policy Objects tab.
3. As shown in Figure 3-19, you'll then see a list of GPOs linked to the node you selected. The GPOs are listed in order of link precedence.

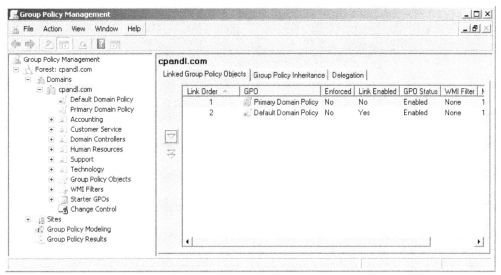

FIGURE 3-19 View the GPOs linked to a particular node.

Another way to examine GPO links is to view all the nodes to which a particular GPO is linked. This will give you an excellent idea of exactly how the GPO is being used.

To view the links per GPO, complete the following steps:

1. In the GPMC, expand the entry for the forest you want to work with, and then expand the related Domains node by double-clicking it.

2. Expand the node for the domain you want to work with. If you don't see the domain you want to work with, right-click Domains and then click Show Domains. You can then select the domains that you want to display.

3. Expand the Group Policy Objects node. Select the GPO you want to examine.

4. In the details pane, select the Scope tab.

5. Under Display Links To This Location, select [Entire Forest] to display all links to the GPO in the enterprise. You can also search all sites in the enterprise or a particular domain by choosing the related option. As shown in Figure 3-20, you'll then see a list of linked locations.

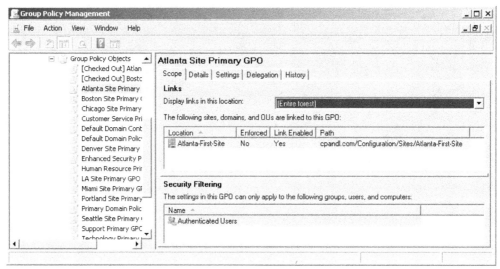

FIGURE 3-20 Determine where a GPO is linked.

Enabling and Disabling GPOs

You can enable or disable GPOs either completely or partially. Completely disabling a GPO is useful if you don't need the GPO now but might need it again in the future or if you're troubleshooting policy processing problems. Partially disabling a GPO is useful when you want the related policy settings to apply to either users or computers but not both.

By partially disabling a policy, you can ensure that only the per-computer policy settings or only the per-user policy settings are applied. In cases in which you are trying to speed up policy processing, you might also want to disable user or computer settings. However, this may result in only minimal performance gains and you should only do this when you've fully determined the impact of this change on your environment.

> **Real World**   Disabling a GPO is different from unlinking a GPO from a container. When you disable processing of a GPO, either completely or partially, the GPO still applies to users and computers according to how the GPO is linked. As a result, Group Policy clients running on computers see the GPO as one that is applicable and might need to be processed.

When you unlink a GPO from a container, the GPO no longer applies to any computers or users in that container. As a result, Group Policy clients running on computers do not see the GPO as one that is applicable and needing to be processed.

You can enable and disable GPOs partially or entirely by completing the following steps:

1. In the GPMC, expand the container for the site, domain, or OU with which you want to work by double-clicking it.

2. Select the GPO you want to work with, and then click the Details tab in the right pane, as shown in Figure 3-21.

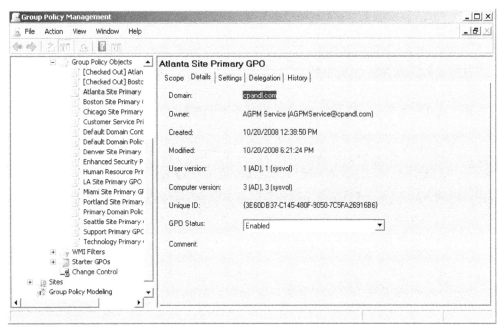

FIGURE 3-21 Specify the desired status for the GPO on the Details tab.

3. Use the GPO Status list to choose one of the following status settings:

   ▪ **Enabled**   Allows processing of the policy object and all its settings.
   ▪ **All Settings Disabled**   Disallows processing of the policy object and all its settings.

- **Computer Configuration Settings Disabled**   Disables processing of Computer Configuration settings; this means that only User Configuration settings are processed.
- **User Configuration Settings Disabled**   Disables processing of User Configuration settings; this means that only Computer Configuration settings are processed.

4. When prompted to confirm that you want to change the status of this GPO, click OK.

Enabling and Disabling GPO Links

In the GPMC, you can stop using a linked GPO in several ways. You can:

- Disable a link to a GPO
- Remove a link to a GPO
- Delete the GPO and all links to it

Disabling a link to a GPO stops the site, domain, or OU from using the related policy settings. It doesn't delete the GPO, however. The GPO remains linked to other sites, domains, or OUs as appropriate. If you disable all links to the GPO from sites, domains, and OUs, the GPO will continue to exist—it will still "live" in the Group Policy Objects container—but its policy settings will have no effect in your enterprise.

> **Tip**   When you access a domain, site, or OU node in the GPMC, the icon for a GPO with an active link is displayed with a black arrow and the icon for a GPO with an inactive link is dimmed.

To disable an active link to a GPO, right-click the GPO in the container to which it is linked and then click Link Enabled. Selecting Link Enabled toggles the option off. In the GPMC, a GPO with an inactive link remains in its previously linked position but is displayed with a dimmed icon. This means you'll see the dimmed icon when you select a container to which the GPO is linked.

To enable a disabled link to a GPO, right-click the GPO in the container to which it is linked and then select Link Enabled. Selecting Link Enabled toggles the option on. In the GPMC, a GPO with an active link is displayed with an icon showing a black arrow.

> **Real World** With respect to GPO processing by clients, disabling a link is similar to unlinking a GPO from a container. Whether you unlink a GPO from a container or disable a link, the GPO no longer applies to any computers or users in that container. As a result, Group Policy clients running on computers do not see the GPO as one that is applicable and needing to be processed.

Removing a GPO Link

A GPO link creates an association between a GPO and the site, domain, or OU to which it is linked. When you disable a link, the association remains and the GPO continues to be displayed (albeit with a dimmed icon) at the level to which it is linked. To break the association between the GPO and a site, domain, or OU, you must remove the link and not simply disable it.

To remove a GPO link, right-click the GPO in the container to which it is linked and then click Delete. When prompted to confirm that you want to delete the link, click OK.

> **Caution** The Group Policy Object container holds the actual GPO rather than linked references to a GPO. Don't select the GPO in the Group Policy Objects container and perform this procedure. If you do, you will permanently delete the GPO.

Deleting GPOs

Deleting a GPO permanently removes the GPO and all links to it. The GPO will not continue to exist in the Group Policy Objects container and will not be linked to any sites, domains, or OUs. The only way to recover a deleted GPO is to restore it from a backup (if a backup copy is available).

> **Note** If a GPO is linked to multiple domains, deleting a GPO from one domain will not delete links in other domains. Therefore, before you remove a GPO, you should determine where the GPO is linked. Note also that Microsoft does not recommend linking a GPO to multiple domains because this could cause performance issues when processing policy.

To delete a GPO, complete the following steps:

1. In the GPMC, expand the entry for the forest you want to work with, and then expand the related Domains node by double-clicking it.

2. Expand the node for the domain you want to work with. If you don't see the domain you want to work with, right-click Domains and then click Show Domains. You can then select the domains you want to display.

3. Expand the Group Policy Objects node. Right-click the GPO, and then select Delete. When prompted to confirm that you want to delete the GPO and all links to the GPO in the current domain, click Yes.

Managing Group Policy Preferences

Most policies have an enabled, disabled, or not configured state, and this makes it easy to establish policy settings. Policy preferences are very different from policy settings, however. To master policy preferences, you need to know:

- How management actions and editing states work
- How to configure the Common tab options
- How to manage preference items

In this section, I'll discuss these concepts.

Configuring Management Actions and Editing States

When you are working with policy preferences, it is very important to keep in mind which type of preference you are working with. For this reason, I've provided a summary of configuration options for preferences in Table 3-1. As the table shows, most preferences support management actions and only a few support editing states.

TABLE 3-1 Preference Configuration Options

PREFERENCE TYPE	SUPPORTS MANAGEMENT ACTIONS	SUPPORTS EDITING STATES
Data sources	Yes	No
Device	No	No
Drive maps	Yes	No
Environment	Yes	No
Files, Ini files	Yes	No
Folder options	No	Yes
Folders	Yes	No
Immediate task	No	No
Internet settings	No	Yes
Local user, local group	Yes	No
Network share	Yes	No
New file type	Yes	No
Power options	No	Yes
Power scheme	Yes	Yes
Regional options	No	Yes
Registry item	Yes	No
Scheduled task	Yes	No
Service	No	No
Shortcuts	Yes	No

Start menu	No	Yes
TCP/IP printer, local printer, shared printer	Yes	No
VPN connection, DUN connection	Yes	No

Based on the table, you can see that policy preferences can be divided into two main classes: those that support management actions, and those that present the graphical user interface from a Control Panel utility. The largest class of preferences is the one that supports the following management actions:

- Create
- Replace
- Update
- Delete

This class of preferences includes those that configure applications, data sources, drive maps, environment variables, files, folders, registry settings, shortcuts, and network shares. With this class of preferences, the action controls how the preference item is applied. With a Create, Replace, or Update action, the item can be removed when it is no longer applied, as discussed in "Removing Preference Items" later in this chapter.

The smallest class of preferences is the one that presents graphical user interfaces from Control Panel utilities. This class of preferences includes those that configure folder options, Internet settings, power options, regional and language settings, and Start menu settings. With this class of preferences, the item is applied according to the editing state of each setting in the related interface. Because the editing state applied cannot be reversed, there is no option to remove when it is no longer applied.

There are a few preferences that support neither management actions nor editing states. With devices, you use the Action list to enable or disable a particular type of device. With immediate tasks, the related preference creates a task. The task runs and is then deleted automatically. With services, you use the related preference to configure an existing service.

Both management actions and editing states are fairly easy to work with. Let's start by looking at the management actions.

Using the Create, Replace, Update, and Delete Actions

With the Create action, you can create a preference item on a user's computer. However, the preference item is created only if it does not already exist. For example, as shown in Figure 3-22, you can create a folder preference item to create a folder with a specific path with any of the following file system attributes: read-only, hidden, or archive.

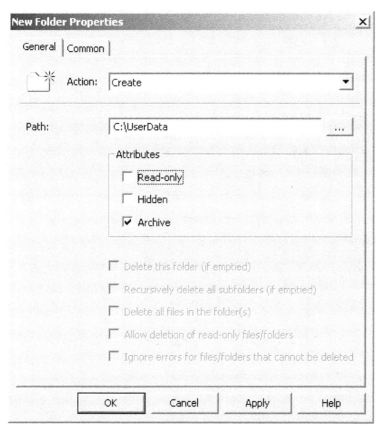

FIGURE 3-22 Create a preference item to add a folder.

You use the Replace action to delete an existing preference item and then re-create it. The Replace action creates a preference item if it doesn't already exist. Continuing the folder preference item example, you could use the Replace action to replace a folder and its contents if the folder exists. The end result of a Replace operation is to delete existing contents and to overwrite existing settings.

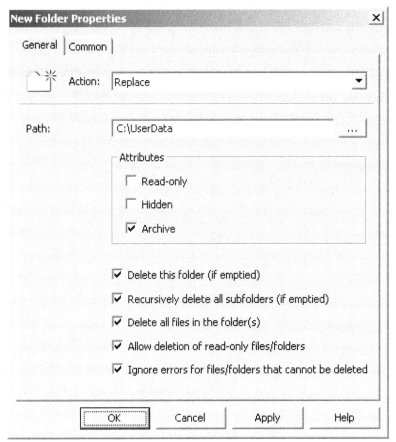

FIGURE 3-23   Create a preference item to replace a folder.

With most preferences, you have additional options that control exactly how the Replace operation works. With folders, as shown in Figure 3-23, you have the following options:

- **Delete This Folder (If Emptied)**   The folder is deleted if it is empty. This occurs only if the preference option to delete all files and recursively delete all subfolders has been processed. If this option is not selected, the Replace operation is prevented from deleting the folder.
- **Delete All Files In The Folder(s)**   This option deletes all files in the folder that are not marked hidden or system. If Recursively Delete All Subfolders is also selected, files that are allowed to be deleted within subfolders are deleted as well. If this option is not selected, the Replace operation is prevented from deleting files within folders.
- **Allow Deletion Of Read-Only Files/Folders**   When this option is selected, the Replace operation clears the read-only attribute on files and folders so that they can be deleted. When this option is not selected, the replace operation is prevented from deleting read-only files and folders.
- **Ignore Error For Files/Folders That Cannot Be Deleted**   The Replace operation ignores error messages that occur because files or folders cannot be deleted. When this option is not selected, an error is returned if the Replace operation encounters any issues deleting files or folders.
- **Recursively Delete All Subfolders (If Emptied)**   When this option is selected, all empty subfolders in the folder that are not marked hidden or system are deleted. When this option is used with the Delete All Files In The Folder option, the Replace operation deletes all files in all subfolders first and then deletes the empty subfolders. When this option is not selected, the Replace operation is prevented from deleting subfolders.

You use the Update action to modify a preference item. The Update action creates a preference item if it does not exist. This action differs from a Replace action in that it only updates settings defined within the preference item. All other settings remain the same.

In other words, updating an item does not delete any related contents. For example, with a folder preference, you can use the Update action to set or clear the read-only, hidden, and archive attributes on a folder (see Figure 3-24).

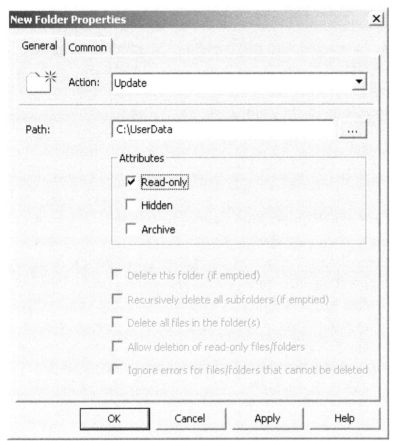

FIGURE 3-24 Create a preference item to update a folder.

With the Delete action, you can delete a preference item on a user's computer (see Figure 3-25). With most preferences, you have additional options that control exactly how the Delete operation works. Often, the additional options will be the same as those available with a Replace operation.

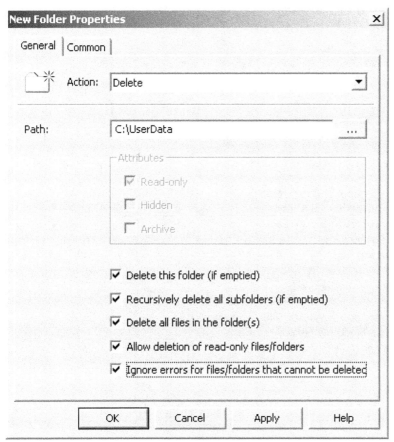

FIGURE 3-25 Create a preference item to delete a folder.

Managing Editing States

Preferences for folder options, Internet settings, power options, regional and language settings, and Start menu settings can be managed using graphical user interfaces from Control Panel utilities. Because each version of the

Windows operating system can have a slightly different interface, the related options are tied to a specific version of Windows.

By default, when you are working with this type of preference, every setting in the interface is processed by the client computer and applied, even if you don't specifically set the related value. This effectively overwrites all existing settings for this interface.

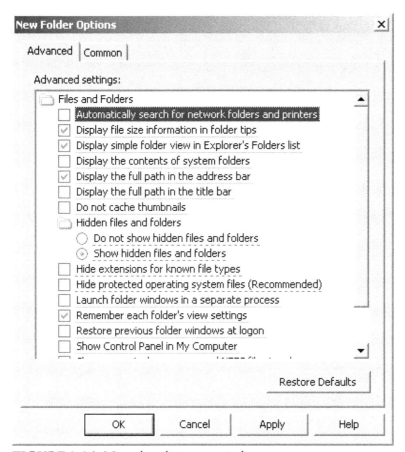

FIGURE 3-26 Note the editing state indicators.

Because of this default overwrite mode, whenever you are configuring this type of preference you need to keep in mind the editing state of interface options. As shown in Figure 3-26, the editing state of each related option is depicted graphically:

- A sold green line indicates that the setting will be delivered and processed on the client.
- A red dashed line indicates that the setting will not be delivered or processed on the client.

When limited space on the interface prevents underlining, the interface uses a green circle as the functional equivalent of a solid green line (meaning that the setting will be delivered and processed on the client) and a red circle as the functional equivalent of a red dashed line (meaning that the setting will not be delivered or processed on the client). Figure 3-27 shows these conventions.

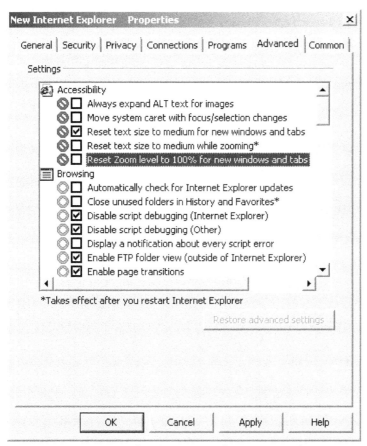

FIGURE 3-27 Note the alternative editing state indicators.

It is important to point out that the value associated with an option is separate from the editing state. Setting or clearing an option will not change the editing state.

You can use the following function keys to manage the editing state of options:

- **F5** Pressing F5 enables processing of all settings on the selected tab. This is useful if you disabled processing of some settings and later decide that you want all settings on a tab to be processed.
- **F6** Pressing F6 enables processing of the currently selected setting on the selected tab. This is useful if you disabled a setting and later decide you want the setting to be processed.
- **F7** Pressing F7 disables processing of the currently selected setting on the selected tab. This is useful to prevent one setting from being processed on the client.
- **F8** Pressing F8 disables processing of all settings on the selected tab. This is useful to prevent all settings on a tab from being processed on the client. It is also useful if you only want a few settings to be enabled.

Controlling Preference Items

Each Group Policy preference extension maintains a separate list of preference items to be processed. When you are editing a GPO, you can manage preference items separately by selecting the preference area and then working with the related preference items in the details pane. Double-click a preference item to display its Properties dialog box. You can then use the Properties dialog box to view or edit settings for the preference item.

Managing Precedence and Processing

A preference extension processes its preference items according to their precedence order. The preference item with the lowest precedence (the one listed last) is processed first, followed by the preference item with the next lowest precedence, and so on until the preference item with the highest precedence (the one listed first) is processed.

Processing occurs in this order to ensure that preference items with higher precedence have priority over preference items with lower precedence. If there is any conflict between the settings applied in preference items, the settings written last win.

In the example shown in Figure 3-28, two preference items for Internet settings have been created. Here, the preference item with the precedence order of 2 is processed first and then the preference item with the precedence order of 1 is processed.

FIGURE 3-28 Preference items have a precedence order.

To change the precedence order, select a preference area in the console tree and then click the preference item that you want to work with in the details pane. You'll then see additional options on the toolbar. These options include:

- Move The Selected Item Up
- Move The Selected Item Down

To lower the precedence of the selected item, click Move The Selected Item Down. To raise the precedence of the selected item, click Move The Selected Item Up.

While you have a preference item selected, you can also use options on the toolbar to disable or enable it for processing. To disable an item, click Disable This Item. To enable an item, click Enable This Item. Other options allow you to:

- Copy or paste the item
- Delete the item
- View properties
- Display the configured settings in an XML file in Internet Explorer
- Add a new item

You have similar options on a shortcut menu when you right-click a preference item.

By default, if processing of one preference item fails, processing of other preference items will continue. To change this behavior, you can select the Stop Processing Items In This Extension If An Error Occurs option on the Common tab. With this option selected, a preference item that fails prevents the remaining preference items within the extension from processing for a particular GPO. This setting doesn't affect processing in other GPOs.

Many preference items have the same set of options on the Common tab. As Figure 3-29 shows, other options on the Common tab include:

- Run In Logged-On User's Security Context
- Remove This Item When It Is No Longer Applied
- Apply Once And Do Not Reapply
- Item-Level Targeting

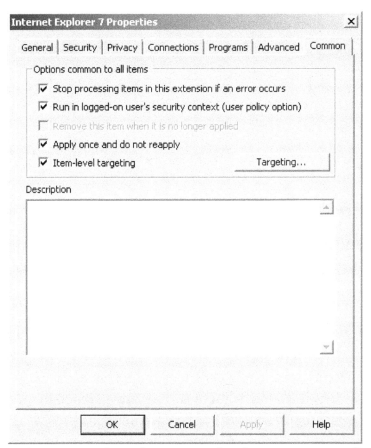

FIGURE 3-29 Control processing of preference items using Common tab options.

Setting the Security Context

By default, the Group Policy client running on a computer processes user preferences within the security context of either the Winlogon account (for early Windows computers) or the System account (for Window Vista, Windows Server 2008 or later computers). In this context, a preference extension is limited to the environment variables and system resources available to the computer.

Alternatively, the client can process user preferences in the security context of the logged on user. This allows the preference extension to access resources as the user rather than as a system service, which may be required when using drive maps or other preferences for which the computer might not have permissions to access resources or might need to work with user environment variables.

To allow the preference extension to run in the logged on user's security context, follow these steps:

1. In the GPMC, right-click the GPO you want to work with and then click Edit.
2. In the Group Policy Management Editor, select the preference area you want to work with in the console tree. In the details pane, you'll see a list of preference items configured for the selected preference area.
3. Double-click a preference item to display its Properties dialog box.
4. On the Common tab, select Run In Logged-On User's Security Context. Click OK.

Removing Preference Items

By default, when the policy settings in a GPO no longer apply to a user or computer, the policy settings are removed because they are no longer set in the Group Policy area of the registry. Default preference items are not removed automatically, however, when a GPO no longer applies to a user or computer.

To change this behavior, you may be able to set the Remove This Item When It Is No Longer Applied option for a preference item. When this option is selected, the preference extension determines whether a preference item that was in scope is now out of scope. If the preference item is out of scope, the preference extension removes the settings associated with the preference item.

If you select Remove This Item When It Is No Longer Applied, the management action is set as Replace. As a result, during Group Policy processing, the preference extension performs a Delete operation followed by a Create operation. Then, if the preference items goes out of scope (meaning it no longer applies) for the user or computer, the results of the preference item are deleted (but not created). Item-level targeting can cause a preference item to go out of scope as well. (Item-level targeting is discussed in more detail in "Using Item-Level Targeting" later in this chapter.)

Generally, preferences that support management actions can be removed when they no longer apply, but preferences that support editing states cannot be removed when they no longer apply. To remove an item when it no longer applies, follow these steps:

1. In the GPMC, right-click the GPO you want to work with and then click Edit.
2. In the Group Policy Management Editor, select the preference area you want to work with in the console tree. In the details pane, you'll see a list of preference items configured for the selected preference area.
3. Double-click a preference item to display its Properties dialog box.
4. On the Common tab, select Remove This Item When It Is No Longer Applied. Click OK.

Applying Preference Items During Refresh

Group Policy stores most policy settings in policy-related branches of the registry. The operating system and compliant applications check the policy-related branches of the registry to determine whether and how various aspects of the operating system are controlled. If a policy setting disables a portion of the user interface, the user is prevented from changing related settings.

Group Policy does not store policy preferences in the policy-related branches of the registry. Instead, it writes preferences to the same locations in the registry that an application or operating system feature uses to store the setting. As a result, users can change settings that were configured using policy preferences. However, by default the results of preference items are rewritten each time Group Policy is refreshed to ensure that preference items are applied as administrators designated.

You can change this behavior by setting the Apply Once And Do Not Reapply option for a preference item. When this option is selected, the preference extension applies the results of the preference item one time and does not reapply the results.

To configure an item so that it isn't reapplied, follow these steps:

1. In the GPMC, right-click the GPO you want to work with and then click Edit.
2. In the Group Policy Management Editor, select the preference area you want to work with in the console tree. In the details pane, you'll see a list of preference items configured for the selected preference area.
3. Double-click a preference item to display its Properties dialog box.
4. On the Common tab, select Apply Once And Do Not Reapply. Click OK.

Using Item-Level Targeting

Item-level targeting allows you to filter the application of a preference item so that the preference item applies only to selected users or computers. Unlike security group filters or Windows Management Instrumentation (WMI) filters, which can be difficult to create and manage, item-level targeting is very easy to work with.

Basically, each targeting item results in a true or false value. If the result is true, the preference item applies and is processed. If the result is false, the preference item does not apply and is not processed.

You can perform item-level targeting on just about any characteristic of a computer as well as several characteristics of users. For example, you can target a preference item so that it applies only to the following:

- Computers with a battery
- Users or computers with a name that matches certain parameters
- A computer CPU speed or RAM greater than a specified amount
- During a specified time or on a specified day of the week or month
- Computers with dial-up, remote access, or Terminal Services connections

- Computers with a certain amount of available disk space on a particular drive
- Computers or users in a particular site or domain
- If an environment variable has a specified value
- If a file or registry value exists in a specified location
- If the computer has an IP or MAC address in a specified range
- If the locale specified is installed
- If an LDAP, WMI, or MSI query returns a specified value.
- A computer with a specified operating system and service pack
- A computer with a PCMCIA slot
- A portable computer in a specified docking state
- When the Group Policy processing mode meets the specified criteria
- When a user or computer is a member of a specified security group

You can also change the value of a targeting item to its opposite by using the Is Not option rather than the default Is option. For example, with Battery Present targeting, you can use Is Not to target computers that do not have a battery.

To achieve very narrowly scoped targeting, you can apply multiple targeting items to a preference item. When you do this, you select a logical operation (AND or OR) to use to combine each targeting item with the preceding ones.

A logical AND is the default setting when you add multiple targeting items. A logical AND is the easiest to work with. For example, if you combine three targeting items with a logical AND operation, the results in the preference item are applied only when all three targeting items evaluate to true.

To configure item-level targeting, follow these steps:

1. In the GPMC, right-click the GPO you want to work with and then click Edit.

2. In the Group Policy Management Editor, select the preference area you want to work with in the console tree. In the details pane, you'll see a list of preference items configured for the selected preference area.

3. Double-click a preference item to display its Properties dialog box.

4. On the Common tab, select Item-Level Targeting, and then click Targeting. This opens the Targeting Editor.

5. In the Targeting Editor, shown in Figure 3-30, click New Item, and then select the targeting item, such as Battery Present. Repeat this process to add other targeting items.

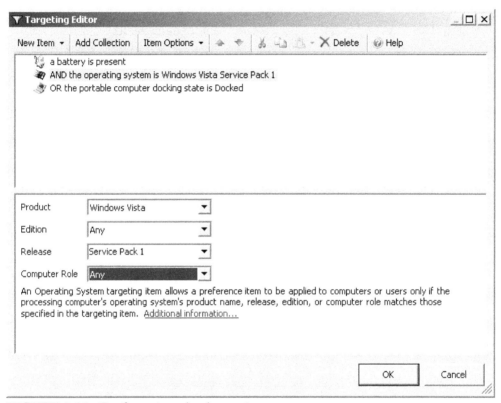

FIGURE 3-30 Configure item-level targeting.

6. To change the value of a targeting item to its opposite, click the targeting item and then select Is Not on the Item Options menu. For example, with Battery Present targeting, you can use Is Not to target a computer without a battery.

7. To connect a targeting item with a logical OR rather than a logical AND, click the targeting item and then select Or on the Item Options menu. For example, you could use OR to ensure the item is processed

when the computer is running Windows Vista or the computer is a docked laptop.

8. Text fields accept variables and wildcards. Press F3 to display a list of variables. Click the variable you want to use to insert it into the text field. Valid wildcards include the asterisk (*) to match multiple characters or the question mark (?) to match a single character.

9. If you need to change the order of a targeting item, click the targeting item to modify it and then click the Move Up or Move Down button on the toolbar.

10. Click OK to return to the Properties dialog box for the preference item. Click OK again to close the Properties dialog box.

Targeting items are evaluated as a logical expression. Using targeting collections, you can create parenthetical groupings within that expression. You can even nest one targeting collection inside another collection to create complex logical expressions.

With a targeting collection, the collection of targeting items must result in the expected value for the item to be applied. With an Is expression, the collection must evaluate to true. With an Is Not expression, the collection must evaluate to false.

After you create your logical expression, you'll need to ensure that the expression makes sense. The Targeting Editor does not evaluate the logic you are trying to apply. It won't flag expressions that might be mutually exclusive as errors. For example, if you use AND expressions to specify that a computer must have one IP address on the 192.168.10.0 network and one IP address on the 192.168.15.0 network, the Targeting Editor will not see the error in your logic. The Targeting Editor will not know that you meant to use an OR expression to indicate that a computer should have an IP address on one network or the other.

Additionally, if you hard code a value when you meant to use an environment variable, the targeting will not work as expected. For example, if you enter a user name rather than using the %UserName% environment variable, the targeting will only apply to that particular user.

Chapter 4. Advanced Group Policy Management

Advanced Group Policy Management (AGPM) is a set of extensions for the Group Policy Management Console that fundamentally changes how you control and work with Active Directory–based Group Policy. As discussed in Appendix A, "Installing Group Policy Extensions and Tools," you need to install the AGPM client and server components before you can use AGPM. AGPM version 3.0 or later supports both policy preferences and policy settings in Group Policy objects (GPOs). After you've installed the AGPM extensions, your GPOs are either uncontrolled or controlled.

Uncontrolled GPOs are not stored in an offline archive and exist only in the production environment. Controlled GPOs exist in two places: a copy of the GPO exists in an offline archive, and the original exists in the production environment.

Controlled GPOs must be checked out of the archive before they can be edited. When a user editing a controlled GPO finishes modifying the GPO, the user checks the GPO back in to the archive. Only an approved administrator can then deploy the updated GPO to the live production environment. Additionally, AGPM allows you to roll back changes to GPOs, to roll forward changes to GPOs, and to recover both GPOs and GPOs links from the AGPM recycle bin. These change control processes are the core features offered by AGPM.

Using Change Control

Advanced Group Policy Management provides extensions for the Group Policy Management Console (GPMC) that introduce new ways to control and work with Active Directory–based Group Policy. Your success with AGPM will depend on how you use the technology. While AGPM provides a change control system, it does not prevent a user with appropriate permissions from circumventing change control. Therefore, as part of deploying AGPM, you need to communicate the importance of working within the change control system and establish guidelines for working with GPOs that require its use.

AGPM uses a client-server architecture. Appendix A provides step-by-step details for installing the AGPM server and client components. You must install the AGPM server component to use AGPM in a domain. Performing a server installation of AGPM installs the AGPM Service on the server and establishes the GPO archive. The AGPM Service enables offline editing by copying GPOs from a domain controller in the current domain and storing them in the archive. The AGPM Service allows you to apply updates to GPOs by copying updated GPOs back to a domain controller in the current domain.

Once you've established an AGPM server for a domain, you can install the AGPM client on computers that you use to manage GPOs. Each Group Policy administrator must have the AGPM client installed on computers that she uses to manage GPOs. You do not need to install the AGPM client on computers of users who will not manage Group Policy.

Connecting to and Using AGPM

When AGPM is added to the GPMC, a Change Control node is displayed under each Domain node. When you select the Change Control node, the GPMC will try to make a connection to the GPO archive on the AGPM server. If the connection is successful, the details pane shows the following top-level tabs (see Figure 4-1):

- **Contents**   Allows you to work with controlled and uncontrolled GPOs by providing five second-level tabs:
- **Controlled**   Lists controlled GPOs. As you add GPOs to the offline archive and control them, they are added to the Controlled tab. If you have appropriate permissions, you can right-click a controlled GPO and then select Check In, Check Out, or Edit to perform the action you want to take. You can also choose commands to rename the GPO, delete the

GPO, deploy the GPO to production, import the original GPO from production, or save the GPO as a template.

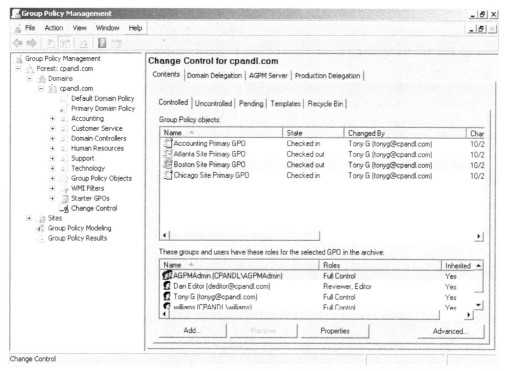

FIGURE 4-1 Use change control to manage GPOs.

> **Tip** When you select a GPO, you can view and manage the AGPM roles assigned to users and groups. Clicking a group and then clicking Properties displays a Properties dialog box that lists the group's current members and allows you to add or remove members. Clicking a user and then clicking Properties displays a Properties dialog box that lists the user's name and contact information and also allows you to modify this information.

- **Uncontrolled** Lists uncontrolled GPOs. When you first deploy AGPM, all your GPOs will be uncontrolled and listed on the Uncontrolled tab. If you have appropriate permissions, you can right-click an uncontrolled GPO and select Controlled to begin controlling the GPO.
- **Pending** Lists controlled GPOs with pending requests from Editors. Anytime there are GPOs with pending requests that need to be

approved, the related GPOs are listed on the Pending tab. If you created the request, you can right-click a pending request and select Withdraw to delete the request. If you have appropriate permissions, you can right-click a pending request and select Approve to approve the request or Reject to reject the request.

Tip When you are working with pending requests, the Withdraw, Approve, and Reject operations can be performed on multiple items. Simply use Shift+Click or Ctrl+Click to select the items on which you want to perform an operation, right-click the selection, and then choose the operation you want.

- **Templates** Lists templates that you've created for new controlled GPOs. A template is similar in purpose to a starter GPO. You use templates to establish baseline preferences and settings for a particular type of new GPO. You can specify a default template for creating controlled GPOs by right-clicking the template and selecting Set As Default.
- **Recycle Bin** Lists controlled GPOs that have been deleted but have not been fully purged from the offline archive. If you have appropriate permissions, you can right-click a deleted GPO and select Destroy to permanently remove the GPO or Restore to restore the GPO to its previous, controlled state.

Note Throughout this text, I'll refer to the AGPM recycle bin simply as the recycle bin. The AGPM recycle bin is separate from the recycle bin used by the operating system.

- **Domain Delegation** Allows you to assign users and groups to each of the AGPM roles. You can also configure the e-mail address and SMTP server for sending approval requests. Only Full Control Administrators can configure domain delegation settings.
- **AGPM Server** Allows you to determine the host name and port of the AGPM server that manages the offline archive for the domain. If AGPM policy is not yet configured in Group Policy, a Full Control Administrator can specify the AGPM server to use by host name and port. Additionally,

this tab allows a Full Control Administrator to control how many old GPO versions to retain.

- **Production Delegation** Allows you to view and manage security permissions for the live production environment. Only Full Control Administrators can configure production delegation settings.

If the GPMC can connect to the AGPM server, the client is configured correctly. If the GPMC cannot connect to the server, you may have incorrectly set the DNS name or port information for the server. As long as AGPM policy is not yet configured, you can change this information on the AGPM Server tab. As shown in Figure 4-2, the FQDN for the server and TCP port typically are listed in the error text. If this information looks to be correct, the issue might be that a firewall port hasn't been opened or that the AGPM Service isn't running.

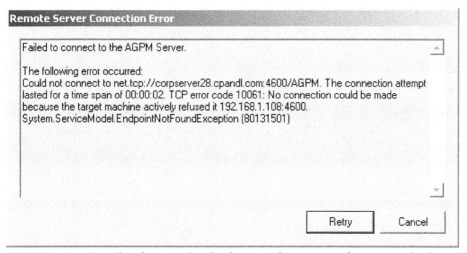

FIGURE 4-2 Resolve the error by checking configuration information, the firewall settings, and the status of the AGPM Service.

If you can connect to the AGPM server but don't have permission to work with the GPO archive, the GPMC connects to the AGPM server but is unable to access the GPO archive. As a result, you get an "insufficient permissions" error as shown in Figure 4-3. To resolve this, you'll need to take one of the following steps:

- Have an AGPM administrator delegate an appropriate domainwide role for your user account or a group of which your user account is a member.
- Add your account to the AGPM administrator group identified as Archive Owner during installation of the AGPM server.

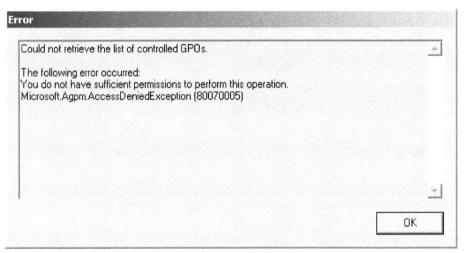

FIGURE 4-3 Resolve this error by ensuring that your account has been assigned an appropriate AGPM role.

Managing GPOs with Change Control

AGPM version 3.0 or later supports both policy preferences and policy settings in GPOs. AGPM includes change management features and fundamentally changes how you control and work with Group Policy. When you are working with Group Policy and not using AGPM, administrative control works like this:

- By default, only members of the Group Policy Creator Owners group can create GPOs.
- To edit or modify an existing GPO, a user must be a member of the Domain Admins group in the domain or of the Enterprise Admins group in the forest, as appropriate for the GPO, or the user must have created the GPO.

- Using delegation, you can grant permissions over the security properties of GPOs to groups or users. Permissions you can grant include the rights to view, create, and manage GPOs.

When you are working with Group Policy and using AGPM, GPOs are either:

- **Uncontrolled** Uncontrolled GPOs are not subject to AGPM change controls. When you are working with the Uncontrolled tab, you'll find that GPOs are listed by name, state, the name of the account that last changed the GPO, last change date, version, GPO status, and WMI filter. Normally the state is listed as Uncontrolled.
- **Controlled** Controlled GPOs are subject to AGPM change controls. When you are working with the Controlled tab, you'll find that GPOs are listed by name, state, the name of the account that last changed the GPO, last change date, version, GPO status, and WMI filter. The Checked In state means that the GPO is checked in and currently under AGPM control. The Checked Out state means that the GPO has been checked out for editing.

Tip Whenever you work with Change Control, it is important to ensure that you are viewing the current state of the tabs and GPOs. To refresh the view, click the Refresh button on the toolbar or select Refresh on the Action menu.

Real World Whenever you work with Group Policy Software Installation packages, keep in mind that AGPM preserves the integrity of these packages. Although you can edit GPOs offline, links between packages, as well as cached client information, are preserved. Therefore, when editing a GPO offline with AGPM, you must configure any Group Policy Software Installation upgrade of a package in another GPO to reference the deployed GPO, not the checked-out copy. Additionally, you must have Read permission for the deployed GPO.

You can work with uncontrolled GPOs in the same ways you work with GPOs when AGPM is not installed. To edit an uncontrolled GPO, select the Group

Policy Objects node in the GPMC, right-click the GPO in the details pane, and then click Edit.

You can view uncontrolled GPOs by selecting the Change Control node in the GPMC, selecting the top-level Contents tab, and then clicking the Uncontrolled tab in the details pane, as shown in Figure 4-4.

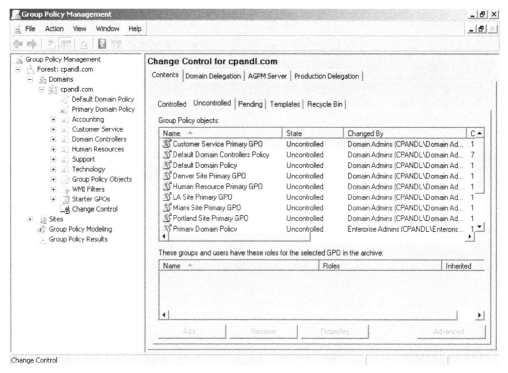

FIGURE 4-4 View uncontrolled GPOs.

To place an uncontrolled GPO under control, you must have appropriate permissions. Users with Reviewer role permissions require prior approval to control GPOs. Users with the Editor, Approver, or Full Control Administrator role can control GPOs without prior approval. For more information on these roles, see "Delegating Change Control Privileges" later in the chapter.

After you elect to control a GPO, the GPMC creates a copy of the GPO in the offline archive. You then use the copy whenever you edit the GPO while working with the Change Control node. Controlling a GPO is the first step in the change control process.

> **Tip** There is no uncontrol option. However, if you no longer want to control a GPO, you can remove control by deleting the GPO from the archive only. To do this, right-click the GPO on the Controlled tab and then click Delete. If you still want to use the GPO in production, don't remove both the archive copy and the live production copy.

With change control in place, GPOs must be checked out prior to editing and checked in after editing. Only one user at a time can check out and edit a controlled GPO. When a GPO is checked out, no one else can check out and edit the GPO within the AGPM change-control framework.

> **Real World** When you check out a GPO under change control, the GPMC lists the production GPO in the Group Policy Objects node with (Checked Out) added to its name. When you check the GPO back in under change control, the GPMC removes the (Checked Out) label.
>
> Change control is only as good as your organization's commitment to using the framework it provides. Change control does not prevent anyone with appropriate access rights from editing GPOs outside the change control framework. For example, anyone who is the creator/owner of a GPO could edit a GPO by right-clicking the GPO in the GPMC's Group Policy Object node and choosing Edit.

The processes related to change control are fairly straight forward. Because of change control, when you are working with GPOs on the Controlled tab, you can perform the following tasks if you have appropriate permissions (see Figure 4-5):

- **Track GPO history** Right-click a controlled GPO and then select History to view its change history, which includes a detailed list of all state changes and unique versions available. History information tells you when changes were made to the GPO, who made the changes, and what changes were made.

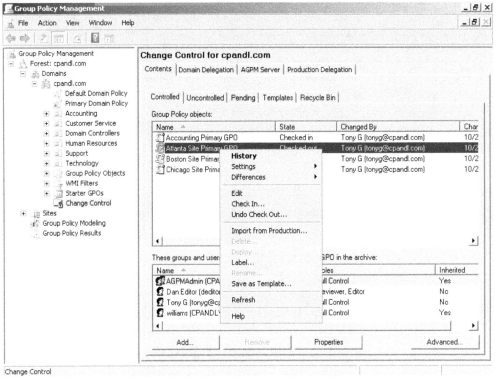

FIGURE 4-5 Manage controlled GPOs on the Controlled tab.

- **Obtain a report on settings**   Right-click a controlled GPO, point to Settings, and then select the type of report you want to generate. If you select HTML Report or XML Report, you'll get a detailed report about the GPO in the format you choose. If you select GPO Links, you'll see a list of the domains and organizational units (OUs) to which the GPO was linked when it was most recently controlled, archived, or checked in. AGPM doesn't manage site links.
- **Obtain a report on the differences in GPO versions**   Right-click a controlled GPO, point to Differences, and then select the type of report you want to generate. If you select HTML Report or XML Report, you'll get a detailed differences report on the GPO in the format you choose.
- **Edit a GPO**   Right-click a controlled GPO that you've previously checked out and then click Edit to edit the GPO in the Group Policy Management Editor.

- **Check in a GPO**   Right-click a controlled GPO that you've previously checked out and then click Check In to check in the GPO and make the edited version of the GPO the current version. When prompted, provide a history comment and then click OK.
- **Check out a GPO**   Right-click a controlled GPO and then click Check Out to check out a GPO so that you can edit it. When prompted, provide a history comment and then click OK.
- **Undo a check out of a GPO**   Right-click a controlled GPO that you previously checked out and then click Undo Check Out to check in the GPO without applying your edits. When prompted to confirm, click Yes.
- **Import a GPO from production**   Right-click a controlled GPO and then click Import From Production to copy the live production version over the current version of the GPO in the archive. This procedure ensures that the archive copy is current and undoes any edits not applied. When prompted, provide a history comment and then click OK.
- **Delete a GPO**   Right-click a controlled GPO that is checked in and then click Delete. Next, to remove the copy of the GPO only from the archive, select Delete GPO From Archive Only and then click OK. Or, to remove the GPO from the archive and from production, select Delete GPO From Archive And Production. The deleted GPO is then moved to the recycle bin.
- **Deploy a GPO**   Right-click a controlled GPO that is checked in and then select Deploy to copy the current version of the GPO in the archive to the live production environment. When prompted to confirm, click Yes. By default, existing links are not modified; only links that existed when the GPO was last archived or checked in but have since been removed are restored. If you don't want to restore previous links, clear the Restore Links check box.

Note   During deployment, no existing links are deleted nor will any OUs be created. Also note that AGPM does not manage site links. Therefore site links will not be modified or restored.

- **Label a GPO**   Right-click a controlled GPO and then click Label to add comments to the history information. When prompted, enter a label and comment and then click OK. The label you provide is entered in the State field, and your comments are entered in the Comment field.

- **Rename a GPO**   Right-click a controlled GPO that is checked in and then click Rename to rename a GPO. In the Rename GPO dialog box, enter the new name for the GPO, add an optional comment, and then click OK.

- **Save a GPO as a Template**   Right-click a GPO on the Controlled or Uncontrolled tab, and then click Save As Template to save the GPO as a template for other new controlled GPOs. In the Create New GPO Template dialog box, enter the name for the GPO template, add an optional comment, and then click OK.

> ***Real World***   With the exception of renaming, all the operations described in the previous list can be performed on multiple GPOs. Simply use Shift+Click or Ctrl+Click to select the GPOs on which you want to perform an operation, right-click, and then choose the operation you want.

Delegating Change Control Privileges

With controlled GPOs, permissions are managed through the AGPM administrative roles. These roles—listed from the role with the least permissions to the role with the most permissions—are as follows:

- **Reviewer**   Role members have read-only access to a GPO for which they've been granted this role. Read-only access allows them to review the GPO edit history and settings but not to make changes.

- **Editor**   Role members have permission to review and edit a GPO for which they've been granted this role. This allows them to perform Reviewer tasks and to make changes to GPOs. Because changes to GPOs are made in the offline archive, changes are not applied until they are officially checked in by an Approver. Additionally, Editors can create GPO templates.

- **Approver**   Role members have permission to review and approve a GPO for which they've been granted this role. This allows them to perform Reviewer tasks and to create, deploy, and delete GPOs. An

Approver checks in a GPO from the archive to make the offline copy of the GPO live in the production environment.

- **Full Control Administrator** Role members have full control over a GPO for which they've been granted this role. This allows them to perform Reviewer, Approver, and Editor tasks. Additionally, Full Control Administrators can modify options and security associated with GPOs.

Table 4-1 summarizes the basic permissions assigned to each role.

TABLE 4-1 Basic Permissions of AGPM Roles

PERMISSION	REVIEWER	EDITOR	APPROVER	FULL CONTROL ADMINISTRATOR
List contents	X	X	X	X
Read settings	X	X	X	X
Edit settings		X		X
Create GPOs in production			X	X
Deploy GPOs to production			X	X
Delete GPOs from production			X	X
Modify options				X
Modify security				X
Create templates		X		X

Because of the additional layer of control, an administrator who wants to work with a particular GPO must not only be a member of the appropriate groups in Active Directory but must also be assigned the appropriate administrative role. For example, if Tony G is to be a Group Policy administrator with full control, Tony needs to be a member of Domain Admins or Enterprise Admins and he needs to be assigned the Full Control Administrator role. However, if Tony G is to be a Group Policy administrator with Editor or Reviewer privileges only, Tony should be assigned the Editor or Reviewer role as appropriate, but he should not be a member Domain Admins, Enterprise Admins, or Group Policy Creator Owners.

Table 4-2 lists the key tasks that members of a particular AGPM role can perform. Note that membership in administrator groups may grant additional privileges that you don't want a Group Policy Reviewer, Editor, or Approver to have. For example, by default, members of Domain Admins and Group Policy Creator Owners can create and manage GPOs in a domain. Therefore, if an Editor or Reviewer is a member of one of these groups, they won't be subject to the limitations of this role.

TABLE 4-2 Key Tasks Members of AGPM Roles Can Perform

TASK	REVIEWER	EDITOR	APPROVER	FULL CONTROL ADMINISTRATOR
Add a GPO to the Controlled tab	Requires approval	Yes	Yes	Yes
Check in a GPO	No	Yes	Yes	Yes
Check out a GPO	No	Yes	No	Yes
Create a GPO in the archive	No	Yes	Yes	Yes
Create a GPO in the archive and in production	No	Requires approval	Yes	Yes
Create a template	No	Yes	No	Yes
Delete a GPO from archive	No	Yes	Yes	Yes
Delete a GPO from archive and production	No	Requires approval	Yes	Yes

Deploy a GPO	No	Requires approval	Yes	Yes
Edit a GPO	No	Yes	No	Yes
Import a GPO from production	No	No	Yes	Yes
Label a GPO	No	Yes	Yes	Yes
Modify GPO options	No	No	No	Yes
Modify GPO security	No	No	No	Yes
Obtain a report on settings	Yes	Yes	Yes	Yes
Obtain a report on the differences in GPO versions	Yes	Yes	Yes	Yes
Rename a GPO	No	Yes	No	Yes
Remove a GPO from the recycle bin	No	No	Yes	Yes
Restore a GPO from the recycle bin	No	Requires approval	Yes	Yes
Save a GPO as a template	No	Yes	No	Yes
Track GPO history	Yes	Yes	Yes	Yes
Undo the check out of a GPO	No	Yes	Yes	Yes

After you mark a GPO as controlled, you must grant AGPM roles to specific users and groups to allow the GPO to be controlled by various users in your organization. The Reviewer, Approver, Editor, and Full Control Administrator roles can be assigned on a per-GPO basis or a per-domain basis. With controlled GPOs, the only account granted an AGPM role by default is the Archive Owner user or group specified when you install the AGPM server components.

> **Note** When you assign the Editor role to someone, he will have the Reviewer and Editor roles. Similarly, when you assign the Approver role to someone, he will have the Reviewer and Approver roles.

By default, the Archive Owner is granted the Full Control Administrator role over all controlled GPOs. This means that if you configured a group as the Archive Owner, you can give someone the Full Control Administrator role throughout the domain simply by adding the user's user account to this group. Using Domain Delegation for AGPM, you can specify other users and groups to have AGPM roles on a domainwide basis. Only Full Control Administrators can configure domain delegation settings.

To delegate privileges on a per-GPO basis, complete the following steps:

1. In the GPMC, select the Change Control node and then select the top-level Contents tab.
2. On the Controlled tab of the Contents panel, select the GPO you want to work with. In the lower pane, you'll see a list of groups and users who have been delegated privileges as well as the role or roles assigned.

> **Note** The Inherited column specifies whether the delegated privilege is inherited. If a delegated privilege is inherited from domain delegation, you cannot edit the inherited role assignment at this level. Otherwise, you can modify the role assignment as necessary.

3. Do one of the following:

- To delegate privileges to a group or user, click Add. Use the Select User, Computer, Or Group dialog box to specify the group or user to which you want to assign an access role and then click OK. In the Add Group Or User dialog box, use the Role list to select the role to grant and then click OK.

> **Tip** The GPMC does not provide a way to change a role assignment directly. If you want to change a user's role, you need to remove the current role assignment and then delegate the new role.

- To remove a noninherited delegated privilege, click the group or user assigned the role and then click Remove. When prompted to confirm, click OK.
- To view or manage the membership of a group that has been delegated privileges, click the group to select it and then click Properties. In the Properties dialog box, you'll see a list of current members. To remove a member, click the user or group, click Remove, and then click Yes when prompted to confirm. To add a member, click Add, use the Select User, Computer, Or Group dialog box to specify the group or user to add, and then click OK.
- To view the security permissions assigned to a group or user, click the group or user to select it, and then select Advanced. Use the Permissions For dialog box and its options to review the assigned security permissions.

To delegate privileges on a domainwide basis, complete the following steps:

1. In GPMC, select the Change Control node and then select the top-level Contents tab.
2. On the Domain Delegation tab of the Contents panel, you'll see a list of groups and users who have been delegated privileges as well as the role or roles assigned.

> **Note** The Inherited column specifies whether the delegated privilege is inherited. By default, the only group or user to inherit privileges at the domain level is the Archive Owner you assigned when you installed

> the AGPM server. You cannot edit an inherited role assignment at this level. Otherwise, you can modify the role assignment as necessary.

3. Do one of the following:

- To delegate privileges to a group or user, click Add. Use the Select User, Computer, Or Group dialog box to specify the group or user to which you want to assign an access role and then click OK. In the Add Group Or User dialog box, use the Role list to select the role to grant and then click OK.
- To remove a noninherited delegated privilege, click the group or user assigned the role and then click Remove. When prompted to confirm, click OK.
- To view or manage the membership of a group that has been delegated privileges, click the group to select it and then click Properties. In the Properties dialog box, you'll see a list of current members. To remove a member, click the user or group, click Remove, and then click Yes when prompted to confirm. To add a member, click Add, use the Select User, Computer, Or Group dialog box to specify the group or user to add, and then click OK.
- To view the security permissions assigned to a group or user, click the group or user to select it and then select Advanced. Use the Permissions For dialog box and its options to review the assigned security permissions.

Managing Workflow and E-mail Notification

AGPM uses workflow methodology to enable Group Policy administrators to notify someone that a task needs to be performed without actually performing the task. The built-in workflow features facilitate communication within the tool as well as through e-mail. The workflow technique used depends on the role or roles assigned to the administrator performing a particular task.

If an administrator has the Reviewer role but not the Editor, Approver, or Full Control Administrator role, he or she must get approval from an Editor, an Approver, or a Full Control Administrator prior to controlling a GPO.

If an administrator has the Editor role and is not also an Approver or a Full Control Administrator, he or she must get approval from an Approver or a Full Control Administrator prior to AGPM finalizing the following tasks:

- Creating a GPO in the archive and in the production environment
- Deleting a GPO from both the production environment and the archive
- Restoring a GPO from the recycle bin to the archive
- Deploying a GPO to the production environment

As part of the workflow, when an Editor tries to create, delete, deploy, or restore a GPO, the GPO is moved from its current location to the Pending tab. On the Pending tab, shown in Figure 4-6, GPOs are listed by name, state, who last changed the GPO, change date, and other values. This allows an Approver or a Full Control Administrator who accesses the Pending tab to determine what needs to be done. The key information to review is the following:

- **Name**   Shows which GPO has a pending action
- **State**   Shows what action is pending
- **Changed By**   Shows who requested the change
- **Change Date**   Shows when the change request was made

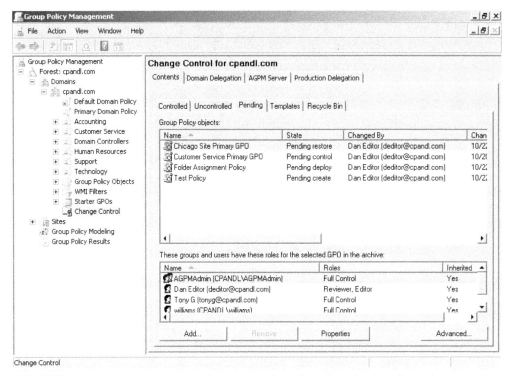

FIGURE 4-6 Requests waiting to be processed are listed on the Pending tab.

If you've configured e-mail notification, approval requests are also sent to a designated approval e-mail address or addresses when an Editor tries to create, delete, or restore a GPO. E-mail notification is not configured by default. To configure e-mail notification, you must be a Full Control Administrator. If you are, you can configure e-mail by completing the following steps:

1. In the GPMC, select the Change Control node in the domain in which you want to manage GPOs.

2. In the details pane, select the Domain Delegation node, as shown in Figure 4-7.

3. Under Send Approval Requests, provide the following information and then click Apply:

   ▪ **From E-Mail Address** Specifies the e-mail alias for the account under which approval requests will be sent. With Microsoft Exchange Server, you need to ensure that the e-mail alias is valid for sending e-mail and might want to set up a related mailbox to ensure this. If you configure a mail-enabled user account (a user account with a mailbox), you can provide the user name and password information for this account in the User Name, Password, and Confirm Password boxes.

- **To E-Mail Address**   Specifies a comma-delimited list of e-mail addresses to which approval requests are sent. With Exchange Server, if an e-mail address is a distribution group, you can notify all the people in the distribution group. For example, if designated Approvers and Full Control Administrators are members of the distribution group, they'll be notified of pending requests.
- **SMTP Server**   Specifies the Simple Mail Transfer Protocol (SMTP) server through which approval requests are routed. This must be a valid SMTP server. Because most SMTP servers block message relay, you need to ensure that the e-mail alias is valid on the SMTP server. Typically, this will mean that the related mailbox exists on the server or that the server is configured to recognize and permit the use of the e-mail address provided in the From E-Mail Address field.
- **User Name**   Sets the user name authorized to connect to the SMTP server and send e-mail messages using the address you've provided for From E-mail Address. With Exchange Server, you should specify the mailbox owner. If the user you specify is not the mailbox owner, the user you specify must have Send On Behalf Of privileges.
- **Password/Confirm Password**   Sets the password for the user account you specified.

Real World   The password you provide is stored within the archive in an encrypted format. The encryption protecting the password causes the password to fail if the archive is moved to another computer. To resolve this, you must re-enter and reconfirm the password and then click Apply.

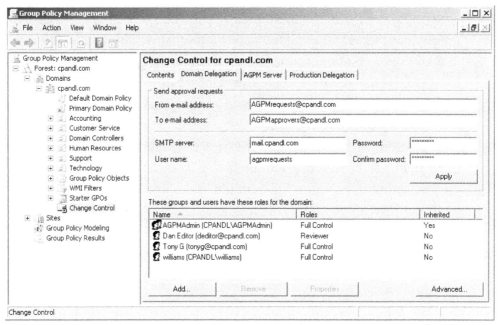

FIGURE 4-7 Configure an e-mail address and SMTP server to use for sending e-mail requests.

To create a GPO, you must be an Approver or a Full Control Administrator. While Approvers and Full Control Administrators can create GPOs without making a formal request, Editors who are not Approvers or Full Control Administrators cannot. Editors create new controlled GPOs by using the following technique:

1. An Editor makes a request stating that he or she wants to create a new controlled GPO by right-clicking Change Control and selecting New Controlled GPO. The Editor sets the name of the GPO and specifies whether to deploy the new GPO to production upon approval or to create it offline without immediately deploying it. The GPO can also be based on a template as a starting point.

2. The new GPO is displayed on the list of GPOs on the Pending tab.

3. An Approver reviews the request and, if appropriate, approves the creation of the GPO. After approval, the GPO is moved to the Controlled tab and made available as appropriate.

Real World Sometimes it seems you cannot create, check out, delete, or deploy controlled GPOs. If you receive Failed and Access Denied errors when trying to create, check out, delete, or deploy controlled GPOs, be sure the domain user account for the AGPM Service is either a member of the Group Policy Creator Owners group or has been delegated permission to create GPOs in the domain. You can verify membership in the Group Policy Creator Owners group by using Active Directory Users And Computers.

You can delegate GPO creation permissions using the GPMC. In the GPMC, select the Group Policy Objects node and then click the Delegation tab in the details pane to determine the users and groups that have been delegated permissions to create (and work with) GPOs. The accounts that are delegated the GPO creation permission by default are Domain Admins, Group Policy Creators Owners, and SYSTEM. To delegate creation permissions to another user or group, click Add, select the account in the dialog box provided, and then click OK.

Additionally, on each individual GPO, the account for the AGPM Service must be delegated the permissions Edit Settings, Delete, and Modify Security. Although these permissions are added by default to any new GPO that you create within AGPM, they are not set on GPOs that are created outside AGPM or prior to installing AGPM. Additionally, an administrator could accidentally remove these permissions. To confirm that the permissions are set, select the GPO under the Group Policy Object node and then click Delegation in the details pane. If the account isn't listed, click Add. Select the account in the Select User, Computer, Or Group dialog box. In the Add Group Or User dialog box, under Permissions, select Edit Settings, Delete, Modify Security, and then click OK.

To check out, edit, check in, or deploy a GPO, you must have appropriate permissions. Editors who are not Approvers or Full Control Administrators check out, edit, check in, and deploy controlled GPOs using a multipart process that works like this:

1. An Editor checks out a GPO from the offline archive by right-clicking it and selecting Check Out. Next, the Editor edits the GPO by right-clicking it and selecting Edit. When finished, he or she checks in the modified GPO to the offline archive by right-clicking the GPO and selecting Check In. The GPO remains visible on the Controlled tab throughout this process.

> **Important**   It is important to remember that AGPM only controls how GPOs are used within the change control system. AGPM does not prevent a user with appropriate permissions from directly editing a GPO in the GPMC and thereby circumventing change control. For this reason, you'll need to communicate the importance of working within the change control system and establish guidelines for working with GPOs that require its use.

2. Checking in a GPO doesn't deploy the GPO; deploying a GPO is a separate process. An Editor makes a request stating that he or she wants to deploy a GPO by right-clicking the GPO on the Controlled tab and selecting Deploy. This copies the GPO to the Pending tab.

3. An Approver reviews the history of the GPO simply by double-clicking the GPO. Using the History window, the Approver can create an HTML report to display a summary of the GPO's policy preferences and policy settings. To determine the changes between versions, the Approver can select each version and then click the Differences button.

4. If the Approver wants to accept the request, he or she can then approve and deploy the GPO by right-clicking the GPO and then clicking Approve. Deploying the GPO copies the current version of the GPO from the offline archive to the live production environment.

5. If the Approver doesn't want to accept the request, he or she can cancel the deployment by right-clicking the GPO and clicking Reject. The Approver can go a step further and reject the changes as well by double-clicking the GPO to access its History window. In the History window, right-click the version to restore and then click Deploy.

Any Editor, Approver, or Full Control Administrator can delete the archive copy of a GPO. However, only an Approver or a Full Control Administrator can delete a GPO from both the archive and production environment without prior approval. Editors who are not Approvers or Full Control Administrators can delete controlled GPOs from both the archive and production by using a multipart process that works like this:

1. An Editor identifies a GPO to delete from production and the archive by right-clicking it, clicking Delete, and then specifying that the GPO should be deleted from the archive and production. The GPO is moved to the Pending tab and displayed on the list of GPOs on the Pending tab.

2. An Approver reviews the deletion request.

3. If the Approver accepts the deletion request, he or she can then approve it simply by right-clicking the GPO and clicking Approve. The GPMC then moves the GPO to the recycle bin.

4. If the Approver doesn't accept the deletion request, he or she can disapprove and cancel the request by right-clicking the GPO and selecting Reject.

Only an Approver or a Full Control Administrator can destroy a GPO by permanently removing it from the recycle bin. Only an Approver or a Full Control Administrator can restore a GPO from the recycle bin without prior approval. For Editors who are not Approvers or Full Control Administrators, restoring controlled GPOs works like this:

1. An Editor identifies a GPO to restore in the recycle bin by right-clicking it and then clicking Restore. This makes a request stating that the GPO should be restored. The GPO is moved to the Pending tab and displayed on the list of GPOs on the Pending tab.

2. An Approver reviews the restoration request.

3. If the Approver accepts the restoration request, he or she can approve it simply by right-clicking the GPO and clicking Approve. Restoring a GPO moves the GPO from the Pending tab to the Controlled tab.

4. If the Approver doesn't accept the restoration request, he or she can then disapprove and cancel the request by right-clicking the GPO and selecting Reject. This action moves the GPO back to the recycle bin.

The administrative template settings for AGPM enable you to control how AGPM works. You can use the AGPM: Configure Logging setting to centrally configure logging and tracing options for AGPM servers and clients to which a GPO with this setting is applied. The setting is available under Computer Configuration\Policies\Administrative Templates\Windows Components\AGPM when editing a GPO in the Group Policy Management Editor. When enabled, trace files are written to %LocalAppData%\Microsoft\AGPM\agpm.log on AGPM clients and %ProgramData%\Microsoft\AGPM\agpmserv.log on AGPM servers.

Other settings are available under User Configuration\Policies\Administrative Templates\Windows Components\Microsoft Management Console\Restricted\Permitted Snap-ins\Extension Snap-ins. In this area, you can:

- Use AGPM: Show Change Control Tab to control the visibility of the Change Control folder in the GPMC.
- Use AGPM: Show History Tab For Linked GPOs to control the visibility of the History tab provided by AGPM when you view a linked GPO in the GPMC.
- Use AGPM: Show History Tab For GPOs to control the visibility of the History tab provided by AGPM when you view a GPO in the GPMC.

To learn about other related settings, see "Configuring Group Policy to Support AGPM" in Appendix A.

Managing Controlled GPOs

With AGPM, your GPOs are either controlled or uncontrolled. With controlled GPOs, you have offline copies of GPOs as well as live GPOs in production, and you have additional management options as discussed in this section. These additional options include:

- Creating and using GPO templates
- Controlling and importing GPOs

- Creating, deploying, and deleting controlled GPOs
- Labeling, restoring, and redeploying controlled GPOs
- Checking out, editing, and checking in controlled GPOs
- Tracking change history and generating reports

Irrespective of AGPM controls, there are certain tasks that you'll use to manage your GPOs in the live production environment. These tasks are discussed in "Managing Your GPOs in Production" in Chapter 3, "Group Policy Management."

Using GPO Templates

A template is a predefined GPO that you use as a baseline for new GPOs. Although GPO templates store both policy preferences and policy settings, you cannot edit a GPO template after you create it. In the enterprise, you can create multiple GPO templates to help other administrators create new GPOs more quickly.

> **Tip** You also can use starter GPOs to help you more easily create new GPOs. However, starter GPOs only store settings within administrative templates. I discuss how to use starter GPOs in "Using Starter GPOs" in Chapter 3.

Creating GPO Templates

To create a GPO template, you must be an Editor or a Full Control Administrator. Editors and Full Control Administrators can create new GPO templates using the following technique:

1. In the GPMC, select the Change Control node in the domain in which you want to manage GPOs.
2. In the details pane, select the top-level Contents node.
3. On the Controlled or Uncontrolled tab, right-click a GPO and then select Save As Template.

4. In the Create New GPO Template dialog box, shown in Figure 4-8, enter a name for the GPO template, add an optional comment if you want, and then click OK.

5. The AGPM Progress window tracks the progress of the template creation process. When the GPMC is finished creating the template, click Close. If an error occurs, note the error, take corrective action, and then repeat this procedure. Most errors you'll see have to do with permissions. You must have appropriate permissions to create GPO templates.

FIGURE 4-8 Specify the name of the new template.

Managing GPO Templates

When you are working with the Change Control node in the GPMC and have selected the top-level Contents tab, GPO templates you've created are available on the Templates tab. As shown in Figure 4-9, when you select a template, the lower pane displays a list of groups and users who have permission to access the template.

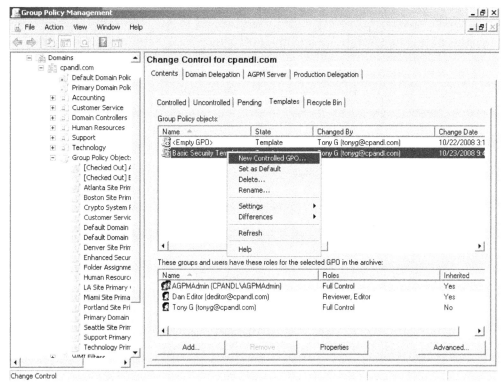

FIGURE 4-9 View available GPO templates.

You can work with templates in much the same way as you work with GPOs. If you right-click a GPO template, you have the following options:

- **New Controlled GPO** Creates a new GPO based on the selected template. Depending on your administrative role, you see the New Controlled GPO dialog box or the Submit Control Request dialog box. The process works exactly as discussed in "Creating Controlled GPOs" later in this chapter.
- **Set As Default** Sets the selected template as the default to be used automatically when creating a new GPO.
- **Delete** Marks the selected template for deletion. To delete a GPO template and move it to the recycle bin, you must have the Approver or Full Control Administrator role. If you do not have permission to delete a GPO, you will be prompted to submit a request, and your pending

delete request will be listed on the Pending tab. The process is similar to the one discussed in "Deleting Controlled GPOs" later in the chapter.

> **Tip** You can delete multiple GPO templates. Simply use Shift+Click or Ctrl+Click to select the GPO templates to delete, right-click, and then click Delete.

- **Rename** Changes the name of the selected template. After you right-click the GPO template, click Rename, and the Rename GPO dialog box is displayed. Enter the new name for the GPO template, add an optional comment if you want, and then click OK.
- **Settings** Generates an HTML-based or XML-based report displaying the settings within the selected GPO template.
- **Differences** Generates an HTML-based or XML-based report comparing the settings between the selected template and another template you identify when prompted.

Delegating Privileges for GPO Templates

You can delegate privileges for a particular GPO template by completing the following steps:

1. In the GPMC, select the Change Control node and then select the top-level Contents tab.

2. On the Templates tab of the Contents panel, select the GPO template you want to work with. In the lower pane, you'll see a list of groups and users who have been delegated privileges as well as the role or roles assigned.

    If a delegated privilege is inherited from domain delegation, you cannot edit the inherited role assignment at this level. Otherwise, you can modify the role assignment as necessary.

3. Do one of the following:

    - To delegate privileges to a group or user, click Add. Use the Select User, Computer, Or Group dialog box to specify the group or user to which you want to assign an access role and then click OK. In the Add

Group Or User dialog box, use the Role list to select the role to grant, and then click OK.

- To remove a noninherited delegated privilege, click the group or user assigned the role and then click Remove. When prompted to confirm, click OK.

- To view or manage the membership of a group that has been delegated privileges, click the group to select it and then click Properties. In the Properties dialog box, you'll see a list of current members. To remove a member, click the user or group, click Remove, and then click Yes when prompted to confirm. To add a member, click Add, use the Select User, Computer, Or Group dialog box to specify the group or user to add, and then click OK.

- To view the security permissions assigned to a group or user, click the group or user to select it, and then select Advanced. Use the Permissions For dialog box and its options to review the assigned security permissions.

Creating Controlled GPOs

The way you create controlled GPOs depends on your AGPM role. While Approvers and Full Control Administrators can create GPOs without making a formal request, Editors who are not Approvers or Full Control Administrators cannot.

Creating GPOs with No Approval Required

If you are an Approver or a Full Control Administrator, you can create a controlled GPO by completing the following steps:

1. In the GPMC, right-click the Change Control node in the domain in which you want to create the controlled GPO. On the shortcut menu, select New Controlled GPO.

2. In the New Controlled GPO dialog box, shown in Figure 4-10, enter a descriptive name for the GPO, such as Customer Service OU Policy. Optionally, enter a comment for the GPO.

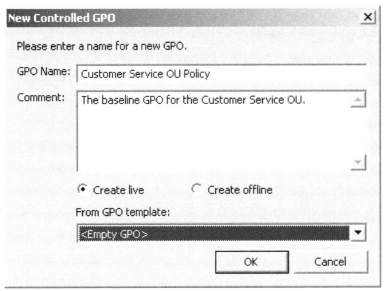

FIGURE 4-10 Create a controlled GPO.

3. Specify where to create the GPO. If you want to create a copy of the GPO in the archive and in the production environment, select Create Live. If you want to create a copy of the GPO in the archive but not in the production environment, select Create Offline.

4. Specify whether to base the GPO on a template. If you want to use a GPO template as the source for the initial settings, use the From GPO Template list to select the GPO template to use. If you do not want to use a GPO template as the source for the initial settings, select <Empty GPO> in the From GPO Template list.

5. Click OK. If you selected <Empty GPO> and an empty template does not yet exist, click OK to create it when prompted.

6. The AGPM Progress window tracks the progress of the GPO creation process. When the GPMC is finished creating the template, click Close. If an error occurs, note the error, take corrective action, and then repeat this procedure. Most errors you'll see have to do with permissions. You must have appropriate permissions to create controlled GPOs.

If you copied the GPO to the archive and to production, the GPO will exist in both places. Otherwise, it will exist only in the archive. To finalize the GPO, you must:

1. Check out the GPO from the archive.
2. Edit the GPO.
3. Check in the GPO to the archive.
4. Deploy the GPO to production. This copies the GPO from the archive to production.
5. Link the GPO to the appropriate containers in Active Directory.

Creating GPOs with Approval Required

If you are an Editor, you must have approval to create a GPO. To create a GPO, you must complete the following steps:

1. In the GPMC, right-click the Change Control node in the domain in which you want to create the controlled GPO. On the shortcut menu, select New Controlled GPO. The GPMC displays the Submit Control Request dialog box, shown in Figure 4-11.
2. If you want to send a courtesy copy of the request to someone, enter the e-mail address in the CC box. You can enter multiple e-mail addresses by separating them with commas.
3. Enter a descriptive name for the GPO, such as Customer Service OU Policy. Optionally, enter a comment for the GPO.
4. Specify where to create the GPO. If you want to create a copy of the GPO in the archive and in the production environment, select Create Live. If you want to create a copy of the GPO in the archive but not in the production environment, select Create Offline.

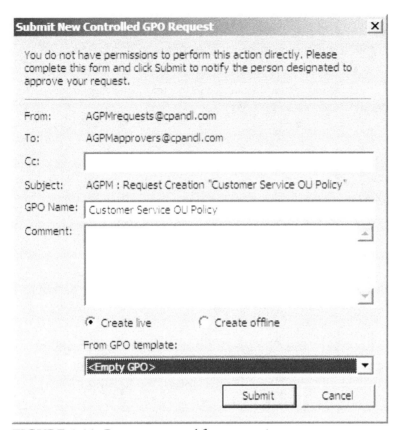

FIGURE 4-11 Request approval for your action.

5. Specify whether to base the GPO on a template. If you want to use a GPO template as the source for the initial settings, use the From GPO Template list to select the GPO template to use. If you do not want to use a GPO template as the source for the initial settings, select <Empty GPO> in the From GPO Template list.

6. Click Submit. If you selected <Empty GPO> and an empty template does not yet exist, click OK to create it when prompted.

7. The AGPM Progress window tracks the progress of the request submission. When the GPMC is finished, click Close. If an error occurs, note the error, take corrective action, and then repeat this procedure. Most errors you'll see have to do with e-mail being improperly configured. Your mail administrator can help you to resolve e-mail errors.

On the Pending tab, you'll see your Pending Create request. Because you created the request, you can right-click the request and then select Withdraw to remove the request at any time (see Figure 4-12). Otherwise, you need to wait for an Approver or a Full Control Administrator to handle your request.

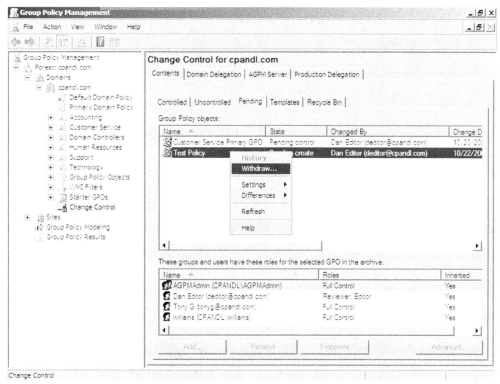

FIGURE 4-12 Review or withdraw your request on the Pending tab.

To reject a pending create request, an Approver or a Full Control Administrator right-clicks the request and then clicks Reject. When prompted, the Approver or Full Control Administrator can enter an optional comment before clicking OK to reject the request. Rejecting the request cancels the pending GPO creation task.

To approve a pending create request, an Approver or a Full Control Administrator right-clicks the request and then clicks Approve. When prompted to confirm, the Approver or Full Control Administrator can enter an optional comment before clicking Yes to authorize the GPO to be created.

When the request is accepted, the GPO is created and the archive copy is made available on the Controlled tab. If the Editor specified that the GPO should be created in production, the GPO is also created in the production environment. To finalize the GPO, you must:

1. Check out the GPO from the archive.
2. Edit the GPO.
3. Check in the GPO to the archive.
4. Deploy the GPO to production. This copies the GPO from the archive to production.
5. Link the GPO to the appropriate containers in Active Directory.

Controlling GPOs

When you select the Change Control node in the GPMC and are working with the top-level Contents tab, uncontrolled GPOs are listed on the Uncontrolled tab. To control an uncontrolled GPO, you must have appropriate permissions. Reviewers require prior approval to control GPOs. Editors, Approvers, and Full Control Administrators can control GPOs without needing prior approval.

> **Real World**   When you create a new controlled GPO using the AGPM extensions, the AGPM Service account is delegated permission to manage the GPO (specifically, the account is granted the Edit Settings, Delete, and Modify Security permissions). To ensure that you can control GPOs created outside AGPM or prior to installing AGPM, you need to ensure that the AGPM Service account is either a member of a group with similar permissions or that you delegate these permissions manually as discussed in "Delegating Control for Working with GPOs" in Chapter 3.

Controlling GPOs with Permissions

If you are an Editor, an Approver, or a Full Control Administrator, you can control a GPO by completing the following steps:

1. In the GPMC, select the Change Control node in the domain you want to work with and then select the top-level Contents node.

2. On the Uncontrolled tab, right-click the GPO you want to control and then select Control.

3. In the Control GPO dialog box, enter a comment for the change history if you want. When you click OK, the GPO is copied to the offline archive and is displayed on the Controlled tab.

Controlling GPOs Without Permissions

If you are a Reviewer, you can control a GPO by completing the following steps:

1. In the GPMC, select the Change Control node in the domain you want to work with and then select the top-level Contents node.

2. On the Uncontrolled tab, right-click the GPO you want to control and then select Control.

3. In the Submit Control Request dialog box, shown in Figure 4-13. Do the following:

   a. If you want to send a courtesy copy of the request to someone, enter the e-mail address in the CC box. You can enter multiple e-mail addresses by separating them with commas. Optionally, enter a comment. Click Submit.

   b. The AGPM Progress window tracks the progress of the request submission. When GPMC is finished, click Close. If an error occurs, note the error, take corrective action, and then repeat this procedure. Most errors you'll see have to do with e-mail being improperly configured. Your mail administrator can help you resolve e-mail errors.

On the Pending tab, you'll see your Pending Control request. Because you created the request, you can right-click the request and then click Withdraw to remove the request at any time. Otherwise, you need to wait for an Editor, an Approver, or a Full Control Administrator to handle your request.

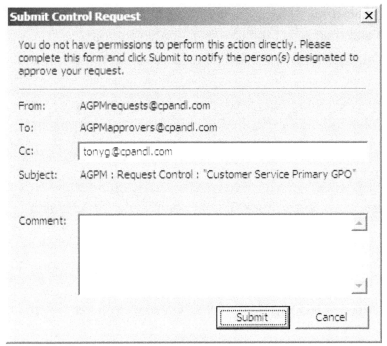

FIGURE 4-13 Request approval for your action.

To reject a pending control request, an Approver, or a Full Control Administrator right-clicks the request and then clicks Reject. When prompted, the Approver or Full Control Administrator can enter an optional comment before clicking OK to reject the request. Rejecting the request cancels the pending control task. This means that the GPO remains uncontrolled and is listed on the Uncontrolled tab.

To approve a pending control request, an Approver or a Full Control Administrator right-clicks the request and then selects Approve. When prompted to confirm, the Editor, Approver, or Full Control Administrator can enter an optional comment before clicking Yes to authorize the GPO to be controlled. When the request is accepted, the GPO is copied to the offline archive from the production environment and made available on the Controlled tab.

Importing GPOs from Production

Importing a GPO from production copies the GPO from the live production environment to the offline archive. This procedure:

- Overwrites the archive copy
- Ensures that the archive copy is current
- Undoes any unapplied edits in the archive copy

Only Approvers and Full Control Administrator can import GPOs from production. If you are an Approver or a Full Control Administrator, you can import a GPO from production by completing the following steps:

1. In the GPMC, select the Change Control node in the domain you want to work with and then select the top-level Contents node.

2. On the Controlled tab, right-click the GPO you want to import from production and then select Import From Production.

3. When prompted, provide a history comment, and then click OK.

4. The AGPM Progress window tracks the progress of the import process. When the GPMC is finished creating the template, click Close. If an error occurs, note the error, and take corrective action as necessary.

> **Note** If you created a GPO in the archive only and haven't previously deployed it to production, a production copy does not exist. Therefore, the Import From Production command is dimmed when you right-click the GPO.

Checking Out, Editing, and Checking In Controlled GPOs

One of the most important features that AGPM provides is the ability for you to edit a GPO offline because it ensures that no one else is modifying the offline copy you are working with. To do this, AGPM implements change controls that require you to check out a GPO prior to editing it.

Only Editors and Full Control Administrators can check out and edit a GPO. An Editor or a Full Control Administrator checks out a GPO from the offline archive by right-clicking it and selecting Check Out. When you check out a GPO, the GPMC does several things:

- Changes the state of the GPO to Checked Out and adds a red highlight to the GPO's icon on the Controlled tab.
- Lists the production GPO in the Group Policy Objects node with (Checked Out) added to its name.
- Allows only the person who checked out the GPO to edit it (within the change control system). However, an Approver or a Full Control Administrator is still able to check in the GPO or undo the checkout of the GPO.
- Opens a copy of the GPO in the Group Policy Management Editor.
- Modifies the GPO's history to note the state change.

The person who checked out the GPO can edit it by right-clicking it and clicking Edit. When finished, he or she can check in the modified GPO to the offline archive by right-clicking the GPO and clicking Check In.

When you check in a GPO, the GPMC does several things:

- Changes the state of the GPO to Checked In and removes the red highlight from the GPO's icon on the Controlled tab.
- Removes the (Checked Out) value from the GPO's name on the Group Policy Objects node.
- Modifies the history to note the state change.
- Establishes the archive copy as the previous version and the version you are checking in as the current version.

> **Tip**   If you double-click a GPO on the Controlled tab, you open a history window. This window has an All States tab, which shows a history of the state changes, and a Unique Versions tab, which shows a list of all unique versions of the GPO that are available. You can restore a particular version from the history to establish it as the current version. You can also compare versions in the history to identify the changes that were made.

Checking in a GPO doesn't deploy the GPO; deploying a GPO is a separate process. You don't have to apply the changes you've made to your copy of the GPO. If you want to discard any changes when you check the GPO back in, right-click the GPO and then click Undo Check Out.

When you undo a check out of a GPO, the GPMC does several things:

- Changes the state of the GPO to Checked In and removes the red highlight from the GPO's icon on the Controlled tab.
- Removes the (Checked Out) value from the GPO's name on the Group Policy Objects node.
- Modifies the history to note the state change.

When a GPO is checked out, an Approver or a Full Control Administrator can check in the GPO or undo the checkout of the GPO.

Deploying Controlled GPOs

Checking in a GPO doesn't deploy the GPO; deploying a GPO is a separate process. When you deploy a GPO, you copy the current version of the GPO from the offline archive to the live production environment.

Real World Group Policy access control lists (ACLs) can be modified through security filtering, WMI filtering, and delegation. For policy to apply, a user must have both Read and Apply Group Policy permissions for the GPO. If a user doesn't have either one, policy stops applying for that object. Read permission is also required in order to manage a GPO.

For AGPM to control the administrative delegation that gets applied to a GPO, AGPM overrides (and rewrites) the security descriptors for a controlled GPO when you deploy it. This ensures that every GPO is configured with an access control list that mandates that the control of that GPO belongs to AGPM, so you can provide access to those that need it within AGPM, not within GPMC.

Permissions are added for the AGPM Service account, and all Deny permissions except the Deny permission for Apply Group Policy are

---

removed. Adding permissions for the AGPM service account ensures that change control works properly for the GPO. Preserving the Deny permission for Apply Group Policy ensures that users or groups can be excluded from having policy applied. Other individual Deny permissions are not preserved, however, to ensure that change control can function as expected.

Deploying a GPO with Permissions

Only Approvers and Full Control Administrators can deploy a GPO without prior approval. If you are an Approver or a Full Control Administrator, you must complete the following steps to deploy a GPO:

1. In the GPMC, right-click the GPO on the Controlled tab and then click Deploy.

Note During deployment, no existing links are deleted nor will any OUs be created. Also note that AGPM does not manage site links. Therefore, site links will not be modified or restored.

2. The Deploy GPO dialog box prompts you to confirm the action, as shown in Figure 4-14. By default, existing links are not modified. Only links that existed when the GPO was last archived or checked in but have since been removed are restored.

Note The Restore Links check box and the Advanced button are grayed out (dimmed) if a production GPO copy that was previously imported had no links or if the online GPO copy has not yet been linked.

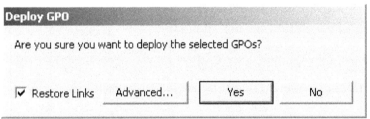

FIGURE 4-14 Confirm that you want to deploy the selected GPO.

3. To review the GPO's links prior to deploying it, click Advanced. As shown in Figure 4-15, the GPO Links For Selected GPOs dialog box shows you where the GPO is linked. Do the following, and then click OK:

* Select the links you want to restore.
* Clear the related check box for links you do not want to restore.

4. If you don't want to restore any previous links, clear the Restore Links check box.

5. Click Yes to deploy the GPO to production.

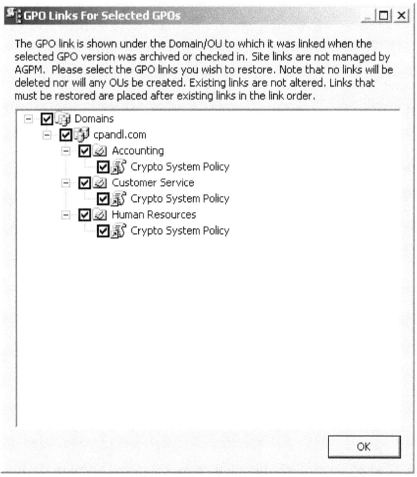

FIGURE 4-15 Review the GPO links as necessary.

Deploying a GPO Without Permissions

Editors who are not Approvers or Full Control Administrators must get approval to deploy a GPO. If you are an Editor, you can deploy a GPO by completing the following steps:

1. In the GPMC, select the Change Control node in the domain you want to work with and then select the top-level Contents node.
2. On the Controlled tab, right-click the GPO you want to control and then click Deploy.
3. In the Submit Control Request dialog box, do the following:
   a. If you want to send a courtesy copy of the request to someone, enter the e-mail address in the CC box. You can enter multiple e-mail addresses by separating them with commas. Optionally, enter a comment. Click Submit.
   b. The AGPM Progress window tracks the progress of the request submission. When the GPMC is finished, click Close. If an error occurs, note the error, take corrective action, and then repeat this procedure. Most errors you'll see have to do with e-mail being improperly configured. Your mail administrator can help you resolve e-mail errors.

On the Pending tab, you'll see the pending deploy request. Because you created the request, you can right-click the request and then click Withdraw to remove the request at any time. Otherwise, you'll need to wait for an Approver or a Full Control Administrator to handle your request.

To reject a pending deploy request, an Approver or a Full Control Administrator right-clicks the request and then selects Reject. When prompted, the Approver or Full Control Administrator can enter an optional comment before clicking OK to reject the request. Rejecting the request cancels the pending deploy task. This means the GPO is returned to the Controlled tab and is not copied to the live production environment.

To approve a pending control request, an Approver or a Full Control Administrator right-clicks the request and then selects Approve. When prompted to confirm, the Approver or Full Control Administrator can enter an optional comment before clicking Yes to authorize the GPO to be deployed. By default, existing links are not modified. Only links that existed when the GPO was last archived or checked in but have since been removed are restored. If you don't want to restore previous links, clear the Restore Links check box before clicking OK.

When the request is accepted, the GPO is copied from the offline archive to the production environment and made available once again on the Controlled tab. During deployment, no existing links are deleted nor will any OUs be created. Also note that AGPM does not manage site links. Therefore, site links will not be modified or restored.

Identifying Differences in GPOs

You can generate difference reports to analyze the differences between Group Policy objects (GPOs), templates, or different versions of a single GPO. Reports can be formatted in HTML or XML, depending on your preference.

If you are a Reviewer, an Editor, an Approver, or a Full Control Administrator, you can :

- **Determine the differences between two GPOs or templates**   Select the two GPOs or templates. Right-click one of the GPOs or templates, click Differences, and then click HTML Report or XML Report to display a differences report summarizing the settings of the GPOs or templates.
- **Determine the differences between a GPO and a template**   Right-click the GPO, click Differences, and then click Template. Select the template and type of report, and then click OK to display a differences report summarizing the settings of the GPO and template.
- **Determine the differences between versions of a GPO**   Double-click the GPO to display its history, and then select the versions to be compared. Right-click one of the versions, click Differences, and then click HTML Report or XML Report to display a differences report summarizing the settings of the GPOs.

- **Determine the differences between a GPO version and a template**
Double-click the GPO to display its history. Right-click the GPO version
to examine, click Differences, and then click Template. Select the
template and type of report, and then click OK to display a differences
report summarizing the settings of the GPO version and template.

Reviewing GPO Links

You can display a diagram showing where GPOs are linked to domains and
organizational units. GPO link diagrams are updated each time you control,
import, or check in a GPO.

If you are a Reviewer, an Editor, an Approver, or a Full Control Administrator,
you can review the links to GPOs. To display GPO links for one or more
GPOs, complete the following steps:

1. In the GPMC, select the Change Control node in the domain you want
   to work with and then select the top-level Contents node.
2. On the Controlled, Pending, or Recycle Bin tab, right-click the GPO you
   want to work with.
3. On the shortcut menu, click Settings and then click GPO links.

To display GPO links for one or more versions of a GPO, complete the
following steps:

1. In the GPMC, select the Change Control node in the domain you want
   to work with and then select the top-level Contents node.
2. On the Controlled, Pending, or Recycle Bin tab, double-click the GPO
   to display its history.
3. In the History window, right-click the GPO version you want to review,
   click Settings, and then click HTML Report or XML Report to display a
   summary of the GPO's settings.

Labeling and Renaming Controlled GPOs

Normally, you add comments to a GPO when you change its state. If you are an Editor, an Approver, or a Full Control Administrator, you can also add comments to a GPO by using labels. In the GPMC, right-click a GPO on the Controlled tab and then select Label. In the Label GPO dialog box, enter a label and comment and then click OK. The label you provide is entered in the State field, and your comments are entered in the Comment field.

Editors and Full Control Administrators can rename controlled GPOs using options on the Controlled tab. To rename a GPO, right-click a GPO that is checked in and then click Rename. In the Rename GPO dialog box, enter the new name for the GPO, add an optional comment if you want, and then click OK.

Uncontrolling GPOs

Once you control a GPO, there is no option to remove control from it. A controlled GPO is simply a GPO with an offline copy in an archive and a live production copy, while an uncontrolled GPO is a GPO with only a live production copy. Therefore, if you no longer want to control a GPO, you can remove control simply by deleting the GPO from the archive but keeping the production copy. Deleting a GPO from the archive moves it to the recycle bin where it can be restored or purged later.

Editors, Approvers, and Full Control Administrators can delete GPOs from the archive. To delete a GPO from the archive and remove control from it, complete the following steps:

1. In the GPMC, select the Change Control node in the domain you want to work with and then select the top-level Contents node.
2. On the Controlled tab, check the status of the GPO you no longer want to control. If the GPO is checked in, you can remove control. Right-click the GPO and then select Delete.

3. In the Delete dialog box, shown in Figure 4-16, select Delete GPO From Archive Only and then click OK.

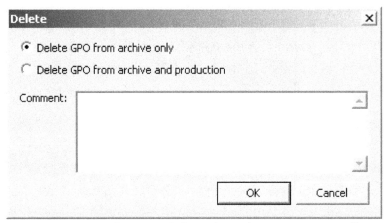

FIGURE 4-16 Delete a GPO from the archive to stop controlling it.

4. Next, when prompted to confirm, click Yes. The GPMC moves the GPO to the recycle bin. If you select the Recycle Bin tab, you'll see the deleted GPO, as shown in Figure 4-17.

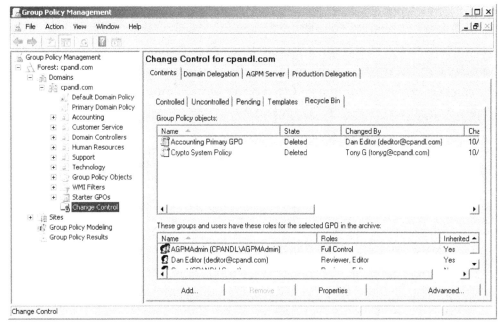

FIGURE 4-17 View deleted GPOs in the recycle bin.

Deleting Controlled GPOs

To delete a controlled GPO and move it to the recycle bin, you must be an Approver or a Full Control Administrator. While Approvers and Full Control Administrators can delete a controlled GPO directly, Editors who are not Approvers or Full Control Administrators must have approval.

> **Note** As I mentioned at the beginning of the chapter, the change control system is only as good as your policies regarding its use. An administrator who has appropriate permissions can delete the production copy of any GPO by right-clicking the GPO under the Group Policy Objects node in the GPMC and choosing Delete. Though this does not delete the archive copy of the GPO, it does go around the change control system.

Deleting a GPO with Permissions

If you are an Approver or a Full Control Administrator and want to delete the GPO from the archive and production, complete the following steps:

1. In the GPMC, select the Change Control node in the domain you want to work with and then select the top-level Contents node.

2. On the Controlled tab, check the status of the GPO you want to delete. If the GPO is checked in, you can delete it by right-clicking it and then clicking Delete.

> **Tip** Before you can delete a checked out GPO, you must check it back in or undo the previous check out. Don't take this step without discussing the issue with the person who checked out the GPO.

3. Next, to remove only the copy of the GPO from the archive, select Delete GPO From Archive Only and then click OK. To remove the GPO from the archive and from production, select Delete GPO From Archive And Production.

4. When prompted to confirm, click Yes. The GPMC moves the GPO to the recycle bin. If you select the Recycle Bin tab, you'll see the deleted GPO.

Deleting a GPO Without Permissions

Editors who are not Approvers or Full Control Administrators must get approval to delete a GPO from both the archive and production. If you are an Editor, you can delete a GPO from both the archive and production by completing the following steps:

1. In the GPMC, select the Change Control node in the domain you want to work with and then select the top-level Contents node.

2. On the Controlled tab, check the status of the GPO you want to delete. If the GPO is checked in, you can delete it by right-clicking it and then selecting Delete.

3. To remove only the copy of the GPO from the archive, select Delete GPO From Archive Only and then click OK. When prompted to confirm, click Yes. The GPMC moves the GPO to the recycle bin. If you select the Recycle Bin tab, you'll see the deleted GPO.

4. To remove the GPO from the archive and from production, select Delete GPO From Archive And Production, and then click OK. When the Submit Control Request dialog box is displayed, do the following:

   a. If you want to send a courtesy copy of the request to someone, enter the e-mail address in the CC box. You can enter multiple e-mail addresses by separating them with commas. Optionally, enter a comment. Click Submit.

   b. The AGPM Progress window tracks the progress of the request submission. When GPMC is finished, click Close. If an error occurs, note the error, take corrective action, and then repeat this procedure. Most errors you'll see have to do with e-mail being improperly configured. Your mail administrator can help you resolve e-mail errors.

On the Pending tab, you'll see your Pending Delete request. Because you created the request, you can right-click the request and then select Withdraw to remove the request at any time. Otherwise, you'll need to wait for an Approver or a Full Control Administrator to handle your request.

To reject a pending delete request, an Approver or a Full Control Administrator right-clicks the request and then selects Reject. When prompted, the Approver or Full Control Administrator can enter an optional comment before clicking OK to reject the request. Rejecting the request cancels the pending delete task. This means the GPO is returned to the Controlled tab and is not deleted from the archive or production.

To approve a pending delete request, an Approver or a Full Control Administrator right-clicks the request and then selects Approve. When prompted to confirm, the Approver or Full Control Administrator can enter an optional comment before clicking Yes to authorize the GPO to be deleted.

When the request is accepted, the GPO is removed from the offline archive and the production environment. A copy of the GPO is placed in the recycle bin and can be viewed by selecting the Recycle Bin tab.

Restoring or Destroying Controlled GPOs

When you delete a GPO or GPO template, the item is moved to the recycle bin within the AGPM archive (see Figure 4-18). The GPO or GPO template will remain in the recycle bin until it is either restored or destroyed. Restoring a deleted GPO or GPO template returns it to the archive. Destroying a GPO or GPO template permanently removes it from the archive.

> **Tip**   If a GPO was deleted from the production environment, restoring it to the archive will not automatically redeploy it to the production environment. To return the GPO to the production environment, you must deploy the GPO as discussed in "Deploying Controlled GPOs" earlier in this chapter.

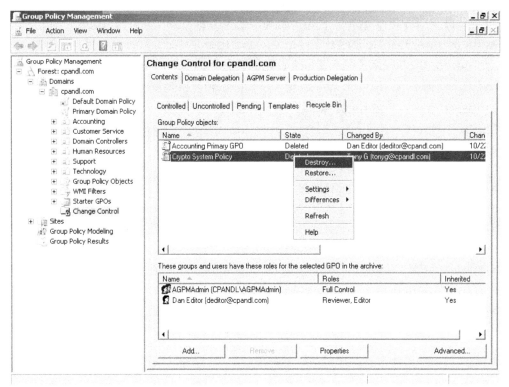

FIGURE 4-18 Destroy or restore GPOs.

Restoring or Destroying Items with Permissions

If you are an Approver or a Full Control Administrator and want to restore or destroy a GPO or GPO template, complete the following steps:

1. In the GPMC, select the Change Control node in the domain you want to work with and then select the top-level Contents node.

2. Select the Recycle Bin tab to display a list of deleted GPOs and GPO templates.

3. Do one of the following:

   ▪ To restore a GPO or GPO template, right-click it and then click Restore. When prompted to confirm, add a comment if you want to, and then click OK. When the AGPM Progress window indicates the operation is complete, click Close. The GPO or GPO template is then restored to its previous location, either the Controlled tab or the Templates tab.

- To destroy a GPO or GPO template, right-click it and then select Destroy. When prompted to confirm, click Yes. When the AGPM Progress window indicates the operation is complete, click Close. The GPO or GPO template is then removed from the recycle bin and permanently deleted.

Restoring or Destroying Items Without Permissions

Editors who are not Approvers or Full Control Administrators cannot permanently delete GPOs or GPO templates. They can, however, request that a GPO or GPO template be restored.

If you are an Editor, you can restore a GPO or GPO template by completing the following steps:

1. In the GPMC, select the Change Control node in the domain you want to work with and then select the top-level Contents node.
2. Select the Recycle Bin tab to display a list of deleted GPOs and GPO templates.
3. Right-click the GPO or GPO template to restore and then click Restore.
4. When the Submit Control Request dialog box is displayed, do the following:

   a. If you want to send a courtesy copy of the request to someone, enter the e-mail address in the CC box. You can enter multiple e-mail addresses by separating them with commas. Optionally, enter a comment. Click Submit.

   b. The AGPM Progress window tracks the progress of the request submission. When GPMC is finished, click Close. If an error occurs, note the error, take corrective action, and then repeat this procedure. Most errors you'll see have to do with e-mail being improperly configured. Your mail administrator can help you resolve e-mail errors.

On the Pending tab, you'll see your pending restore request. Because you created the request, you can right-click the request and then select Withdraw to remove the request at any time. Otherwise, you'll need to wait for an Approver or a Full Control Administrator to handle your request.

To reject a pending delete request, an Approver or a Full Control Administrator right-clicks the request and then selects Reject. When prompted, the Approver or Full Control Administrator can enter an optional comment before clicking OK to reject the request. Rejecting the request cancels the pending restore task. This means the GPO or GPO template is returned to the Recycle Bin tab.

To approve a pending restore request, an Approver or a Full Control Administrator right-clicks the request and then selects Approve. When prompted to confirm, the Approver or Full Control Administrator can enter an optional comment before clicking Yes to authorize the GPO to be deleted.

When the request is accepted, the GPO or GPO template is restored to its previous location, either the Controlled tab or the Templates tab.

Controlling GPO Versions and History

After you install AGPM, the GPMC tracks the history of each GPO you've created. When you are working with GPOs in the Group Policy Object node or GPO links within other nodes, you can view this history by selecting the GPO or GPO link in the left pane and then clicking the History tab in the details pane. When you are working with the Change Control node and its top-level Contents tab, you can display the history of a GPO by double-clicking the GPO or by right-clicking a GPO and then clicking History.

Working with GPO History

History provides a record of events in the lifetime of the selected GPO. Whether you are working with the History tab or the History window, there are two related subtabs:

- **All States**   Tracks changes in the state of the GPO. State changes that occurred in production are identified with the label Production.
- **Unique Versions**   Tracks the unique versions of the GPO that are checked into the archive. The version deployed to the production

environment, shortcuts to unique versions, and informational states are omitted from this list.

When you are working with GPO history, you can compare multiple versions of a GPO or obtain a report of the settings within a version of a GPO. Both of these tasks are discussed in "Identifying Differences in GPOs" earlier in the chapter.

By default, every version of every controlled GPO is retained in the archive. However, you can configure the AGPM Service to limit the number of versions retained for each GPO and automatically delete the oldest version when that limit is exceeded. To do this, complete the following steps:

1. In the GPMC, select the Change Control node and then select the top-level Contents tab.

2. After you select the AGPM Server tab, do one of the following:

- To limit the number of versions of a GPO maintained in the archive, select the Delete Old Versions check box. Specify how many versions to retain, and then click Apply.
- To retain all the versions of a GPO in the archive, clear the Delete Old Versions check box and then click Apply.

When a GPO version is deleted, a record of that version remains in the history of the GPO, but the GPO version itself is deleted from the archive. The maximum number of unique versions to store for each GPO does not include the current version, so entering 0 retains only the current version. The limit can be no more than 999 versions.

Preventing or Enabling Deletion of History Versions

In the History window or on the History tab, you can prevent a GPO version from being deleted by marking it as not deletable. To specify whether a version of a GPO is deletable, right-click it and then do one of the following:

- Click Do Not Allow Deletion to prevent the version from being deleted from the history.
- Click Allow Deletion to allow the version to be deleted from the history.

Rolling Back to a Previous Version of a GPO

As an Approver or a Full Control Administrator, you can roll back changes to a GPO by redeploying an earlier version of the GPO from its history. Deploying an earlier version of a GPO overwrites the version of the GPO currently in production.

To deploy a previous version of a GPO to the production environment, complete the following steps:

1. In the GPMC, select the Change Control node and then select the top-level Contents tab.

2. On the Controlled tab, double-click the GPO you want to work with to display its history.

3. Right-click the version to be deployed, and then click Deploy. When prompted to confirm, click Yes. When the AGPM Progress window indicates the operation is complete, click Close. In the History window, click Close.

The version you deployed becomes the current version in production.

Chapter 5. Searching and Filtering Group Policy

Because Group Policy is so extensive, it sometimes can be difficult to find what you are looking for in the Group Policy Management Console (GPMC) and related policy editors—whether it's a set of policies, a particular Group Policy object (GPO), or an object that Group Policy is affecting. Rather than search through every single GPO and every related policy setting in those GPOs, you can save time and be much more effective by using one of several filtering techniques, including filtering policy settings to streamline the view and searching policy objects, links, and configuration settings for various conditions, values, and keywords.

By default, a linked GPO applies to all users and computers in the container to which it is linked. But sometimes you don't want a GPO to apply to a user or computer in a particular container, and this is where processing filters come in handy. You can apply two types of processing filters to GPOs:

- **Security group filters**   Control the security groups to which a policy object is applied
- **Windows Management Instrumentation (WMI) filters**   Control the computers to which a policy object is applied

Processing filters are very different from view filters. You filter the view to make it easier to find what you are looking for in the GPMC and related editors. You filter the way policy is processed to change how policy is applied.

Finding Policy Settings

When you are viewing or editing a GPO, all policy settings for all Administrative templates are displayed in the Group Policy Management Editor by default. Because so many policy settings are available and many of them might not be applicable in your environment or might not be suited to your current needs, this default view can make finding the policy settings you want to work with difficult.

Filtering Techniques for Policy Settings

To reduce the policy set and make it more manageable, you can filter the view so that only the policy settings you want to work with are shown. For example, if you are looking for a particular group of policy settings, such as those that are configured for or can be used with computers running Windows 7 with Service Pack 2 or later, you can filter the view to show only those policy settings.

The one drawback is that this type of filtering applies only to settings within the Administrative templates. Anytime you are actively editing a GPO, you can filter the Administrative templates by using any combination of the following techniques:

- Show or hide policy settings that can be fully managed
- Show or hide policy settings that are currently configured
- Show or hide policy settings that have comments
- Show only the policy settings that contain a specific keyword
- Show only the policy settings that apply to a specific requirement regarding the operating system, application, or system configuration

> **Note** Filtering policy settings only affects their display in the Group Policy Management Editor. Filtered policy settings are still applied as intended throughout the site, domain, or organizational unit (OU).

Policy settings within the Administrative templates are either managed by the Group Policy service or they are not. When a policy setting is managed by the Group Policy service, it is added and applied when it is in scope for a computer or a user and removed if it later falls out of scope for a computer or a user. When a policy setting is unmanaged, it is added and applied when it is in scope for a computer or a user but is not removed if it later falls out of scope.

Showing or hiding managed settings is useful if you want to ensure that you are working with nonlegacy policy settings. As legacy policy settings typically modify different sections of the Windows registry than do template settings for current versions of Windows, it is recommended that you not use legacy Administrative templates, and the option not to use them is selected by default. If you want to work with legacy Administrative templates and their settings, you must clear this filter option.

Showing or hiding policy settings that are currently configured is useful when you want to determine what policy settings have or have not been applied. By filtering policy to show only configured settings, you see only policy settings that are enabled or disabled, and policy settings that are set as "not configured" are hidden. Conversely, when you filter policy to show only nonconfigured settings, you see only policy settings that are set as "not configured," and policy settings that are enabled or disabled are hidden from view.

Every policy setting in the Administrative templates has a comment property. This property allows any administrator to enter text associated with a specific policy setting. When you are trying to find comments from other administrators or comments you made previously, you can show policy settings with comments. If you are trying to add documentation to policy settings, you might also want to search for policy settings that are configured but have no comments.

Keyword and requirements filters let you narrow the match criteria even further. Keyword filters are inclusive. You use them to select items you want to display rather than to hide items you don't want to display.

You can filter keywords in one of the following ways:

- **Any**   Matches policy settings that include any of the words in the filter. Choose Any to separately match any of the keywords. For example, if you enter **security**, **key**, and **computer**, any policy setting that contains the word *security*, the word *key*, or the word *computer* is a match for the keyword filter.

- **All**   Matches policy settings that include all the words in the filter. Choose All to match only settings that have all the keywords. For example, if you enter **security**, **key**, and **computer**, only policy settings that contain all three words are a match for the keyword filter.
- **Exact**   Matches policy settings that are exact matches for a keyword phrase. Choose Exact to exactly match a keyword phrase. For example, if you enter **security key on computer**, only policy settings that contain this exact phrase are a match for the keyword filter.

The keyword filter can search within any combination of the following:

- **Policy setting title**   Used to search within the title of a policy setting
- **Explain text**   Used to search within the explanatory text associated with a policy setting
- **Comment**   Used to search within the comment text associated with a policy setting

You use requirements filters when you want to view only the policy settings that work with specific technologies and operating systems. By filtering policy settings in this way, you see only the policy settings that meet your specified operating system, application, or system configuration requirements. For example, you could filter policy to:

- View only the policy settings that are supported by Windows 7 with Service Pack 2 or later.
- View only the policy settings that apply to Windows Internet Explorer 10.
- View only the policy settings that apply to Internet Explorer 10 on Windows 7 Professional with Service Pack 2 or later.

As you can see, this makes it easy to find policy settings that match very stringent criteria.

Filtering Policy Settings

When you are viewing or editing a policy object in the Group Policy Management Editor, you can filter the related policy settings to find the policy settings you want to work with. Filtering works only with the Administrative templates. When you apply a filter, the filter applies to both Computer Configuration and User Configuration settings.

To filter policy settings, complete the following steps.

1. In the Group Policy Management Editor, expand Policies and then expand Computer Configuration or User Configuration as appropriate.

2. Right-click Administrative Templates, and then choose Filter Options to open the Filter Options dialog box, shown in Figure 5-1.

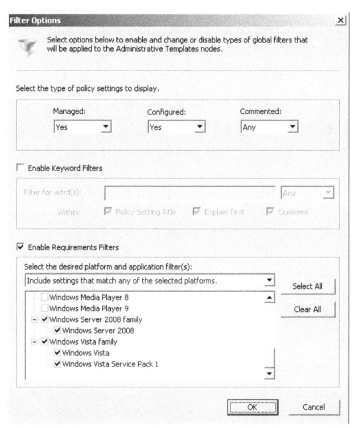

FIGURE 5-1 Use the available options to define your filter.

3. To filter by managed or unmanaged policy settings, choose one of the following options from the Managed list:

- **Any**   Displays both managed and unmanaged settings
- **Yes**   Displays only managed settings
- **No**   Displays only unmanaged settings

4. To filter by configured state, choose one of the following options from the Configured list:

- **Any**   Displays both configured and not configured settings
- **Yes**   Displays only settings that are configured
- **No**   Displays only settings that are not configured

5. To filter based on whether a policy setting has comments, choose one of the following options from the Comment list:

- **Any**   Displays both commented and uncommented policy settings
- **Yes**   Displays only settings that have comments
- **No**   Displays only settings that do not have comments

6. To filter policy settings by keyword, do the following:

a. Select the Enable Keyword Filters check box.

b. Enter one or more keywords in the Filter For Word(s) box.

c. In the Search Criteria list, make a selection. Choose Any to match any of the words in the Filter For Word(s) box. Choose All to match only settings that have all the words in the Filter For Word(s) box. Choose Exact to exactly match the phrase in the Filter For Word(s) box.

d. Select the appropriate check boxes next to Within. Select Policy Setting Title to search the title of the policy setting. Select Explain Text to search the explanatory text of the policy setting. Select Comment to search the comment of the policy setting.

7. To filter policy settings by requirements, do the following:

a. Select the Enable Requirements Filters check box.

b. In the Select The Desired Platform And Application Filter(s) list, make a selection. Choose Include Settings That Match Any Of The Selected Platforms to display policy settings that match any of the technologies or platforms you select. Choose Include Settings That Match All Of The Selected Platforms to display policy settings that match all the technologies and platforms you select.

c. Select the technologies and platforms you want to match.

8. Click OK to apply your filter settings and close the Filter Options dialog box.

When you apply a filter, the view of the Administrative Templates node is filtered and a filter icon is added to the Administrative Templates node and any subnodes under Computer Configuration and User Configuration that contain policy settings that match the filter criteria, as shown in Figure 5-2. You can navigate the matching nodes as you do normally. If you select the All Settings node under either Computer Configuration or User Configuration, you'll see a complete list of the policy settings that match your filter criteria for either Computer Configuration or User Configuration, as appropriate. To remove the filter, right-click Administrative Templates and then select Filter On to clear the filtering flag.

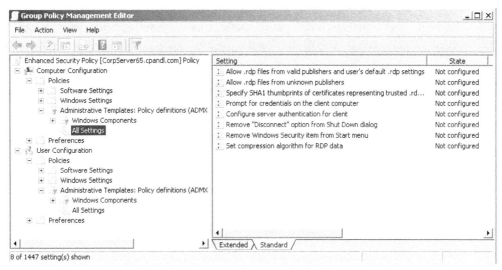

FIGURE 5-2 Review the policy settings that match the filter criteria.

Searching for GPOs

Clearly, being able to search within individual GPOs is helpful. Still, you'll often want to perform similar searches on a larger scope, such as searching all GPOs in a domain or forest for specific values or configuration criteria. To search all GPOs in a domain or forest, you can use the search feature in the Group Policy Management Console (GPMC).

Search Techniques for Policy Objects, Links, and Settings

If you want to find a specific policy object, link, or setting, the GPMC search feature is the right tool for you. You can use the search feature to find virtually any value associated with a policy object. The search feature can search all GPOs in the currently selected domain or in all the domains of a selected forest.

You can search for any of the following items:

- **GPO Name**   Allows you to search for a policy object by name. For example, if you know that a policy object has the word *Sales* in its name but you don't know in which domain the object exists, you can search for all policy objects with names that contain this keyword.
- **GPO Links**   Allows you to search for policy objects that are linked or not linked in a particular domain. For example, if you want to find all policy objects that are linked in a particular domain, you can search for all policy object links that exist in that domain. Or, if you want to find all policy objects that aren't currently linked to a domain, you can search for all policy object links that do not exist in that domain.
- **Security Groups, Users, or Computers**   Allows you to search for security groups, users, or computers that have directly assigned (explicit) or inherited (implicit) Group Policy management privileges in a particular domain or in all domains in a forest. For example, you might need to know whether the ServiceTechs group has explicit permission to edit Group Policy settings or whether the user MikeP has permission to read

Group Policy settings in a particular domain or in any domain of the current forest.

- **Linked WMI Filter** Allows you to search for a linked Windows Management Instrumentation (WMI) filter in a particular domain. This allows you to determine whether a filter with specific criteria is or is not being applied.

- **User Configuration** Allows you to quickly determine whether certain policy preferences and policy settings under User Configuration are configured. You can search all areas of policy preferences and the following areas of policy settings: Deployed Printer Connections, Folder Redirection, Internet Explorer Branding, Internet Explorer Zonemapping, Microsoft Offline Files, Policy-based QoS, Registry, Scripts, and Software Installation. For example, you might need to find policy objects in a particular domain that have Folder Redirection configured, and you can use this search feature to do so.

- **Computer Configuration** Allows you to quickly determine whether certain policy preferences and policy settings under Computer Configuration are configured. You can search all areas of policy preferences and the following areas of policy settings: 802.3 Group Policy, Deployed Printer Connections, EFS Recovery, Internet Explorer Zonemapping, Internet Protocol Security Policies, Microsoft Disk Quota, Microsoft Offline Files, Policy-based QoS, Registry, Scripts, and Security. For example, you might need to find policy objects in a particular domain that have a 802.3 wireless networking policy configured, and you can use this search feature to do so.

- **GUID** Allows you to search for a policy object by its globally unique identifier (GUID). This is useful if you already know the full GUID of a policy object that you need to locate. A typical scenario where you might know the GUID and not know the policy object location is when you are troubleshooting a problem with Group Policy and see errors that reference the GUID of a policy object.

As part of your search, you define the conditions under which matches are found. Conditions are dynamic and based on the search item you select.

Conditions can be inclusive or exclusive. You use inclusive conditions to select items you want to display. You use exclusive conditions to hide items you don't want to display.

Conditions include:

- **Contains/Does Not Contain**   Allows you to search based on specific values that are either contained or not contained in the search item. For example, if you are sure the policy object you are looking for doesn't have the word *Security* in its name (while most other policy objects you've created do), you can search for a GPO Name that does not contain the value Security.
- **Is/Is Not**   Allows you to search for a value that is or is not being used. For example, you may want to search to determine whether a linked WMI filter is or is not being applied to policy objects.
- **Is Exactly/Equals**   Allows you to search for an exact value associated with a search item. For example, if you are sure the policy object you are looking for is named Support Policy, you can search for a GPO Name that has that exact value.
- **Exist In/Does Not Exist In**   Allows you to search for GPO links that either exist in or do not exist in the selected domain. This allows you to obtain a list of policy objects linked in the domain or a list of policy objects linked outside the domain.
- **Has This Explicit Permission/Does Not Have This Explicit Permission** Allows you to search for security groups, users, and computers that have or do not have an explicit permission in Group Policy. Explicit permissions are directly assigned. For example, if TimC has been delegated the Edit Settings permission on the TechServices Policy GPO, he has explicit Edit Settings permission with regard to this object.
- **Has This Effective Permission/Does Not Have This Effective Permission**   Allows you to search for security groups, users, and computers that have or do not have an effective permission in Group Policy. Effective permissions are indirectly assigned. For example, a

member of the Domain Admins group has the effective permission to apply settings.

After you select a search item and a search condition for that search item, you specify the value to match. As summarized in Table 5-1, each search item has different types of values you can match. By combining search items and defining conditions for each, you can narrow the search to find the policy objects you are looking for.

TABLE 5-1 Value for Search Items

Computer Configuration	Specifies the policy area to match. Choose the policy area to match from the list provided. If you set the condition as Contains, the GPO must have this area of policy configured to match the search criteria. If you set the condition as Does Not Contain, the GPO must not have this area of policy configured to match the search criteria.
GPO Links	Specifies whether to look for links in the current domain or all available sites. If you set the condition as Exists In, the links in the domain or sites specified match the search criteria. If you set the condition as Does Not Exist In, the links that do not exist in the domain or sites specified match the search criteria.
GPO Name	Sets the text to match in the GPO name. If you set the condition as Contains, the name must contain the text to match. If you set the condition as Does Not Contain, the name must not contain the text to match. If you set the condition as Is Exactly, the name must be exactly as you enter it to match.
GUID	Sets the globally unique identifier (GUID) to match. As the only applicable condition is Equals , the GUID you enter must match a GPO's GUID exactly to match the search criteria.
Linked WMI Filter	Sets the WMI filter to match. Choose the WMI filter name to match from the list provided. If you set the condition Is, the GPO must have the filter applied to match the search criteria. If you set the condition Is Not, the GPO must not have the filter applied to match the search criteria.

Security Groups, Users, or Computers	Sets the delegated permissions to match. Choose the delegated permission to match from the list provided. If you set the condition as Has This Explicit Permission, a security group, user, or computer must have this explicit permission to match the search criteria. If you set the condition as Does Not Have This Explicit Permission, a security group, user, or computer must not have this explicit permission to match the search criteria.
User Configuration	Sets the policy area to match. Choose the policy area to match from the list provided. If you set the condition as Contains, the GPO must have this area of policy configured to match the search criteria. If you set the condition as Does Not Contain, the GPO must not have this area of policy configured to match the search criteria.

Performing Searches for GPOs

To search Group Policy for any of the previously discussed search criteria, complete these steps:

1. Open the GPMC. If you want to search all the domains in a particular forest, right-click the entry for the forest you want to work with and then click Search. If you want to search a specific domain, right-click the domain and then click Search.

2. In the Search For Group Policy Objects dialog box, shown in Figure 5-3, select a search item on the Search Item list, such as GPO Name or User Configuration.

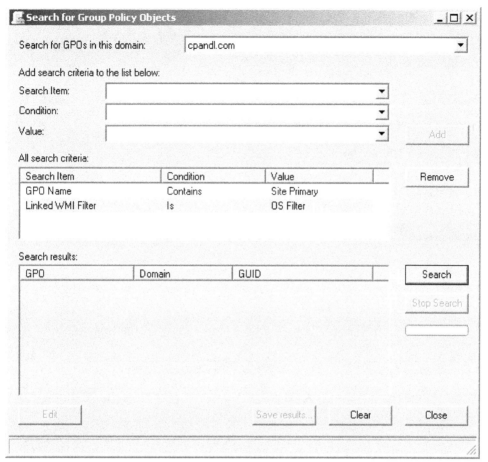

FIGURE 5-3 Use specific search conditions and values to search Group Policy.

3. Use the Condition list to set the search condition.

4. Select or enter a search value in the Value field.

5. Click Add to add the search criteria.

6. As necessary, repeat steps 2 through 5 to add additional search criteria. Keep in mind that additional search criteria further restrict the result set. A policy object must match all search criteria to be displayed in the search results.

7. Click Search to search for policy objects that meet your search criteria.

As shown in Figure 5-4, the search results are displayed in the lower pane of the Search For Group Policy Objects dialog box. GPOs are listed by name, domain, and GUID.

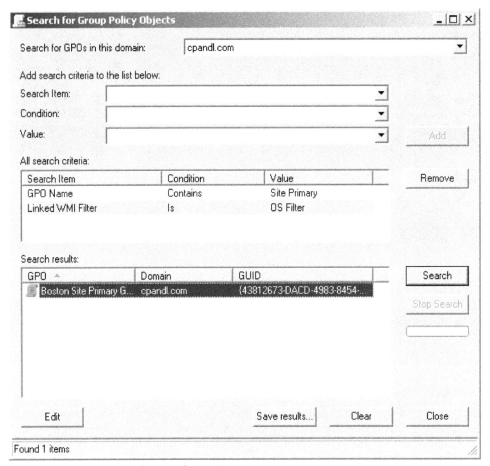

FIGURE 5-4 Review the search results.

You can view or edit the settings of any policy object listed by selecting it in the Search Results list and then clicking Edit. If you have a long list of GPOs and want to save the list, complete the following steps:

1. Click Save Results.
2. Use the Save GPO Search Results dialog box to select a save location for the list.

3. Enter a file name.

4. Click Save. Each GPO is saved to a separate line within a comma-separated values (CSV) text file. Within each line, commas are used to separate the name, domain, and GUID values.

Using Security Group Filters

You'll often need to determine or control whether and how Group Policy applies to a particular security group, user, or computer. By default, GPOs apply to all users and computers in the container to which a particular GPO is linked.

Security Group Filtering

When you've delegated Group Policy management permissions to users or have administrators whose accounts are defined at the domain or OU level, you might not want a policy object to be applied to such accounts. For example, if you've delegated administrator privileges and Group Policy management permissions to Debby, you might want to enable her to install programs and perform other tasks that standard users cannot because of restrictions you've defined in Group Policy. In this case, you must take special steps to ensure that a Group Policy object isn't applied to Debby.

A linked GPO applies to users and computers because of the security settings on the GPO. Two GPO permissions determine whether a policy object applies to a security group, user, or computer:

- **Read**   If this permission is allowed, the security group, user, or computer can read the policy for the purposes of applying it to other groups, users, or computers (not for the purposes of viewing policy settings; View Settings is an explicit permission that must be granted).
- **Apply Group Policy**   If this permission is allowed, the GPO is applied to the security group, user, or computer. The settings of an applied GPO take effect on the group, user, or computer.

> **Note** Additional permissions are also assigned to administrators and the operating system. All members of the Enterprise Admins and Domain Admins groups, as well as the Local System account, have permission to edit or delete GPOs and manage their security.

A security group, user, or computer must have both Read and Apply Group Policy permissions for a policy object to be applied. By default, all users and computers have these permissions for all new GPOs. They inherit these permissions from their membership in the implicit group Authenticated Users. An authenticated user is any user or computer that has logged on to the domain and been authenticated.

To set the permissions so that a GPO applies only to specific users, security groups, or computers (rather than to all authenticated users), you must remove Authenticated Users from the permissions set and then add new security group filters for users who are to receive the GPO. Only members of these groups within the site, domain, or OU where the GPO is linked receive the GPO; members of the groups in other sites, domains, or OUs do not receive the GPO.

Examining Security Group Filters

In the GPMC, you can determine which groups, users, and computers have been assigned both Read and Apply Group Policy permissions by completing the following steps:

1. In the GPMC, expand the entry for the forest you want to work with and then expand the related Domains node.

2. Expand the node for the domain you want to work with. If you don't see the domain you want to work with, right-click Domains and then click Show Domains. You can then select the domains you want to display.

3. Expand the Group Policy Objects node, and then select the GPO you want to work with.

4. In the details pane, click the Scope tab. On the Scope tab, the Security Filtering pane shows which groups, users, and computers have been assigned both Read and Apply Group Policy permissions. By default, only the Authenticated Users group is listed.

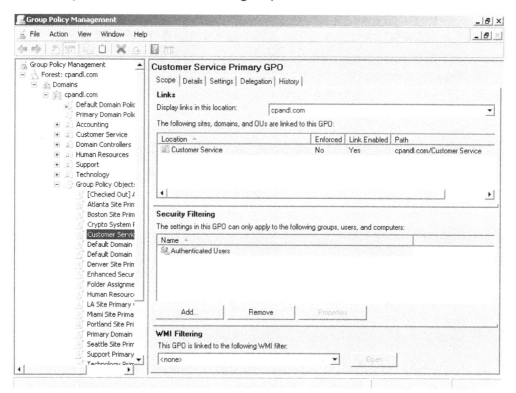

FIGURE 5-5 Review the security filtering configuration.

Real World You can add or remove groups, users, and computers directly from the Security Filtering panel by using the Add and Remove options. Adding a group, user, or computer grants Read and Apply Group Policy permissions. Removing a group, user, or computer removes Read and Apply Group Policy permissions. However, the Security Filtering panel doesn't give you the complete picture of the security permissions that have been assigned to the GPO. For this reason, I describe how you should work with the Delegation tab in the sections that follow. On the Delegation tab, you see the exact set of allowed permissions for all users and groups. This lets you see at a glance how permissions are applied.

Applying Security Group Filters

By default, Authenticated Users, Creator Owner, System, Domain Admins, Enterprise Admins, and Enterprise Domain Controllers have access permissions for GPOs. If you install Advanced Group Policy Management (AGPM), the AGPM service account also has permissions for GPOs.

To change permissions so that a GPO applies only to specific security groups, users, or computers, complete the following steps:

1. In the GPMC, expand the entry for the forest you want to work with and then expand the related Domains node.

2. Expand the node for the domain you want to work with. If you don't see the domain you want to work with, right-click Domains and then click Show Domains. You can then select the domains you want to display.

3. Expand the Group Policy Objects node, and then select the GPO you want to work with.

4. In the details pane, click the Delegation tab to see a list of users and groups that have some level of permissions for the selected policy object.

5. Click Advanced. In the Security Settings dialog box, shown in Figure 5-6, you'll see the list of users and groups that have permissions on the selected GPO. When you select a user or group, you'll see the individual permissions assigned.

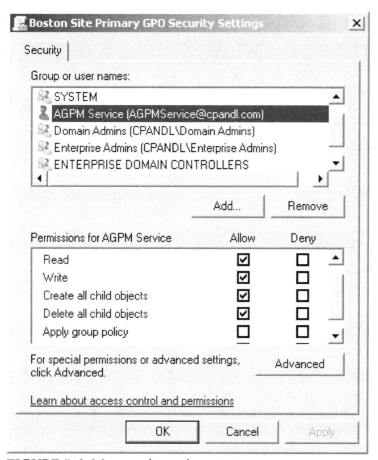

FIGURE 5-6 Manage advanced permissions.

6. If the Authenticated Users group is listed, select it and then click Remove. When prompted to confirm, click OK.

7. Click Add. Use the Select Users, Computers, Or Groups dialog box to select a security group, user, or computer that should have permissions on the selected GPO. Click OK.

8. In the Security Settings dialog box, select the security group, user, or computer you just added. Then do one of the following:

  ▪ If the policy object should be applied to the security group, user, or computer, the minimum permissions should be set to allow Read and Apply Group Policy.

- If the policy object should not be applied to the security group, user, or computer, the minimum permissions should be set to allow Read and deny Apply Group Policy.

> **Caution**   Don't change other permissions unless you are sure of the consequences. A better way to manage other permissions is to follow the techniques discussed in "Delegating Privileges for Group Policy Management" in Chapter 3, "Group Policy Management."

9. Remove and add other groups, users, and computers as appropriate. When you are finished, click OK to apply the security settings.

To remove security group filters and apply the GPO to all authenticated users, complete the following steps:

1. In the GPMC, expand the Group Policy Objects node and then select the GPO you want to work with.

2. In the details pane, click the Delegation tab to see a list of users and groups that have some level of permissions for the selected policy object.

3. Click Advanced. In the Security Settings dialog box, shown earlier in Figure 5-6, you'll see the list of users and groups that have permissions on the selected GPO. When you select a user or group, you'll see the individual permissions assigned.

4. If the Authenticated Users group is not listed, click Add. In the Select Users, Computers, Or Groups dialog box, enter **Authenticated Users** and then click OK.

5. With the Authenticated Users group selected, you should see that this group has been granted Read permission by default. Under Allow, select Apply Group Policy as well to assign this permission to the Authenticated Users group.

6. Remove any additional groups, users, or computers you added previously by selecting each in turn and then clicking Remove. When prompted to confirm, click OK.

7. When you are finished, click OK to apply the security settings.

Using WMI Filters

Windows desktops and Windows servers support Windows Management Instrumentation (WMI). WMI is a management framework that you can use to query a computer to determine its attributes. For example, you can create a WMI query to determine the operating system running on a computer or the amount of available memory.

WMI queries by themselves are helpful, especially when used in scripts. To really tap into their power, however, you can use them with WMI filters. A WMI filter consists of one or more WMI queries that determine whether certain criteria are true. When you link a WMI filter to a GPO, you can use it to control policy application by forcing Group Policy to evaluate your queries with regard to the computers to which the GPO applies. If all the queries return true, meaning that a target computer meets the search criteria, the settings in the GPO are applied. If any of the queries return false, meaning that a target computer does not meet the search criteria, the settings in the GPO are not applied.

WMI filters provide a powerful solution for targeting GPOs to specific users and computers. However, because they are evaluated every time Group Policy is processed, they can increase the amount of time it takes to process policy.

Creating WMI Queries

WMI filters apply only to computers running Windows desktop and Windows Server operating systems. WMI filters are most useful as tools for exception management. By filtering for particular criteria, you can target particular GPOs to specific users and computers.

You create and manage WMI filters by using the GPMC. Most WMI filters use the Root\CimV2 namespace, and this option is populated by default in the GPMC. In the GPMC, you can link a GPO to only one WMI filter at a time. However, each WMI filter can be linked to many GPOs.

WMI filters are evaluated on a destination computer after the list of potential GPOs is determined and filtered based on security group membership. Because a WMI filter applies to every policy setting in the GPO, you must create separate GPOs if you have different filtering requirements for different policy settings.

You can use WMI filters to target Group Policy settings based on just about any measurable characteristic of a computer, including:

- Amount of memory installed
- Available hard disk space
- Processor type or speed
- Network adapter type or speed
- Operating system version, service pack level, or hotfix
- Registry key or key value
- System services that are running

You create WMI queries using the WMI Query Language. The basic syntax is:

```
Select * from WMIObjectClass where Condition
```

In this syntax, *WMIObjectClass* is the WMI class you want to work with, and *Condition* is the condition you want to evaluate. The *Select* statement returns objects of the specified class. A condition has three parts:

- The name of the object property you are examining
- An operator, such as = for equals, > for greater than, or < for less than
- The value to evaluate

Operators can also be defined by using Is or Like. The Is operator is used to exactly match criteria. The Like operator is used to match a keyword or text string within a value. In the following example, you create a filter to target computers running Windows 7:

```
Select * from Win32_OperatingSystem where Caption like "%7%"
```

The Win32_OperatingSystem class tracks the overall operating system configuration. The Win32_OperatingSystem class is one of two WMI object classes that you'll use frequently. The other is Win32_ComputerSystem. The Win32_ComputerSystem class tracks the overall computer configuration.

In Windows PowerShell, you can use the Get-WMIObject cmdlet to get a WMI object that you want to work with. By redirecting the object to Format-List *, you can list all the properties of the object and their values. When working with WMI, you should work with the root namespace, specified by setting the –Namespace parameter to root/cimv2. By using the –Computer parameter, you can specify the computer you want to work with. If you want to work with the local computer, use a dot (.) instead of a computer name.

Following this, you can examine the Win32_OperatingSystem object and its properties to obtain summary information regarding the operating system configuration of a computer by entering the following command at the Windows PowerShell prompt:

```
Get-WmiObject -Class Win32_OperatingSystem -Namespace root/cimv2
-ComputerName . | Format-List *
```

To save the output in a file, simply redirect the output to a file. In the following example, you redirect the output to a file in the working directory named os_save.txt:

```
Get-WmiObject -Class Win32_OperatingSystem -Namespace root/cimv2
-ComputerName . | Format-List * > os_save.txt
```

The detailed operating system information, obtained by using this command, is shown in Listing 5-1. Table 5-2 provides a summary of the operating system properties and their meanings.

LISTING 5-1 Verbose Operating System Configuration Output

```
Status              : OK
Name                : Microsoft® Windows Server® 2008 R2 Enterprise
|C:\Windows|\Device\Harddisk1\Partition1
FreePhysicalMemory  : 679172
```

```
FreeSpaceInPagingFiles: 3749368
FreeVirtualMemory       : 2748020
__GENUS                 : 2
__CLASS                 : Win32_OperatingSystem
__SUPERCLASS            : CIM_OperatingSystem
__DYNASTY               : CIM_ManagedSystemElement
__RELPATH               : Win32_OperatingSystem=@
__PROPERTY_COUNT        : 65
__DERIVATION            : {CIM_OperatingSystem,
                          CIM_LogicalElement,
                          CIM_ManagedSystemElement}
__SERVER                : CORPSERVER84
__NAMESPACE             : root\cimv2
__PATH                  :
\\CORPSERVER84\root\cimv2:Win32_OperatingSystem=@
BootDevice              : \Device\HarddiskVolume1
BuildNumber             : 7601
BuildType               : Multiprocessor Free
Caption                 : Microsoft® Windows Server®
                          2008 R2 Enterprise
CodeSet                 : 1252
CountryCode             : 1
CreationClassName       : Win32_OperatingSystem
CSCreationClassName     : Win32_ComputerSystem
CSDVersion              : Service Pack 1
CSName                  : CORPSERVER84
CurrentTimeZone         : -420
DataExecutionPrevention_32BitApplications : True
DataExecutionPrevention_Available        : True
DataExecutionPrevention_Drivers    : True
DataExecutionPrevention_SupportPolicy    : 3
Debug                   : False
Description             :
Distributed             : False
EncryptionLevel         : 256
ForegroundApplicationBoost       : 2
InstallDate             : 20080917143704.000000-480
LargeSystemCache        :
LastBootUpTime          : 20080804124518.375199-420
LocalDateTime           : 20080804183034.619000-420
Locale                  : 0409
Manufacturer            : Microsoft Corporation
MaxNumberOfProcesses    : 4294967295
MaxProcessMemorySize    : 8589934464
MUILanguages            : {en-US}
```

```
NumberOfLicensedUsers:
NumberOfProcesses    : 95
NumberOfUsers        : 3
OperatingSystemSKU   : 10
Organization         :
OSArchitecture       : 64-bit
OSLanguage           : 1033
OSProductSuite       : 274
OSType               : 18
OtherTypeDescription :
PAEEnabled           :
PlusProductID        :
PlusVersionNumber    :
Primary              : True
ProductType          : 2
QuantumLength        : 1
QuantumType          : 1
RegisteredUser       : Windows User
SerialNumber         :
ServicePackMajorVersion        : 1
ServicePackMinorVersion        : 0
SizeStoredInPagingFiles        : 3974528
SuiteMask            : 274
SystemDevice         : \Device\HarddiskVolume2
SystemDirectory      : C:\Windows\system32
SystemDrive          : C:
TotalSwapSpaceSize           :
TotalVirtualMemorySize       : 7591744
TotalVisibleMemorySize       : 3667328
Version              : 6.1.7601
WindowsDirectory     : C:\Windows
Scope     : System.Management.ManagementScope
Path      : \\Server52\root\cimv2:
            Win32_OperatingSystem=@
Options   : System.Management.ObjectGetOptions
ClassPath   : \\CorpServer52\root\cimv2:
              Win32_OperatingSystem
Properties           : {BootDevice...}
SystemProperties     : {___GENUS, ___CLASS,
                        ___SUPERCLASS...}
Qualifiers           : {dynamic, Locale, provider, Singleton...}
Site        :
Container            :
```

TABLE 5-2 Properties of Win32_OperatingSystem

BootDevice	Disk drive from which the Win32 operating system boots.
BuildNumber	Build number of the operating system.
BuildType	Type of build used for the operating system, such as "retail build", "checked build", or "Multiprocessor Free".
Caption	Operating system name.
ClassPath	WMI object class path.
CodeSet	Code page value used by the operating system.
Container	The container associated with the object.
CountryCode	Country code used by the operating system.
CreationClassName	Name of the class from which the object is derived.
CSCreationClassName	Name of the class from which the computer system object is derived.
CSDVersion	Indicates the latest service pack installed on the computer. The value is NULL if no service pack is installed.
CSName	Name of the computer system associated with this object class.
CurrentTimeZone	Number of minutes the operating system is offset from Coordinated Universal Time. The value is positive, negative, or zero.
DataExecutionPrevention_32BitApplications	Indicates whether Data Execution Prevention (DEP) is enabled for 32-bit applications.
DataExecutionPrevention_Available	Indicates whether DEP is supported by the system hardware.

DataExecutionPrevention_Drivers	Indicates whether DEP is enabled for device drivers.
DataExecutionPrevention_SupportPolicy	Specifies the DEP support policy being used. Values are 0 = none, 2 = on for essential Windows programs and services only, 3 = on for all programs except those specifically excluded.
Debug	Indicates whether the operating system is a checked (debug) build. If TRUE, the debugging version of User.exe is installed.
Description	Description of the Windows operating system.
Distributed	Indicates whether the operating system is distributed across multiple computer system nodes. If so, these nodes should be grouped as a cluster.
EncryptionLevel	Level of encryption for secure transactions, as 40-bit, 128-bit, or n-bit.
ForegroundApplicationBoost	Sets the priority of the foreground application. Application boost is implemented by giving an application more processor time. Values are: 0 = none, 1 = minimum, 2 = maximum (default).
FreePhysicalMemory	Physical memory (in kilobytes) currently unused and available.
FreeSpaceInPagingFiles	Amount of free space (in kilobytes) in the operating system's paging files. Swapping occurs when the free space fills up.
FreeVirtualMemory	Virtual memory (in kilobytes) unused and available.
InstallDate	Date when the operating system was installed.

LargeSystemCache	Indicates whether memory usage is optimized for programs or the system cache. Values are: 0 = memory usage is optimized for programs, 1 = memory usage is optimized for the system cache.
LastBootUpTime	When the operating system was last booted.
LocalDateTime	Local date and time on the computer.
Locale	Language identifier used by the operating system.
Manufacturer	Operating system manufacturer. For Win32 systems, this value will be "Microsoft Corporation".
MaxNumberOfProcesses	Maximum number of process contexts the operating system can support. If there is no fixed maximum, the value is 0.
MaxProcessMemorySize	Maximum memory (in kilobytes) that can be allocated to a process. A value of zero indicates that there is no maximum.
MUILanguages	User interface languages supported.
Name	Name of the operating system instance.
NumberOfLicensedUsers	Number of user licenses for the operating system. A value of 0 = unlimited, a value of −1 = unknown.
NumberOfProcesses	Current number of process contexts on the system.
NumberOfUsers	Current number of user sessions.
OperatingSystemSKU	Operating system product type indicator.
Options	Lists the management object options.
Organization	Company name set for the registered user of the operating system.

OSArchitecture	Operating system architecture, as 32-bit or 64-bit.
OSLanguage	Language version of the operating system installed.
OSProductSuite	Operating system product suite installed.
OSType	Type of operating system. Values include: 1 = other, 18 = Windows NT or later.
OtherTypeDescription	Sets additional description; used when OSType = 1.
Path	Identifies the full WMI path to the object class.
PAEEnabled	Indicates whether physical address expansion (PAE) is enabled.
PlusProductID	Product number for Windows Plus! (if installed).
PlusVersionNumber	Version number of Windows Plus! (if installed).
Primary	Indicates whether this is the primary operating system.
ProductType	Operating system product type. Values are: 1 = workstation, 2 = domain controller, 3 = server.
Properties	Lists all the properties of the object.
Qualifiers	Lists any qualifiers for the object.
QuantumLength	Number of clock ticks per unit of processor execution. Values are: 1 = unknown, 2 = one tick, 3 = two ticks.

QuantumType	Length type for units of processor execution. Values are: 1 = unknown, 2 = fixed, 3 = variable. With variable length, foreground and background applications can have different values. With fixed length, the foreground and background values are the same.
RegisteredUser	Name set for the registered user of the operating system.
Scope	Lists the management object scope.
SerialNumber	Operating system product serial number.
ServicePackMajorVersion	Major version number of the service pack installed on the computer. If no service pack has been installed, the value is 0 or NULL.
ServicePackMinorVersion	Minor version number of the service pack installed on the computer. If no service pack has been installed, the value is 0 or NULL.
Site	Site associated with the object.
SizeStoredInPagingFiles	Total number of kilobytes that can be stored in the operating system's paging files. A value of 0 indicates that there are no paging files.
Status	Current status of the object. Values include: "OK", "Error", "Unknown", "Degraded", "Pred Fail", "Starting", "Stopping", and "Service".
SuiteMask	Bit flags that identify the product suites available on the system.
SystemDevice	Physical disk partition on which the operating system is installed.
SystemDirectory	System directory of the operating system.
SystemDrive	Physical disk partition on which the operating system is installed.

SystemProperties	Lists the system properties.
TotalSwapSpaceSize	Total swap space in kilobytes. This value may be unspecified (NULL) if swap space is not distinguished from page files.
TotalVirtualMemorySize	Virtual memory size (in kilobytes).
TotalVisibleMemorySize	Total amount of physical memory (in kilobytes) that is available to the operating system.
Version	Version number of the operating system.
WindowsDirectory	Windows directory of the operating system.

The detailed operating system information tells you a great deal about the operating system running on the computer. The same is true for computer configuration details, which can be obtained by entering the following command at a Windows PowerShell prompt:

```
Get-WmiObject -Class Win32_ComputerSystem -Namespace root/cimv2
-ComputerName . | Format-List *
```

Listing 5-2 provides an example of the output from this command, and Table 5-3 provides a summary of the computer configuration properties and their meaning. As discussed previously, you can redirect the output to a save file.

LISTING 5-2 Computer Configuration Information

```
AdminPasswordStatus          : 1
BootupState                  : Normal boot
ChassisBootupState           : 3
KeyboardPasswordStatus       : 2
PowerOnPasswordStatus        : 1
PowerSupplyState             : 3
PowerState                   : 0
FrontPanelResetStatus        : 2
ThermalState                 : 3
Status                       : OK
Name                         : CORPSERVER84
PowerManagementCapabilities  :
PowerManagementSupported     :
```

```
__GENUS                     : 2
__CLASS                     : Win32_ComputerSystem
__SUPERCLASS                : CIM_UnitaryComputerSystem
__DYNASTY                   : CIM_ManagedSystemElement
__RELPATH                   :
Win32_ComputerSystem.Name="CORPSERVER84"
__PROPERTY_COUNT            : 58
__DERIVATION                : {CIM_UnitaryComputerSystem,
CIM_ComputerSystem, CIM_System,CIM_LogicalElement...}
__SERVER                    : CORPSERVER84
__NAMESPACE                 : root\cimv2
__PATH      :\\CORPSERVER84\root\cimv2:
            Win32_ComputerSystem.Name="CORPSERVER84"
AutomaticManagedPagefile    : True
AutomaticResetBootOption    : True
AutomaticResetCapability    : True
BootOptionOnLimit           :
BootOptionOnWatchDog        :
BootROMSupported            : True
Caption                     : CORPSERVER84
CreationClassName           : Win32_ComputerSystem
CurrentTimeZone             : -420
DaylightInEffect            : True
Description                 : AT/AT COMPATIBLE
DNSHostName                 : CORPSERVER84
Domain                      : imaginedlands.com
DomainRole                  : 5
EnableDaylightSavingsTime   : True
InfraredSupported           : False
InitialLoadInfo             :
InstallDate                 :
LastLoadInfo                :
Manufacturer                : Dell Inc.
Model                       :
NameFormat                  :
NetworkServerModeEnabled    : True
NumberOfLogicalProcessors   : 2
NumberOfProcessors          : 1
OEMLogoBitmap               :
OEMStringArray              : {www.dell.com}
PartOfDomain                : True
PauseAfterReset             : -1
PCSystemType                : 5
PrimaryOwnerContact         :
PrimaryOwnerName            : Windows User
```

```
ResetCapability          : 1
ResetCount               : -1
ResetLimit               : -1
Roles                    : {LM_Workstation, LM_Server,
Primary_Domain_Controller, Timesource...}
SupportContactDescription :
SystemStartupDelay       :
SystemStartupOptions     :
SystemStartupSetting     :
SystemType               : x64-based PC
TotalPhysicalMemory      : 3755343872
UserName                 : IMAGINEDL\williams
WakeUpType               : 6
Workgroup                :
Scope                    : System.Management.ManagementScope
Path                     : \\Server52\root\cimv2:
             Win32_ComputerSystem.Name="Server52"
Options                  : System.Management.ObjectGetOptions
ClassPath                : \\Server52\root\cimv2:
                           Win32_ComputerSystem
Properties               : {AdminPasswordStatus...}
SystemProperties         : {___GENUS, ___CLASS,
                           ___SUPERCLASS...}
Qualifiers               : {dynamic, Locale,
                           provider, UUID}
Site                     :
Container                :
```

TABLE 5-3 Computer Configuration Entries and Their Meaning

AdminPasswordStatus	Status of the Administrator password. Values are: 1 = disabled, 2 = enabled, 3 = not implemented, 4 = unknown.
AutomaticManagedPagefile	Indicates whether the computer's page file is being managed by the operating system.
AutomaticResetBootOption	Indicates whether the automatic reset boot option is enabled.
AutomaticResetCapability	Indicates whether the automatic reset is enabled.
BootOptionOnLimit	System action to be taken when the ResetLimit value is reached. Values are: 1 = reserved, 2 = operating system, 3 = system utilities, 4 = do not reboot.

BootOptionOnWatchDog	Reboot action to be taken after the time on the watchdog timer has elapsed. Values are: 1 = reserved, 2 = operating system, 3 = system utilities, 4 = do not reboot.
BootROMSupported	Indicates whether a boot ROM is supported.
BootupState	Indicates how the system was started. Values are: "Normal boot", "Fail-safe boot", and "Fail-safe with network boot".
Caption	System name.
ChassisBootupState	Bootup state of the system chassis. Values are: 1 = other, 2 = unknown, 3 = safe, 4 = warning, 5 = critical, 6 = nonrecoverable.
ClassPath	Windows Management Instrumentation (WMI) object class path.
Container	Container associated with the object.
CreationClassName	Name of class from which object is derived.
CurrentTimeZone	Number of minutes the computer is offset from Coordinated Universal Time.
DaylightInEffect	Indicates whether daylight saving mode is on.
Description	Description of the computer.
DNSHostName	Name of the server according to DNS.
Domain	Name of the domain to which the computer belongs.
DomainRole	Domain role of the computer. Values are:0 = stand-alone workstation, 1 = member workstation, 2 = stand-alone server, 3 = member server, 4 = backup domain controller, 5 = primary domain controller.
EnableDaylightSavingsTime	Indicates whether daylight saving time (DST) is enabled. If True, the system changes to an hour ahead or behind when DST starts or ends. If False, the system does not change to an hour ahead or behind when DST starts or ends.

FrontPanelResetStatus	Hardware security settings for the reset button on the computer. Values are: 0 = disabled, 1 = enabled, 2 = not implemented, 3 = unknown.
InfraredSupported	Indicates whether an infrared (IR) port exists on the computer system.
InitialLoadInfo	Data needed to find either the initial load device (its key) or the boot service to request the operating system to start up.
InstallDate	Date when the computer was installed.
KeyboardPasswordStatus	Indicates the keyboard password status. Values are: 0 = disabled, 1 = enabled, 2 = not implemented, 3 = unknown.
LastLoadInfo	Array entry of the InitialLoadInfo property, which holds the data corresponding to booting the currently loaded operating system.
Manufacturer	Computer manufacturer's name.
Model	Product name given by the manufacturer.
Name	Computer name.
NameFormat	Identifies how the computer system name is generated.
NetworkServerModeEnabled	Indicates whether network server mode is enabled.
NumberOfLogicalProcessors	Number of processor cores. If the computer has two processors with four cores each, the number of logical processors is eight. If the computer has hyperthreading architecture, the number of logical processors may also be higher than the number of physical processors.
NumberOfProcessors	Number of enabled processors on the computer.
OEMLogoBitmap	Identifies the bitmap for the OEM's logo.
OEMStringArray	List of descriptive strings set by the OEM.
PartOfDomain	Indicates whether the computer is part of a domain. If True, the computer is a member of a domain. If False, the computer is a member of a workgroup.

Options	Lists the management object options.
Path	Identifies the full WMI path to the object class.
PauseAfterReset	Time delay (in milliseconds) before a reboot is initiated after a system power cycle or reset. A value of -1 indicates there is no time delay.
PCSystemType	Indicates the type of computer. Values are: 0 = unspecified, 1 = desktop, 2 = mobile, 3 = workstation, 4 = enterprise server, 5 = small office and home office (SOHO) server, 6 = appliance PC, 7 = performance server, 8 = role maximum.
PowerManagementCapabilities	Power management capabilities of a logical device. Values are: 0 = unknown, 1 = not supported, 2 = disabled, 3 = enabled, 4 = power saving modes entered automatically, 5 = power state settable, 6 = power cycling supported, 7 = timed power on supported.
PowerManagementSupported	Indicates whether the device's power can be managed.
PowerOnPasswordStatus	Power on password status. Values are:0 = disabled, 1 = enabled, 2 = not implemented, 3 = unknown.
PowerState	Indicates the current power state of the computer. Values are: 0 = unknown, 1 = full power, 2 = power save – low power mode, 3 = power save – standby, 4 = power save – unknown, 5 = power cycle, 6 = power off, 7 = power save – warning.
PowerSupplyState	State of the enclosure's power supply when last booted. Values are: 1 = other, 2 = unknown, 3 = safe, 4 = warning, 5 = critical, 6 = nonrecoverable.
PrimaryOwnerContact	Contact information for the computer's owner.
PrimaryOwnerName	Name of the system owner.
Properties	Lists all the properties of the object.
Qualifiers	Lists any qualifiers for the object.

ResetCapability	Value indicates whether a computer can be reset using the Power and Reset buttons (or other hardware means). Values are: 1 = other, 2 = unknown, 3 = disabled, 4 = enabled, 5 = nonrecoverable.
ResetCount	Number of automatic resets since the last intentional reset. A value of -1 indicates that the count is unknown.
ResetLimit	Number of consecutive times a system reset will be attempted. A value of -1 indicates that the limit is unknown.
Roles	System roles.
Scope	Lists the management object scope.
Site	The site associated with the object.
Status	Current status of the computer. Values are: "OK", "Error", "Degraded", "Unknown", "Pred Fail", "Starting", "Stopping", "Service".
SupportContactDescription	List of the support contact information for the computer.
SystemProperties	Lists the system properties.
SystemStartupDelay	Startup delay in seconds.
SystemStartupOptions	List of the startup options for the computer.
SystemStartupSetting	Index of the default start profile.
SystemType	System architecture type, such as "X86-based PC" or "64-bit Intel PC".
ThermalState	Thermal state of the system chassis when last booted. Values are: 1 = other, 2 = unknown, 3 = safe, 4 = warning, 5 = critical, 6 = nonrecoverable.
TotalPhysicalMemory	Total byte size of physical memory.
UserName	Name of the user currently logged on.

WakeUpType	Event that caused the system to power up. Values are: 0 = reserved, 1 = other, 2 = unknown, 3 = APM timer, 4 = modem ring, 5 = LAN remote, 6 = power switch, 7 = PCI PME#, 8 = AC power restored.
Workgroup	When a computer is a member of a workgroup, the workgroup name is listed here.

In addition to targeting operating system or computer configuration properties, you might want to target computers based on the amount of disk space and file system type. In the following example, you target computers that have more than 100 megabytes (MB) of available space on the C, D, or G partition:

```
Select * from Win32_LogicalDisk where (Name = " C:"  OR Name = " D:"
OR Name = " G:" ) AND DriveType = 3 AND FreeSpace > 104857600 AND
FileSystem = " NTFS"
```

In the preceding example, DriveType = 3 represents a local disk and FreeSpace units are in bytes (100 MB = 104,857,600 bytes). The partitions must be located on one or more local fixed disks, and they must be running the NTFS file system.

In Windows PowerShell, you can examine all the properties of the Win32_LogicalDisk object by entering the following command at the Windows PowerShell prompt:

```
Get-WmiObject -Class Win32_LogicalDisk -Namespace root/cimv2
 -ComputerName . | Format-List *
```

As you'll see, there are many properties you can work with, including Compressed, which indicates whether a disk is compressed. Other important WMI object classes include:

- **Win32_BIOS**   Displays information about the BIOS configuration on the computer
- **Win32_NetworkAdapterConfiguration**   Displays information about the network adapter configuration on the computer

- **Win32_PageFile**   Displays information about the page file configuration on the computer
- **Win32_PhysicalMemory**   Displays information about the physical memory configuration on the computer
- **Win32_Process**   Displays information about all the processes running on the computer
- **Win32_Processor**   Displays information about the computer's CPU
- **Win32_Service**   Displays information about all the services configured on the computer

Using the techniques I've discussed previously, you can examine the properties of any or all of these objects by using Windows PowerShell. If you do, you will find that Win32_PhysicalMemory has a Capacity property that tracks the total physical memory in bytes. Knowing this, you could easily create a WMI filter to target computers with 256 MB of RAM or more. The WMI query to handle the task is the following:

```
Select * from Win32_PhysicalMemory where Capacity > 262000000
```

I used the value 262000000 because there are 262,144,000 bytes in 256 MB, and we want the computer to have at least this capacity.

To display a complete list of WMI objects, enter the following command at the Windows PowerShell prompt:

```
Get-WmiObject –list -Namespace root/cimv2 -ComputerName .
 | Format-List name
```

Because the list of available objects is so long, you'll definitely want to redirect the output to a file. In the following example, you redirect the output to a file in the working directory called FullWMIObjectList.txt:

```
Get-WmiObject –list -Namespace root/cimv2 -ComputerName .
 | Format-List name > FullWMIObjectList.txt
```

Rather than viewing all WMI classes, you may want to see only the Win32 WMI classes. To view only the Win32 WMI classes, use the following command:

```
Get-WmiObject -list | where {$_.name -like "*Win32_*"}
```

Managing WMI Filters

Creating and applying WMI filters is a two-step process. First you define the WMI filter and set the desired query. Then you link the WMI filter to GPOs as appropriate. If you later decide that you don't want to link a WMI filter to a GPO, you can unlink the filter to remove it. After you remove the link to the WMI filter, the GPO will no longer filter policy application based on the queries defined in the filter.

Creating a WMI Filter

Because WMI filters let you easily target specific types of computers, they are often overused. However, this approach is not necessarily a good one. WMI filters work well when you have a few management exceptions. They don't work well when you deploy them widely. If you create multiple WMI filters, each targeted to separate GPOs, you may negatively impact performance. Why? Too many WMI filters can slow down Group Policy processing because each filter must be evaluated whenever policy is applied. To avoid problems, test your WMI filters carefully and deploy them strategically.

To create a WMI filter, complete the following steps:

1. In the GPMC, expand the entry for the forest you want to work with and then expand the related Domains node.
2. Expand the WMI Filters node to display a list of currently configured filters in the details pane, as shown in Figure 5-7. If an existing WMI filter is linked to one or more GPOs, the names of the GPOs are listed under the Linked GPO column.

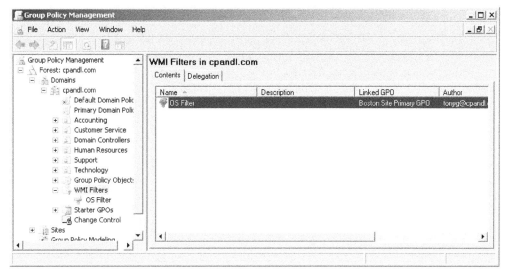

FIGURE 5-7 List currently configured WMI filters.

3. Right-click the WMI Filters node in the domain in which you want to add a WMI filter, and then click New.

4. In the New WMI Filter dialog box, shown in Figure 5-8, type a name for the new WMI filter in the Name box, and then type a description of the filter in the Description box.

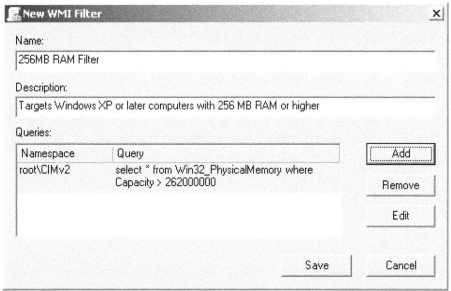

FIGURE 5-8 Create the WMI query.

5. Click Add. In the WMI Query dialog box, the default namespace is root\CimV2. In most cases, you do not need to change the namespace. If you need to change this value, click Browse, select the namespace you need to use from the list, and then click OK.

6. In the WMI Query dialog box, define a WMI query in the Query box, and then click OK.

7. To add additional queries to the filter, repeat steps 4 through 6.

8. After you add all the necessary WMI queries, click Save. The WMI filter will then be available to be linked.

Viewing and Editing WMI Filters

When you select the WMI Filters node in the GPMC, you see a list of the currently configured WMI filters in the details pane. If a WMI filter is linked to one or more GPOs, the names of the GPOs are listed in the Linked GPO column.

To view and manage individual filters, expand the WMI Filters node in the console tree and then select the WMI filter you want to work with. In the details pane, you'll then see the configuration details for the selected WMI filter. As shown in Figure 5-9, the General tab displays:

- The description you entered for the WMI filter
- The queries you defined for the WMI filter
- The GPOs that are linked to the WMI filter

If you want to edit the filter definition, click Edit Filter. You are then able to see the filter name and description. You are also able to add, remove, or edit WMI queries. When you are finished, click Save to save the changes. Any query changes are reflected the next time clients process group policy.

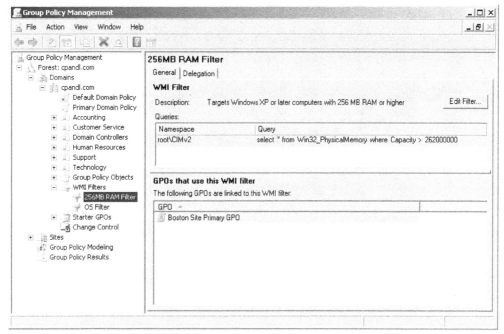

FIGURE 5-9 Review the WMI filter details.

Applying or Removing a WMI Filter

To apply a WMI filter, you must link it to a GPO. Each GPO can have only one linked WMI filter at a time. If you no longer want a GPO to process a WMI filter, you can remove the link.

To add or remove a link to a WMI filter, complete the following steps:

1. In the GPMC, expand the entry for the forest you want to work with and then expand the related Domains node.

2. Expand the node for the domain you want to work with. If you don't see the domain you want to work with, right-click Domains and then click Show Domains. You can then select the domains you want to display.

3. Expand the Group Policy Objects node and then select the GPO you want to work with.

4. In the details pane, click the Scope tab. On the Scope tab, the WMI Filtering pane shows whether the GPO is linked to a WMI filter (see Figure 5-10).

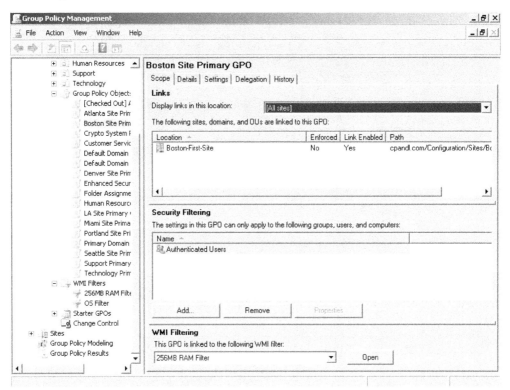

FIGURE 5-10 Link a WMI filter to a GPO.

5. Do one of the following:

- If you want to add a link to a WMI filter, select the WMI filter from the drop-down list provided. When prompted to confirm that you want to change to the selected filter, click Yes.
- If you want to remove a link to a WMI filter, select <None> from the drop-down list provided. When prompted to confirm that you want to remove the previously selected filter, click Yes.

Chapter 6. Maintaining and Migrating the SYSVOL

The SYSVOL is a collection of folders that contain copies of a domain's public files, including system policies, logon scripts, and important elements of Group Policy objects (GPOs). The SYSVOL directory must be available and the appropriate subdirectories must be shared on a server before the server can advertise itself on the network as a domain controller. Shared subdirectories within the SYSVOL are replicated to every domain controller in the domain.

In Group Policy, only the Group Policy template (GPT) is replicated through SYSVOL replication. Active Directory replication handles replication of the Group Policy container (GPC), which is stored in the domain's directory database. For Group Policy to be effective, both the GPT and the GPC must be available on a domain controller.

Migrating the SYSVOL

When a domain is operating at the Windows Server 2008 domain functional level, domain controllers can use Distributed File System (DFS) Replication for replication of the SYSVOL share. As discussed in "Replication Changes" in Chapter 2, "Deploying Group Policy," DFS Replication technology significantly improves replication of the SYSVOL. For files that are larger than 64 kilobytes (KB), DFS Replication uses an algorithm called *remote differential compression* (RDC) to detect changes to the data, and this enables DFS Replication to replicate only the changes, in the form of file blocks, without having to replicate entire files. To ensure rapid propagation of changes, the DFS Replication service actively monitors the SYSVOL. If a change occurs to any file in the SYSVOL, the service automatically replicates the file updates to the SYSVOL folders on the other domain controllers in the domain.

SYSVOL Migration Essentials

Distributed File System (DFS) Replication is the default file replication service only for domains that are initially created on domain controllers running

Windows Server 2008 or later, and set to operate at the Windows 2008 or higher domain functional level. In domains operating at the Windows Server 2003 functional level or lower, File Replication Service (FRS) is the default replication service for SYSVOL replication. Domains raised to the Windows Server 2008 domain functional level from a lower functional level use FRS as the default replication service for SYSVOL replication as well.

To implement DFS Replication of the SYSVOL throughout a domain, you must:

1. Upgrade your domain controllers to Windows Server 2008 or later.
2. Raise the domain functional level to Windows Server 2008 or later.
3. Initiate SYSVOL migration to move from using FRS replication of the SYSVOL to DFS Replication.

> **Note** This procedure is required only for existing domain controllers and when DFS Replication of the SYSVOL has not yet been implemented. Once you upgrade the domain, any computer you promote to a domain controller afterward will use DFS Replication automatically.

Upgrading your domain controllers and raising the domain function level are steps that you should take only after careful planning. You can use *Active Directory Administration: The Personal Trainer* to help you plan and perform the upgrade.

> **Tip** On your management desktop, you can install the DFSR management tools as part of the Remote Server Administration tools. See "Installing the Remote Server Administration Tools" in Appendix A, "Installing Group Policy Extensions and Tools," for details.

You initiate a SYSVOL migration from FRS replication to DFS Replication by running the DFS Replication Migration utility (Dfsrmig.exe). This utility is included with Windows Server 2008 and Windows Server 2008 R2. You run the DFS Replication Migration utility on one domain controller in a domain you've prepared for migration, and this initiates SYSVOL migration globally for all domain controllers in the domain. Once you initiate a global migration, you use the utility to manage the migration through the following migration states:

- **Start** In this state, the migration is ready to start. FRS is still responsible for replicating the contents of the SYSVOL share between domain controllers.
- **Preparing** A transitional state in which the DFS Replication service is preparing to make a copy of the contents of the SYSVOL share.
- **Waiting for Initial Sync** A transitional state in which the DFS Replication service is waiting for the initial sync to complete. This process builds up entries for all files in the SYSVOL_DFSR folder in the Jet database used by Active Directory.
- **Prepared** In this state, the DFS Replication service has successfully made a copy of the contents of the SYSVOL share and then initiated replication of its copy of the SYSVOL folder with the DFS Replication service running on peer domain controllers that have migrated to the Prepared state as well. However, FRS is still responsible for replicating the contents of the SYSVOL share between domain controllers.
- **Redirecting** A transitional state in which the DFS Replication service is preparing to take control of SYSVOL replication.
- **Redirected** In this state, the DFS Replication service has taken control of SYSVOL replication. The Netlogon service is now sharing and advertising the SYSVOL copy maintained by the DFS Replication service. FRS is still replicating the old SYSVOL folder with instances of the FRS service running on peer domain controllers.
- **Eliminating** A transitional state in which the domain controller is in the process of retiring the FRS service.
- **Eliminated** In this state, the FRS service is retired and the DFS Replication service has assumed sole responsibility for replicating the contents of the SYSVOL share between all domain controllers in the domain.

At the Prepared and Redirected states, you have the opportunity to ensure that DFS Replication is working properly. If you suspect there is a problem, you can roll back migration to the Start or Prepared states. Note that it is not possible to roll back the migration once the Eliminated state has been reached.

You should only perform a migration of the SYSVOL from FRS replication to DFS Replication after careful planning and testing. As part of your implementation plan, you should plan to notify other administrators when you start the migration and when the migration is complete. Notification is important because you don't want other administrators to make changes that will modify the contents of the SYSVOL during the migration. If any changes are made to the SYSVOL share during the transition from the Prepared to the Redirected state, you need to copy the changes from SYSVOL to the SYSVOL_DFSR share on any replicated writable domain controller.

Checking the SYSVOL Replication Status

When domain controllers are using FRS replication, the Netlogon service shares and advertises the SYSVOL copy maintained by the FRS replication service. If you enter **net share** at a command prompt, you'll see two related shares, as shown in this example:

```
D:\Users\williams>net share

Share name    Resource        Remark
-------------------------------------------------------
C$            C:\             Default share
D$            D:\             Default share
IPC$                          Remote IPC
ADMIN$        C:\Windows      Remote Admin
NETLOGON C:\Windows\SYSVOL\sysvol\imaginedlands.com\SCRIPTS
Logon server share

SYSVOL C:\Windows\SYSVOL\sysvol    Logon server share

The command completed successfully.
```

Here, the path to the NETLOGON share is C:\Windows\SYSVOL\sysvol\imaginedlands.com\SCRIPTS, and the path to the SYSVOL share is C:\Windows\SYSVOL\sysvol. This is the default configuration for the SYSVOL when FRS replication is being used.

When domain controllers are using DFS Replication, the Netlogon service shares and advertises the SYSVOL copy maintained by the DFS Replication service. If you enter **net share** at a command prompt, you'll see two related shares, as shown in this example:

```
 D:\Users\williams>net share

Share name    Resource        Remark
----------------------------------------------------
C$            C:\             Default share
D$            D:\             Default share
IPC$                          Remote IPC
ADMIN$        C:\Windows      Remote Admin
NETLOGON C:\Windows\SYSVOL_DFSR\sysvol\imaginedlands.com\SCRIPTS
Logon server share

SYSVOL C:\Windows\SYSVOL_DFSR\sysvol   Logon server share

The command completed successfully.
```

Here, the path to the NETLOGON share is C:\Windows\SYSVOL_DFSR\sysvol\imaginedlands.com\SCRIPTS, and the path to the SYSVOL share is C:\Windows\SYSVOL_DFSR\sysvol. This is the default configuration for the SYSVOL when DFS Replication is being used.

Knowing this, you can easily determine whether a domain controller is using FRS replication or DFS Replication. If you see C:\Windows\SYSVOL\sysvol, the domain controller is still using FRS replication. If you see C:\Windows\SYSVOL_DFSR\sysvol, the domain controller is using DFS Replication.

Performing the SYSVOL Migration

The DFS Replication Migration utility (Dfsrmig.exe) has several options. The key options are:

- **/SetGlobalState**   Sets a desired global state for the migration.
- **/GetGlobalState**   Gets the current global state for the migration.

You follow the /SetGlobalState option with a value that specifies the desired state. Values you use to set the state are:

- for Start state
- for Prepared state
- for Redirected state
- for Eliminated state

> **Real World**   The migration of a large Active Directory environment can take a long time. Because of site replication schedules, you may have to wait for intersite replication to occur before remote domain controllers in other sites process the migration directive. Because a writable domain controller acting on behalf of a read-only domain controller sets the migration states for the read-only domain controller, you may have to wait for the writable domain controller to replicate the desired state and for the read-only domain controller to establish the desired state.

Using the DFS Replication Migration utility (Dfsrmig.exe), you migrate the SYSVOL from FRS replication to DFS Replication by going through each migration state. You move domain controllers to the Prepared state first, then to the Redirected state, and finally to the Eliminated state.

Step 1: Migrating to the Prepared State

You move all domain controllers in a domain to the Prepared state by entering the following command at an elevated, administrator command prompt: **dfsrmig /SetGlobalState 1**. Dfsrmig will report the following:

```
Current DFSR global state: 'Start'New DFSR global state: 'Prepared'

Migration will proceed to 'Prepared' state. DFSR service will copy
the contents of SYSVOL to SYSVOL_DFSR folder.

If any DC is unable to start migration then try manual polling. OR
Run with option /CreateGlobalObjects. Migration can start anytime
between 15 min to 1 hour. Succeeded.
```

Caution You should run Dfsrmig only on a domain controller
running Windows Server 2008 and in a domain operating at the
Windows Server 2008 domain functional level.

Real World During this or any other stage of the migration, you can
use the following techniques to help you resolve problems:

Remotely query the Service Control Manager running on a domain
controller to determine whether the DFS Replication service is running.
Use the following command to determine the status of the service: **sc
\\ComputerName query dfsr,** where *ComputerName* is the host name
of the domain controller. For example, run the command **sc
\\CorpServer84 query dfsr**.

Force Active Directory replication on a domain controller by running
the following command at an elevated command prompt on the
domain controller: **repadmin /syncall**.

Manually poll Active Directory to trigger the migration by running the
following command at an elevated command prompt: **dfsrdiag PollAd
/Member:ComputerName,** where *ComputerName* is the host name of
the domain controller—for example, **dfsrdiag PollAd
/Member:CorpServer84**.

Next, at an elevated, administrator command prompt, enter the following
command to check the migration state: **dfsrmig /GetMigrationState**. The
output of this command tells you the exact status of the migration to the
Prepared state. Any domain controllers not in sync with this global state are
listed by name and domain-controller type. Once all domain controllers have
reached this state, the output from the command will be similar to the
following:

```
All Domain Controllers have migrated successfully to Global state
('Prepared')
Succeeded.
```

If you want to double-check, you have several ways to confirm that all domain controllers are prepared. As part of moving to the Prepared state, the DFS Replication service will copy the contents of the SYSVOL to the SYSVOL_DFSR folder. If the SYSVOL_DFSR folder has been created under %SystemRoot%, this confirms that the migration to the Prepared state worked properly. When the DFS Replication service on each domain controller reaches the Prepared state, Information event 8014 will be registered in its event log as well.

Once all domain controllers have successfully reached the Prepared state, check the replication status by entering the following command: **repadmin /replsum**. Proceed only if the domain has a healthy status for Active Directory replication.

> **Note**   Rather than continuing, if necessary, you can roll back to the Start state by entering the following command: **dfsrmig /SetGlobalState 0**. You then need to restart this procedure at step 1.

Step 2: Migrating to the Redirected State

If all domain controllers have successfully reached the Prepared state, you can move the domain controllers to the Redirected state by entering the following command: **dfsrmig /SetGlobalState 2**. Dfsrmig will report the following:

```
 Current DFSR global state: 'Prepared'
New DFSR global state: 'Redirected'

Migration will proceed to 'Redirected' state. The SYSVOL share will
be changed to SYSVOL_DFSR folder.

If any changes have been made to the SYSVOL share during the state
transition from 'Prepared' to 'Redirected', please robocopy the
changes from SYSVOL to SYSVOL_DFSR on any replicated RWDC.
Succeeded.
```

Next, at an elevated, administrator command prompt, enter the following command to check the migration state: **dfsrmig /GetMigrationState**. As before, the output of the command tells you the exact status of the migration to the Redirected state, such as:

```
 All Domain Controllers have migrated successfully to Global state
('Redirected')
Succeeded.
```

If you want to double-check, you can confirm in several ways that all domain controllers are redirected. As part of moving to the Redirected state, the path to the SYSVOL share is changed to the SYSVOL_DFSR folder, and you can confirm this by entering **net share** at a command prompt. If the SYSVOL is being shared and the share path points to the path that is being replicated by the DFS Replication service (meaning it includes the SYSVOL_DFSR folder), this confirms that the migration to the Redirected state was successful. When the DFS Replication service on each domain controller reaches the Redirected state, Information event 8017 will be registered in its event log as well.

Once all domain controllers have successfully reached the Redirected state, check the replication status by entering the following command: **repadmin /replsum**. Proceed only if the domain has a healthy status for Active Directory replication.

> **Note** Rather than continuing, if necessary, you can roll back to the Start state by entering **dfsrmig /SetGlobalState 0** or to the Prepared state by entering **dfsrmig /SetGlobalState 1**. You would then need to restart this procedure at step 1 or step 2, respectively.

Step 3: Migrating to the Eliminated State

If any changes were made to the SYSVOL share during the state transition from Prepared to Redirected, you must use Robocopy to copy the changes from SYSVOL to the SYSVOL_DFSR share on any replicated writable domain controller prior to proceeding to the Eliminated state.

Once all domain controllers in the domain have successfully reached the Redirected state, you can move the domain controllers to the Eliminated state by entering the following command: **dfsrmig /SetGlobalState 3**. Dfsrmig will report the following:

```
 Current DFSR global state: 'Redirected'
New DFSR global state: 'Eliminated'

Migration will proceed to 'Eliminated' state. It is not possible to
revert this step.

If any RODC is stuck in the 'Eliminating' state for too long then run
with option /DeleteRoNtfrsMembers.
Succeeded.
```

> **Caution**   Once you initiate the Eliminated state, you cannot roll back to a previous state.

Next, at an elevated, administrator command prompt, enter the following command to check the migration state: **dfsrmig /GetMigrationState**. As before, the output of the command tells you the exact status of the migration to the Eliminated state, such as:

```
 All Domain Controllers have migrated successfully to Global state
('Eliminated')
Succeeded.
```

If you want to double-check, you can confirm in several ways that all domain controllers have eliminated the SYSVOL. As part of moving to the Eliminated state, the %SystemRoot%\Sysvol folder is removed, which you can confirm in Windows Explorer. When the DFS Replication service on each domain controller reaches the Eliminated state, Information event 8019 will be registered in its event log. In the DFS Management console, you'll see the Domain System Volume when you select the Replication node, as shown in Figure 6-1.

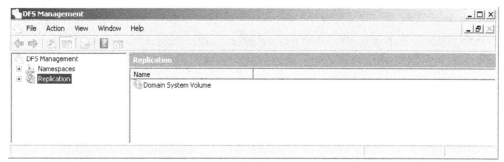

FIGURE 6-1 Use DFS Management to check DFS Replication.

Once the migration is complete, only DFS Replication is replicating the SYSVOL share throughout the domain. This means the SYSVOL share that is advertised by domain controllers corresponds to the SYSVOL_DFSR folder that is replicated by the DFS Replication service. New domain controllers that are established after completing the migration will default to using the DFS Replication service for replicating the contents of the SYSVOL share.

Maintaining the SYSVOL

Because Active Directory replicates the SYSVOL for you, you really don't need to manage the SYSVOL on a daily basis. That said, you may occasionally need to perform maintenance tasks as your network changes. This section discusses the key maintenance tasks you might need to perform.

Managing SYSVOL Storage

The location of the SYSVOL folder and subfolders is configurable. When domain controllers use FRS replication, the default location for the SYSVOL root is %SystemRoot%\Sysvol. When domain controllers use DFS Replication, the default location for the SYSVOL root is %SystemRoot%\Sysvol_dfsr.

Within the SYSVOL, you'll find a domain subfolder. For a SYSVOL replicated with FRS, this folder is located at %SystemRoot%\Sysvol\domain. For a SYSVOL replicated with DFS, this folder is located at %SystemRoot%\Sysvol_dfsr\domain. The domain subfolder contains the policies, scripts, and starter GPOs for the domain.

Within the SYSVOL, you'll find a sysvol*DomainName* subfolder, where *DomainName* is the name of the domain in which the domain controller is located. For SYSVOLs replicated with FRS, this folder is located at %SystemRoot%\\Sysvol\\sysvol*DomainName*. For SYSVOLs replicated with DFS, this folder is located at %SystemRoot%\\Sysvol_dfsr\\sysvol*DomainName*. The SYSVOL uses a junction point to make this folder appear to be the same as the domain subfolder. However, the sysvol*DomainName* subfolder is in fact a junction point that points to the domain-specific subfolder of the domain folder.

Within the SYSVOL, you'll find a staging folder, which is used to manage changes to SYSVOL content. The way the staging area works depends on the replication technique you are using. With FRS replication, %SystemRoot%\\Sysvol\\staging is a junction point that points to %SystemRoot%\\Sysvol\\domain\\staging. With DFS Replication, %SystemRoot%\\Sysvol_dfsr\\Sysvol*DomainName*\\DfsrPrivate is a junction point that points to a subfolder of %SystemDrive%\\System Volume Information\\DFSR\\Private. The DFSR\\Private folder in turn contains the following subfolders:

- **ConflictAndDeleted** Caches files and folders where conflicting changes were made on two or more domain controllers. When a file is modified by two or more domain controllers, the most recently updated file wins the conflict, and DFS Replication moves the losing file or files to this folder. This folder also stores files that are deleted from replicated folders.
- **Deleted** Tracks deletions that have been processed, unless you are moving deleted files automatically to the ConflictAndDeleted folder as per the default configuration.
- **Installing** Tracks installations that have been processed.
- **Staging** Acts as a queue for changes that need to be replicated to other domain controllers, as well as for new files that need to be replicated.

Real World In the ConflictAndDeleted folder, you'll find a log of files with conflicting changes and their original locations. This log is in the file ConflictAndDeletedManifest.xml.

The ConflictAndDeletedManifest.xml file stores information about the current contents of the ConflictAndDeleted folder. The DFS Replication service writes to the ConflictAndDeletedManifest.xml file when files are added or removed from the ConflictAndDeleted folder. If no conflicts or deletions are occurring, the ConflictAndDeleted folder will be empty and the ConflictAndDeletedManifest.xml file will not exist (because it was deleted by the DFS Replication service).

The SYSVOL folders are hidden and designated as protected by the operating system. To view them in Windows Explorer, you need to open the Folder Options utility by double-clicking Folder Options in Control Panel. Then, on the View tab, select Show Hidden Files And Folders, clear Hide Protected Operating System Files, and then click OK. Once you do this, you'll be able to see the SYSVOL folders I discuss.

If you want to work in the System Volume Information folder, you need to work a bit harder, because this folder is secured and only the System account has access by default. In Windows Explorer, open the Properties dialog box for the System Volume Information folder by double-clicking the folder. On the Security tab, click Edit. In the Permissions For dialog box, click Add and then enter the name of the user to whom you want to give access to the folder. Typically, this is the account with which you are logged on. Click OK. If you receive notifications concerning subfolders that you are locked out of, click Continue repeatedly until you can finally click OK to close the Properties dialog box. Now, you can open the System Volume Information folder and take a look around.

Whether FRS or DFS Replication is used, the staging folder has a default storage quota of 4 gigabytes (GB). As your installation of Active Directory Domain Services (AD DS) grows in size and complexity, the amount of disk space needed for the SYSVOL typically will grow. Because of this, you may need to modify the storage quota. You'll also need to ensure that the volume on which the SYSVOL is created has adequate space to store the related files. You can reduce the amount of data stored on the SYSVOL by creating a central store, as discussed in "SYSVOL Changes" in Chapter 2.

System maintenance tasks that modify disk configuration can affect the SYSVOL. Therefore, when you maintain disk configurations, even if the maintenance occurs on a different disk drive, you should verify that the maintenance does not affect the SYSVOL. Why? Logical drive letters can change after you add and remove disks. FRS replication and DFS Replication locate the SYSVOL by using paths that are stored in AD DS. If drive letters change after you add or remove disk drives, you need to manually update the paths in the registry and AD DS or restore the original configuration.

You should relocate the SYSVOL only when required by disk-space maintenance or upgrades. To relocate the SYSVOL, you must:

1. Copy the entire folder structure (including any hidden folders) to the new location.
2. Update the related junction points.
3. Update the path values that are stored in the registry and in AD DS.

Performing these procedures maintains the relationships between the paths, the folders, and the junction points and ensures proper domain controller operations. As an alternative to relocating the SYSVOL, you can relocate the Staging folder while leaving the rest of the SYSVOL in its original location. For more information, see "Relocating the Staging Folder" later in this chapter.

Managing Storage Quotas for DFS Replication

As discussed previously, the DfsrPrivate folder contains subfolders that are used by the DFS Replication service to manage replication. The Staging folder has a default storage quota of 4 GB. Subfolders within the ConflictAndDeleted folder have default storage quotas of 660 megabytes (MB).

If staging-area disk space is low, DFS Replication will have problems cleaning up the staging area. This will result in related low disk space and error events being generated in the event logs. You can avoid this problem in most cases by using a central store. You can also modify the storage quotas used by DFS Replication if necessary.

Each domain controller has separate settings for DFS Replication and storage quotas. To change the storage configuration used by DFS Replication, you must modify the configuration separately on each domain controller in the domain by completing the following steps:

1. Open DFS Management by clicking Start, All Programs, Administrative Tools, DFS Management.
2. In the console tree, expand the Replication node and then select Domain System Volume. As shown in Figure 6-2, you'll see detailed information for the Domain System Volume, including:

- **Local Path**   Shows the full file path to the replicated folder.
- **Membership Status**   Shows the replication group membership status as either enabled or disabled.
- **Member**   Shows the member server on which replication is configured.
- **Replicated Folder**   Shows the name of the replicated folder.
- **Staging Quota**   Shows the storage quota for the staging folder.

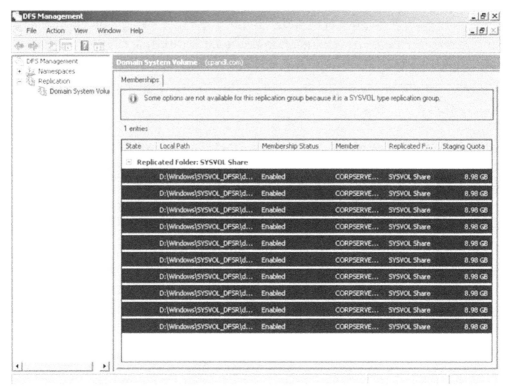

FIGURE 6-2 Use DFS Management to check DFS Replication.

3. In the details pane, right-click the DFS Replication member entry you want to manage and then click Properties.

4. On the Staging tab, shown in Figure 6-3, use the Quota combo box to set the quota you want for the Staging folder, and then click Apply. The default quota is 4,096 MB. The minimum quota you can set is 10 MB, and the maximum quota that you can set is 4,294,967,295 MB (or 4 terabytes).

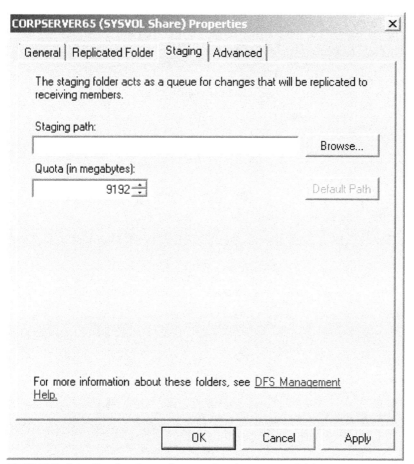

FIGURE 6-3 Set the desired quota for the staging folder.

5. On the Advanced tab, shown in Figure 6-4, use the Quota combo box to set the quota for subfolders within the ConflictAndDeleted folder, and then click Apply. The default quota is 660 MB. The minimum quota you can set is 10 MB and the maximum quota that you can set is 4,294,967,295 MB (or 4 terabytes).

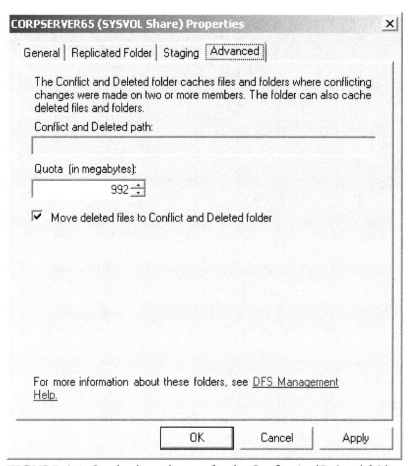

FIGURE 6-4 Set the desired quota for the ConflictAndDeleted folder.

6. Click OK to close the Properties dialog box.

> **Real World**   By default, the ConflictAndDeleted folder has a
> maximum allowed size of 660 megabytes (MB). This size limit is
> enforced by a disk quota and can be changed as discussed in this
> section. Typically, the size of the ConflictAndDeleted folder will rarely
> approach this limit. However, if the ConflictAndDeletedManifest.xml file
> becomes corrupted, it can in some situations cause the
> ConflictAndDeleted folder to exceed its quota and might also prevent
> the DFS Replication service from replicating files.
>
> To resolve this problem, you can initiate a cleanup of the
> ConflictAndDeleted folder and the ConflictAndDeletedManifest.xml file.

To do this, you need the globally unique identifier (GUID) of the SYSVOL share, which you can obtain by entering the following command at a command prompt:

```
wmic /namespace:\\root\microsoftdfs path
dfsrreplicatedfolderconfig get
replicatedfolderguid,replicatedfoldername
```

To initiate cleanup, enter the following command at a command prompt:

```
wmic /namespace:\\root\microsoftdfs path
dfsrreplicatedfolderinfo where
"replicatedfolderguid='<GUID>'" call
cleanupconflictdirectory
```

where *GUID* is the GUID of the replicated folder that has a corrupted ConflictAndDeletedManifest.xml file.

If no conflicts or deletions are occurring when you run the command, the ConflictAndDeleted folder will be empty and the ConflictAndDeletedManifest.xml file will not exist (because it was deleted by the DFS Replication service). If conflicts or deletions are occurring when you run the command, some files will remain in the ConflictAndDeleted folder, including the ConflictAndDeletedManifest.xml file. However, the size will be much smaller and the total size of the ConflictAndDeleted folder should be below the quota limit.

Relocating the Staging Folder

Within the SYSVOL, the Staging folder acts as a queue for changes that need to be replicated to other domain controllers and for new files that need to be replicated. When you are using DFS Replication to replicate the SYSVOL, the location of the Staging folder can be configured by using DFS Management. However, before you do this, be sure to notify domain administrators that they should not make any changes in the SYSVOL directory until the move is complete.

Each domain controller has separate settings for DFS Replication and the Staging folder. To relocate the Staging folder, you must modify the configuration on each domain controller separately by completing the following steps:

1. Open DFS Management by clicking Start, All Programs, Administrative Tools, DFS Management.

> **Caution** Changing the location of the Staging folder creates a nonstandard configuration that will make working with the SYSVOL more difficult. Whenever you work with the SYSVOL, you'll need to remember that the Staging folder is in a separate location and handle this accordingly. Any disk drive on which you locate the Staging folder must be backed up to ensure that you can recover the domain controller.

2. In the console tree, expand the Replication node and then select Domain System Volume.

3. In the details pane, right-click the DFS Replication member entry you want to manage and then select Properties.

4. On the Advanced tab, click Browse. Use the Browse For Folder dialog box to select the new location for the Staging folder. If necessary, you can use the dialog box to create a folder in a particular location as well.

5. Because the DFS Replication service obtains the location of the Staging folder on startup, you must restart the DFS Replication server. To reset the DFS Replication service, stop the service by using the command **sc stop dfsr**, and then start the service by using **sc start dfsr**. The stop and start commands must be entered at an elevated, administrator command prompt. Alternatively, you can use the Services utility to restart the service.

If you later want to restore the Staging folder to its original location, you'll need to browse to the related folder in the SYSVOL (%SystemRoot%\SYSVOL_DFSR \Sysvol*DomainName*\DfsrPrivate) and then select Staging, where *DomainName* is the fully qualified name of the domain, such as imaginedlands.com.

Identifying Replication Partners

When you are trying to determine whether replication is working properly, it is often helpful to locate a domain controller's replication partners. One way to do this is to examine the connection objects for a domain controller by using Active Directory Sites And Services. To do this, however, you must know the site in which the domain controller is located. If you don't know the site in which the domain controller is located, you can use the DSQUERY SERVER command to determine this information. At a command prompt enter **dsquery server –name *ServerName*,** where *ServerName* is the name of the domain controller—for example, *dsquery –server –name CorpServer65*. The output of the command lists the site in which the domain controller is located.

To identify replication partners by examining connection objects, complete the following steps:

1. Open Active Directory Sites And Services by clicking Start, All Programs, Administrative Tools, Active Directory Sites And Services.

2. In the console tree, double-click the Sites container to display the list of sites.

3. Double-click the site that contains the domain controller whose connection objects you want to determine.

4. Double-click the Servers folder to display the list of servers in the selected site.

5. Double-click the server object for the domain controller whose replication partners you want to identify. This displays the server's NTDS Settings object.

6. Click the NTDS Settings object to display the list of connection objects in the details pane. These objects represent inbound connections that are used for replication to the server. The From Server column displays the names of the domain controllers that are source replication partners for the selected domain controller.

Rebuilding the SYSVOL

A domain controller cannot function without a properly shared and replicating SYSVOL. If you suspect that the SYSVOL is not configured properly, you can rebuild the SYSVOL on the domain controller. However, you should do this only when all other domain controllers in the domain have a healthy and functioning SYSVOL. Additionally, do not attempt to rebuild the SYSVOL until you resolve any problems that may be occurring with DFS Replication in a domain.

One way to rebuild the SYSVOL is to perform a nonauthoritative restore of the domain controller from a backup on which the SYSVOL was working properly. For details, see "Backing Up and Recovering Active Directory" in Chapter 9, "Maintaining and Recovering Active Directory," in *Active Directory Administrator's Pocket Consultant*.

You also can rebuild the SYSVOL on a domain controller by performing the following procedures:

1. Identify the target domain controller. This is the domain controller for which you are repairing the SYSVOL.

    > **Caution** This procedure won't work in all deployments of Active Directory and probably will need to be modified to work in your environment. Before you try this procedure in a live production environment, you should thoroughly test this procedure on a development or test network. Further, if the SYSVOL configurations of the source and target aren't the same, you need to update the locations where folder paths are specified in junction points in the file system, in Netlogon parameters in the registry, and in attributes in Active Directory Domain Services (AD DS). The latter two tasks are beyond the scope of this book.

2. Identify a source replication partner as discussed in "Identifying Replication Partners" earlier in the chapter. You will import the SYSVOL from the source replication partner.

3. Compare the SYSVOL configuration on the target and source domain controllers. Ensure that both use the same locations for directory paths and junction points. For example, if both use the default paths on the C drive for SYSVOL storage, the configurations are identical and you can proceed. Otherwise, you should not use this technique to rebuild the SYSVOL.

4. Create a copy of the current SYSVOL directory structure for both the target and source by entering the following commands at an elevated command prompt on both servers:

```
cd %systemroot%
dir /s /ad sysvol_dfsr > save.txt
```

5. If you open Save.txt in Notepad and search twice for Junction, you'll find the exact paths to both junction points the SYSVOL is using. The path for the System Volume Information\DFSR\Private folder includes two GUIDs separated by a hyphen.

6. On the source replication partner and the target domain controller, use the Services utility or the SC command to ensure that the DFS Replication Service and the Netlogon service have been started and are running. Then, verify that the related shares are being shared by entering **net share** at a command prompt.

7. Verify that replication is working between the source replication partner and the target domain controller by entering **dcdiag /test:replications** at a command prompt.

8. Restart the target domain controller in Directory Services Restore Mode. Restarting in Directory Services Restore Mode takes the target domain controller offline, meaning it functions as a member server and not as a domain controller. During installation of Active Directory Domain Services, you set the Administrator password for logging on to the server in Directory Services Restore Mode.

9. You can restart a domain controller in Directory Services Restore Mode manually by pressing the F8 key during domain controller startup. You must then log on by using the Directory Services Restore Mode password for the local Administrator account.

10. In Directory Services Restore Mode, the DFS Replication service is stopped automatically. You also need to stop the Netlogon service.

Use the Services utility or the SC command to do this. Note that both services restart automatically when you restart the domain controller normally after you complete the procedure to import the SYSVOL folder structure.

11. On the target domain controller, delete the contents of the %SystemRoot%\SYSVOL_DFSR folder but retain the folder itself.

12. Using Robocopy, copy the entire SYSVOL folder structure from the source replication partner to the target domain controller. You use Robocopy to ensure that file ownership and access control list settings are retained on the SYSVOL folders and files. At an elevated command prompt, enter the following command:

```
robocopy SourceShare DestinationShare /copyall /mir /b
 /r:0 /xd "DfsrPrivate" /xf "DfsrPrivate"
```

where SourceShare is the full UNC path to the SYSVOL share you are copying on the source replication server, and DestinationShare is the full UNC path to the SYSVOL share on the target domain controller. The additional parameters have the following usage:

- **/copyall** copies the following file information: data, attributes, time stamps, NTFS access control list (ACL), owner information, and auditing information.
- **/mir** mirrors the directory tree that you are copying.
- **/b** copies files in backup mode to override file and folder permission settings (ACLs).
- **/r:0** specifies performing 0 (zero) retries on failed copies.
- **/xd "DfsrPrivate"** excludes the DfsrPrivate directory from the copy.
- **/xf "DfsrPrivate"** excludes the DfsrPrivate file from the copy.

13. Verify that the security settings on the copied SYSVOL are the same as on the original SYSVOL. You can use Windows Explorer to examine file and folder security settings. If there's a problem with the security settings, repeat steps 9 and 10.

14. Verify that the folder structure was copied correctly and that the required junction points still exist. One way to do this is to enter the following commands at an elevated command prompt:

```
cd %systemroot%
dir /s /ad sysvol_dfsr > current.txt
```

> When you open the Current.txt file in Notepad, you can examine the directory structure.

15. Restore the default junction points as necessary, and verify that the default junction points are configured correctly. The default junction points are C:\Windows\SYSVOL_DFSR\domain\DfsrPrivate and C:\Windows\SYSVOL_DFSR\Sysvol*DomainName,* where *DomainName* is the fully qualified name of the domain, such as C:\Windows\SYSVOL_DFSR\Sysvol\imaginedlands.com.

16. Restart the target domain controller normally. Restarting the server normally will ensure that the target domain controller starts in normal operating mode. In this mode, the DFS Replication service and the Netlogon service should start automatically.

17. Check the Directory Service event log to ensure that it contains no errors related to replication, the SYSVOL, or Netlogon. Test replication on the target domain controller to ensure that replication is working as expected. If you are unable to successfully complete this procedure, you need to perform a nonauthoritative restore of the domain controller from backup.

Real World To restore the junction points, you must know the volume GUIDs. I recommend copying and pasting the GUIDs from the Save.txt file you created earlier on the target domain controller. When the target domain controller is using a default configuration of the SYSVOL, enter the following commands at an elevated command prompt to create and then verify the first junction point using the GUIDs:

```
cd %SystemRoot%\SYSVOL_DFSR\domain

mklink /J DfsrPrivate "C:\System Volume
Information\DFSR\Private\GUID"

dir /a:L
```

To create and verify the second junction point, enter the following commands at an elevated command prompt:

```
cd %SystemRoot%\SYSVOL_DFSR\Sysvol

mklink /J DomainName C:\Windows\Sysvol\DomainName

dir /a:L
```

> Here, *DomainName* is the fully qualified name of the domain, such as imaginedlands.com.

Generating Replication Diagnostics Reports

When domain controllers are using FRS replication, you can use the Ultrasound utility to monitor FRS replication. When domain controllers are using DFS Replication, you can use the DFS Management console to monitor DFS Replication. Using the Diagnostic Reports features of DFS Management, you also can implement monitoring to detect low disk space and other potential issues that might cause DFS Replication to fail.

Using the DFS Management console, you can:

- Generate a health report. A health report shows the overall health of replication and replication efficiency.
- Perform a propagation test. A propagation test checks replication progress by creating a test file in a replicated folder.
- Generate a propagation report. A propagation report tracks the replication progress for the test file created during a propagation test.

> **Note** The amount of time required to test replication and generate reports will vary based on DFS Replication health, the number of replicated folders, available server resources, network connectivity, and other factors.

Generating Replication Health Reports

With DFS Replication, you can create health reports to determine the health of the replication architecture and to determine replication efficiency. To generate a health report, complete the following steps:

1. Click Start, point to Administrative Tools, and then click DFS Management.

2. In the console tree, under the Replication node, right-click Domain System Volume, and then click Create Diagnostic Report.

3. When the Diagnostic Report Wizard starts, choose Health Report, as shown in Figure 6-5, and then click Next.

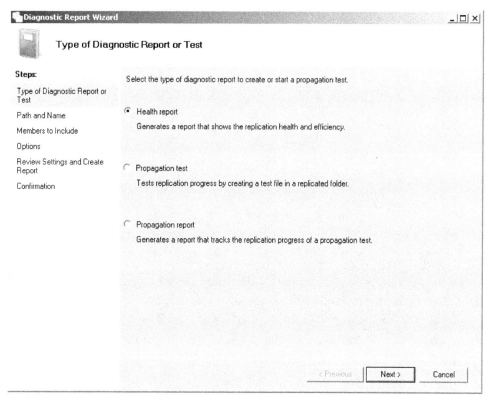

FIGURE 6-5 Generate a health report for DFS Replication.

4. On the Path And Name page, shown in Figure 6-6, configure the save path for the report by using the Report Path options. Then enter a name for the report in the Report Name box as appropriate. Click Next.

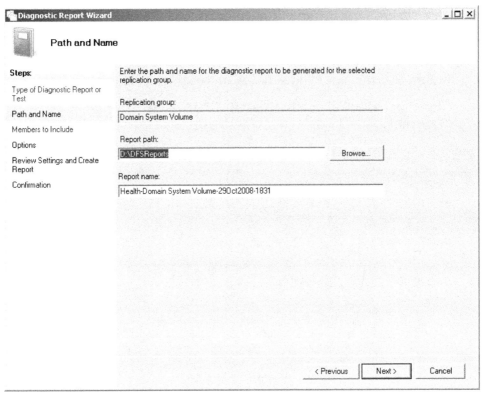

FIGURE 6-6 Specify the save path and report name.

5. On the Members To Include page, use the options provided to select servers to include in the report. Generally, you'll want to limit the number of servers you include to allow the test to be completed faster.

6. To include an excluded server, click it in the Excluded Members list and then click Add. To exclude an included member, click in the Included Members list and then click Remove. Click Next.

7. On the Options page, shown in Figure 6-7, specify whether to count backlogged files in the report. Counting backlogged files is important because the more files that domain controllers have in their back log, the further behind they are with their replication.

8. If you include backlogged files, use the Reference Member list to select a reference member that has the most up-to-date files. Files on the reference member will be compared to files on other members to determine whether other servers have a backlog of files.

9. If you want to count replicated files and their sizes on each member, select the Count The Replicated Files And Their Sizes check box. Click Next.

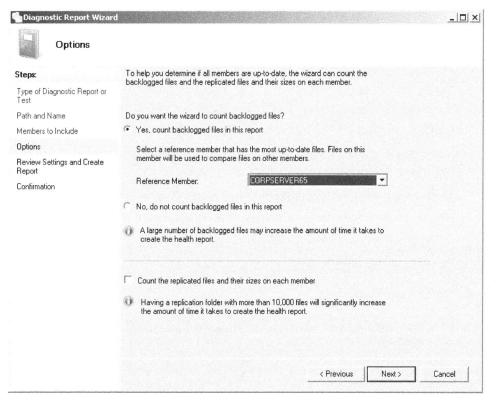

FIGURE 6-7 Optimize the report settings.

10. Review the options you've selected, and then click Create to generate the health report. The more options and included servers selected, the longer it will take to generate the report.

11. When the wizard finishes generating the report, it opens the report in Windows Internet Explorer. Review the results and note the save location of the health report for future reference.

Performing Propagation Tests

A propagation test checks replication progress by creating a test file in a replicated folder and then using a related reporting mechanism to check how long the test file took to propagate. To get a good understanding of how replication is working, you'll need to run several propagation tests. Ideally, you'll run the tests at different times of day and under different conditions.

To perform a propagation test, complete the following steps:

1. Click Start, point to Administrative Tools, and then click DFS Management.

2. In the console tree, under the Replication node, right-click Domain System Volume, and then click Create Diagnostic Report.

3. When the Diagnostic Report Wizard starts, choose Propagation Test and then click Next.

4. On the Start A New Propagation Test page, shown in Figure 6-8, select SYSVOL Share from the Replicated Folder list. From the Propagation Server list, select the server to test.

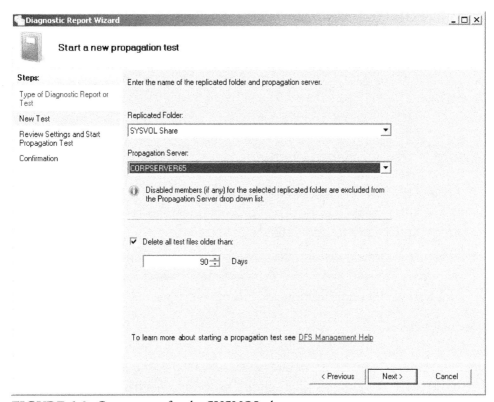

FIGURE 6-8 Create a test for the SYSVOL share.

5. By default, any existing test files that are older than 90 days will be deleted. This is typically what you want to happen. Click Next.

6. Review the options you've selected and then click Create to perform the propagation test. Click Close.

7. When the wizard finishes, it does not automatically generate a related report. You must create this report separately as discussed in the next section. However, keep in mind that to get useful reports, you should run several propagation tests under different conditions and at different times.

Generating Propagation Reports

A propagation report tracks the replication progress for test files created during propagation tests. The report is designed to help you identify replication problems, such as whether the domain is experiencing high replication latency between domain controllers.

To generate a propagation report, complete the following steps:

1. Click Start, point to Administrative Tools, and then click DFS Management.

2. In the console tree, under the Replication node, right-click Domain System Volume, and then click Create Diagnostic Report.

3. When the Diagnostic Report Wizard starts, choose Propagation Report and then click Next.

4. On the Report Options page, shown in Figure 6-9, select SYSVOL Share from the Replicated Folder list. From the Propagation Server list, select a server you previously tested.

5. Use the combo box provided to set the number of test files to include. By default, the wizard will include a maximum of five test files in the report. Click Next.

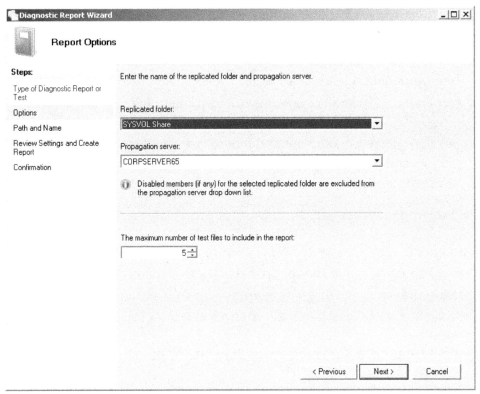

FIGURE 6-9 Select the replicated folder and server you previously tested.

6. On the Path And Name page, configure the save path for the report by using the Report Path options. Then enter a name for the report in the Report Name box, as appropriate. Click Next.

7. Review the options you've selected, and then click Create to generate the propagation report.

8. When the wizard finishes generating the report, it opens the report in Internet Explorer. Review the results and note the save location of the propagation report for future reference.

Troubleshooting Replication Issues

During normal Active Directory operations, changes made to the directory, policy, and SYSVOL on one domain controller are replicated to that domain controller's replication partners. To determine whether replication is working properly, you can use the Domain Controller Diagnostics Tool (Dcdiag.exe) to perform a series of replication tests. To do this, follow these steps:

1. Start an elevated, administrator command prompt by clicking Start, right-clicking Command Prompt, and then clicking Run As Administrator.

2. At the command prompt, enter the following command: **dcdiag /s:*ServerName* /test:replications**, where *ServerName* specifies the name of the domain controller that you want to examine.

3. The output of the diagnostics testing provides a wealth of information that can help you diagnose and resolve replication issues. If any test fails, open Event Viewer and check for replication errors in the Directory Service log.

Using an elevated, administrator command prompt, you can verify successful replication by entering **repadmin /showrepl**. If you are not running Repadmin on the domain controller whose replication you are checking, you can specify a destination domain controller in the command. For example, if you want to check CorpServer98, enter the following command:

```
repadmin /showrepl CorpServer98
```

As shown in Sample 6-1, Repadmin lists inbound neighbors for the current or specified domain controller. These inbound neighbors identify the distinguished name of each directory partition for which inbound directory replication has been attempted, the site and name of the source domain controller, and whether replication succeeded.

SAMPLE 6-1. Confirming replication with neighbors.

```
 LA-First-Site\CORPSERVER98
DSA Options: IS_GC DISABLE_OUTBOUND_REPL IS_RODC
Site Options: (none)
DSA object GUID: a465bbc1-c3d9-46ec-96fc
DSA invocationID: c045996c-b163-45b7-80d3


==== INBOUND NEIGHBORS ======================================

DC=imaginedlands,DC=com
```

```
 Atlanta-First-Site\CORPSERVER65 via RPC
 DSA object GUID: a9d16546-c45a-4609-8c1e
 Last attempt @ 2008-12-11 12:14:18 was successful.


CN=Configuration,DC=imaginedlands,DC=com
 Atlanta-First-Site\CORPSERVER65 via RPC
 DSA object GUID: a9d16546-c45a-4609-8c1e
 Last attempt @ 2008-12-11 12:14:18 was successful.


CN=Schema,CN=Configuration,DC=imaginedlands,DC=com
 Atlanta-First-Site\CORPSERVER65 via RPC
 DSA object GUID: a9d16546-c45a-4609-8c1e
 Last attempt @ 2008-12-11 12:14:18 was successful.


DC=DomainDnsZones,DC=imaginedlands,DC=com
 Atlanta-First-Site\CORPSERVER65 via RPC
 DSA object GUID: a9d16546-c45a-4609-8c1e
 Last attempt @ 2008-12-11 12:14:18 was successful.


DC=ForestDnsZones,DC=imaginedlands,DC=com
 Atlanta-First-Site\CORPSERVER65 via RPC
 DSA object GUID: a9d16546-c45a-4609-8c1e
 Last attempt @ 2008-12-11 12:14:18 was successful.
```

The example shows the replication status for five directory partitions:

- **DC=imaginedlands,DC=com**   A domain partition
- **CN=Configuration,DC=imaginedlands,DC=com**   The forestwide Configuration partition
- CN=Schema,CN=Configuration,DC=imaginedlands,DC=com   The forestwide Schema partition
- **DC=DomainDnsZones,DC=imaginedlands,DC=com**   The DNS application partition for domain-level zones
- **DC=ForestDnsZones,DC=imaginedlands,DC=com**   The DNS application partition for forest-level zones

If you find problems with replication, you can try to force Active Directory replication by running the following command at an elevated command prompt on the domain controller: **repadmin /syncall**. You also can force the DFS Replication service to poll Active Directory by running the following command at an elevated command prompt: **dfsrdiag PollAd /Member:*ComputerName***, where *ComputerName* is the host name of the domain controller—for example, **dfsrdiag PollAd /Member:CorpServer84**. Manually polling Active Directory in this way can trigger replication if changes are waiting to be replicated.

As part of troubleshooting, you should ensure that the DFS Replication service and the Netlogon service are running and configured properly. If you suspect there is a problem with the DFS Replication service, you can use the following command to determine the status of the service on the local computer: **sc query dfsr**. To reset the DFS Replication service, stop the service by using **sc stop dfsr** and then start the service by using **sc start dfsr**. The stop and start commands must be entered at an elevated, administrator command prompt.

> **Note** To work with a remote computer, you must specify the UNC path as part of the command, such as **sc *ComputerName* query dfsr**, where *ComputerName* is the host name of the domain controller—for example, **sc \\CorpServer84 query dfsr**.

If you suspect a problem with the Netlogon service, you can use the following command to determine the status of the service on the local computer: **sc query netlogon**. To reset the Netlogon service, stop the service by using **sc stop netlogon** and then start the service by using **sc start netlogon**. The stop and start commands must be entered at an elevated, administrator command prompt.

To verify that the SYSVOL shares are configured properly, enter the following command at a command prompt: **net share**. With FRS replication, the default path to the NETLOGON share is C:\Windows\SYSVOL\sysvol\imaginedlands.com\SCRIPTS, and the path to the SYSVOL share is C:\Windows\SYSVOL\sysvol. With DFS Replication, the default path to the NETLOGON share is C:\Windows\SYSVOL_DFSR\sysvol\imaginedlands.com\SCRIPTS, and the path to the SYSVOL share is C:\Windows\SYSVOL_DFSR\sysvol.

Next, in Windows Explorer, verify that the folder locations actually exist on the system currently identified as the system drive. If the drive letter of the system drive changed, you need to manually update the paths in the registry and AD DS, or restore the original configuration.

Because security settings on the SYSVOL can also affect replication, you should verify that the proper permissions are set for SYSVOL replication. To do this, follow these steps:

1. Start an elevated, administrator command prompt by clicking Start, right-clicking Command Prompt, and then clicking Run As Administrator.

2. At the command prompt, enter the following command: **dcdiag /s:ServerName /test:netlogons**, where *ServerName* specifies the name of the domain controller to check.

3. In the output of the Netlogon test, look for a message that states that "*ComputerName* passed test NetLogons," where *ComputerName* is the name of the domain controller. If you do not see this message, check the permissions on the related folders.

Chapter 7. Managing Group Policy Processing

The Group Policy client running on a computer is responsible for processing policy and requesting updates to policy. To ensure that policy changes you make are applied as expected, you need a strong understanding of:

- How inheritance works and how inheritance can be modified.
- How policy is processed and refreshed, and how you can modify these processes.
- How policy processing changes when users connect over slow links, and how you can manage slow-link processing.
- How you can plan policy changes so that no surprises occur when you move computers or when users log on from different locations.

Understanding processing rules will help you master Group Policy and also help prepare you for the unexpected. After reading this chapter, you'll know when, why, and how Group Policy applies to users and computers.

Managing Group Policy Inheritance

When you work with Group Policy, it is important to note the level of support for the policies you are working with. A policy supported by all computers running Windows 7 or later means that computers running Windows 7, Windows Server 2008 R2 and later versions of the Windows operating system support this policy.

When you create or modify GPOs, the policy preferences and settings you configure affect users and computers. Through inheritance, a GPO applied to a parent container is inherited by a child container. This means that a policy preference or setting applied to a parent object is passed down to a child object. Thus, inheritance ensures that every computer and user object in a domain, no matter which container it is stored in, is affected by Group Policy.

Most policy settings have three configuration options: Not Configured, Enabled, or Disabled. Not Configured is the default state for most policy settings. If a policy setting is enabled, the policy setting is enforced and is applied to all users and computers that are subject to the policy either directly or through inheritance. If a policy setting is disabled, the policy setting is not enforced and is not applied to users and computers that are subject to the policy either directly or through inheritance.

Most policy preferences have four configuration options: Create, Replace, Update, or Delete. The Create option creates the preference only if the preference does not already exist. The Replace option deletes the preference if it exists and then re-creates it, or creates the preference if it doesn't yet exist. The Update option modifies the preference if it exists or creates the preference if it does not exist. The Delete option deletes the preference if it exists.

You can change the way inheritance works in four key ways. You can:

- Change link order and precedence
- Override inheritance (as long as there is no enforcement)
- Block inheritance (to prevent inheritance completely)
- Enforce inheritance (to supersede and prevent overriding or blocking)

The sections that follow describe how to manage Group Policy inheritance using these techniques.

Changing Link Order and Precedence

The order of inheritance for Group Policy goes from the site level to the domain level to the organizational unit (OU) level. When multiple policy objects are linked to a particular level, the link order determines the order in which policy is applied. Linked policy objects are always applied in link-ranking order. Lower-ranking policy objects are processed before higher-ranking policy objects.

In the Group Policy Management Console (GPMC), you can determine the GPOs that are in scope for a particular OU by selecting the OU in the console tree and then selecting the Linked Group Policy Objects tab in the details pane, as shown in Figure 7-1. These policies will be processed from the lowest link order to the highest. Support Desktop Policy (with link order 3) will be processed before Support Networking Policy (with link order 2). Support Security Policy (with link order 1) will be processed last.

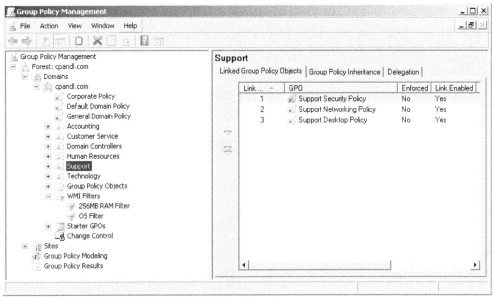

FIGURE 7-1 Review the link-ranking order.

What effect does link order have on policy settings? Well, because Support Networking Policy settings are processed after Support Desktop Policy settings, Support Desktop Policy settings have higher precedence and take priority. Because Support Security Policy settings are processed last, Support Security Policy settings have the highest precedence and take priority over both Support Desktop Policy and Support Networking Policy.

To go beyond the scope of the OU and view how domain policy affects the OU, select the OU in the console tree and then select the Group Policy Inheritance tab, as shown in Figure 7-2. This tab doesn't display site-linked GPOs; site-linked GPOs are listed under the Sites node.

The precedence order shows exactly how policy objects are being processed for the container you've selected in the console tree. As with link order, lower-ranking policy objects are processed before higher-ranking policy objects. Here, General Domain Policy (with precedence 6) will be processed first, then Corporate Policy (with precedence 5), and so on. Support Security Policy is processed last, so any policy settings configured in this policy object are final and will override those of other policy objects (unless inheritance blocking or enforcing is used).

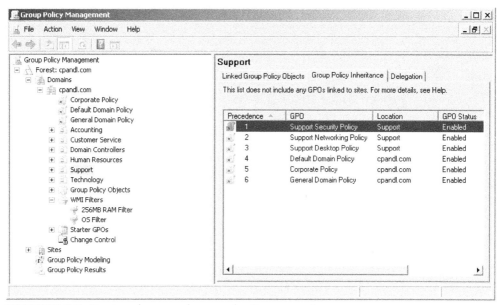

FIGURE 7-2 Review the precedence order for processing.

When multiple policy objects are linked at a specific level, you can easily change the link order (and thus the precedence order) of the policy objects linked at that level. To change the precedence order, complete these steps:

1. In the GPMC, select the container for the site, domain, or OU you want to work with.

2. In the details pane, the Linked Group Policy Objects tab should be selected by default. Click the policy object you want to work with.

3. Click the Move Link Up or Move Link Down button as appropriate to change the link order of the selected policy object.

4. When you have finished changing the link order, confirm that policy objects are being processed in the expected order by checking the precedence order on the Group Policy Inheritance tab.

Overriding Inheritance

As discussed previously, policy is inherited by lower-level containers from top-level containers. If multiple policy objects modify the same areas of policy, the order in which the policy objects are applied determines which policy settings take effect. Essentially, the order of inheritance goes from the site level to the domain level to the OU level. Although the Group Policy Inheritance tab doesn't actually show this, this means that Group Policy settings for a site are passed down to domains, and the settings for a domain are passed down to OUs.

You can override policy inheritance in several ways. With policy settings, you can:

- **Disable an enabled (and inherited) policy setting**   When a policy setting is enabled in a higher-level policy object, you can override inheritance by disabling the policy setting in a lower-level policy object. You thus override the policy setting that is enabled in the higher-level container. For example, if the user policy Prohibit Use Of Internet Connection Sharing On Your DNS Domain is enabled for a site, users in the site should not be able to use Internet Connection Sharing. However, if domain policy specifically disables this user policy, users in the domain can use Internet Connection Sharing. On the other hand, if the domain policy is set to Not Configured, that setting will not be modified and will be inherited as specified for the higher-level container.

- **Enable a disabled (and inherited) policy setting**   When a policy setting is disabled in a higher-level policy object, you can override inheritance by enabling the policy setting in a lower-level policy object. By enabling the policy setting in a lower-level policy object, you override the policy setting that is disabled in the higher-level container. For example, if the user policy Allow Shared Folders To Be Published is disabled for a domain, users in the domain should not be able to publish shared folders in Active Directory. However, if the Support Team OU policy specifically enables this user policy, users in the Support Team OU can publish shared folders in Active Directory. Again, if the OU policy is set to Not Configured, the policy setting will not be modified and will be inherited from the higher-level container.

With policy preferences, you can:

- **Delete a created (and inherited) preference**   When a policy preference is created in a higher-level policy object, you can override inheritance by deleting the policy preference in a lower-level policy object. You thus override the policy preference that is created in the higher-level container. For example, if you create a folder using Folder preferences within a site, users in the site should have this folder. However, if domain policy specifically deletes this folder, users in the domain will not have this folder. On the other hand, if the domain policy doesn't set this Folder preference, that preference will not be modified and will be inherited as specified from the higher-level container.

- **Create a deleted (and inherited) policy preference**   When a policy preference is deleted in a higher-level policy object, you can override inheritance by creating the policy preference in a lower-level policy object. By enabling the policy preference in a lower-level policy object, you override the policy preference that is deleted in the higher-level container. For example, if you delete an environment variable by using Environment preferences within a site, users in the site should not have the environment variable. However, if domain policy specifically creates this environment variable, users in the domain will have this environment variable. On the other hand, if the domain policy doesn't set this Environment preference, that preference will not be modified and will be inherited as specified from the higher-level container.

As you can see, overriding inheritance is a basic technique for changing the way inheritance works. As long as a policy is not blocked or enforced, this technique will achieve the effects you want.

Blocking Inheritance

Sometimes you will want to block inheritance so that policy preferences and settings from higher-level containers are not applied to users and computers in a particular container. When inheritance is blocked, only configured policy preferences and settings from policy objects linked at that level are applied. This means that all GPOs from all high-level containers are blocked (as long as there is no policy enforcement).

By using blocking, you can ensure that domain or OU administrators have full control over the policies that apply to users and computers under their administration. At the domain level, domain administrators can use inheritance blocking to block inherited policy settings from the site level. At the OU level, OU administrators can use inheritance blocking to block inherited policy settings from both the domain level and the site level.

That said, the way you use blocking or enforcement will depend largely on your organizational structure and how much control is delegated to your administrators. Some organizations choose to centrally manage Group Policy. Others delegate control to divisions, branch offices, or departments within the organization. There is no one-size-fits-all solution. A balance between central management and delegation of control might work best.

Consider the following scenarios to see how blocking can be used:

- If you want a domain to be autonomous and don't want the domain to inherit any site policies, you can configure the domain to block inheritance from higher-level containers. Because inheritance is blocked, only the configured policy preferences and settings from policy objects linked to the domain are applied. Blocking inheritance of site policy doesn't affect inheritance of the domain policy objects by OUs, but it does mean that OUs in that domain will not inherit site policies either.
- If you want an OU to be autonomous and don't want the OU to inherit any site or domain policies, configure the OU to block inheritance from higher-level containers. Because inheritance is blocked, only the

configured policy preferences and settings from policy objects linked to the OU are applied. If the OU contains other OUs, inheritance blocking won't affect inheritance of policy objects linked to this OU, but the child OUs will not inherit site or domain policies.

In the GPMC, you can block inheritance by right-clicking the domain or OU that should not inherit settings from higher-level containers and then clicking Block Inheritance. If Block Inheritance is already selected, selecting it again removes the setting. When you block inheritance in the GPMC, a blue circle with an exclamation point is added to the container's node in the console tree. This notification icon provides a quick way to tell whether any domain or OU has the Block Inheritance setting enabled. If you select the container and then select the Group Policy Inheritance tab in the details pane, you'll also see that higher-level policy objects are no longer being inherited, as shown in Figure 7-3.

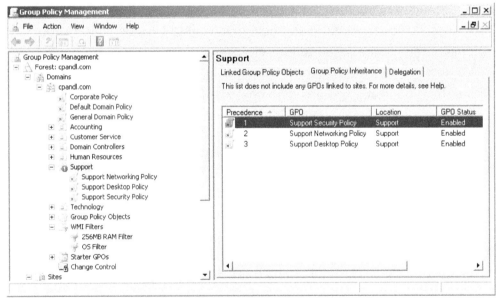

FIGURE 7-3 Inheritance blocking is enabled.

> **Note** Blocking inheritance does not affect local GPOs. If you do not want local GPOs to be applied, you should disable them. To disable processing of Local Group Policy objects on computers running Windows Vista, Windows Server 2008 or later, you can enable the Turn Off Local Group Policy Objects Processing policy setting in an Active Directory–based Group Policy object that the computer processes. In Group Policy, this setting is located under Computer Configuration. Expand Policies\Administrative Templates\System\Group Policy, and then double-click the Turn Off Local Group Policy Objects Processing policy entry.

Enforcing Inheritance

Sometimes you might want to enforce inheritance and prevent administrators who have authority over a container from overriding or blocking inherited Group Policy settings. When inheritance is enforced, all configured policy preferences and settings from higher-level policy objects are inherited and applied regardless of how they are configured in lower-level policy objects. Thus, enforcement of inheritance is used to supersede overriding and blocking of policy preferences and settings.

Forest administrators can use inheritance enforcement to ensure that configured policy settings from the site level are applied and to prevent overriding or blocking of policy settings by both domain and OU administrators. Domain administrators can use inheritance enforcement to ensure that configured policy settings from the domain level are applied and to prevent overriding or blocking of policy settings by OU administrators.

Enforcing Group Policy inheritance dramatically affects the way that Group Policy is processed and applied. By default, a site policy has the lowest precedence, and as such it is the first policy processed. Any of the other policy objects can override or block its preferences or settings because they are processed later. On the other hand, an enforced site policy can have the highest precedence, and as such it will be the last policy processed. This means that no other policy objects can override or block its preferences or settings.

Consider the following scenarios to see how inheritance enforcement can be used:

- As a forest administrator, you want to ensure that domains inherit a particular site policy, so you configure the site policy to enforce inheritance. All configured policy preferences and settings from the site policy are thus applied regardless of whether domain administrators have tried to override or block policy from the site level. Enforcement of the site policy also affects inheritance for OUs in the affected domains. They will inherit the site policy regardless of whether overriding or blocking has been used.
- As a domain administrator, you want to ensure that OUs within the domain inherit a particular domain policy, so you configure the domain policy to enforce inheritance. All configured policy preferences and settings from the domain policy are thus applied regardless of whether OU administrators have tried to override or block policy from the domain level. Enforcement of the domain policy also affects inheritance for child OUs within the affected OUs. They will inherit the domain policy regardless of whether overriding or blocking has been used.

In the GPMC, you can enforce policy inheritance by expanding the container to which the policy is linked, right-clicking the link to the GPO that you want to enforce, and then clicking Enforced. If Enforced is already selected, selecting it again removes enforcement.

When you enforce inheritance in the GPMC, a lock icon is added to the link to the GPO. This notification icon provides a quick way to tell whether any linked GPO has its inheritance enforced. If you select a link to the GPO in the console tree and then select the Scope tab in the details pane, you'll also see a Yes entry in the Enforced column under Links, as shown in Figure 7-4.

Note If multiple GPOs are enforced at the same level, the settings of a GPO with higher precedence will be applied over a GPO with lower precedence. For example, if you've linked three GPOs to the site level and enforced all three GPOs, the settings in the GPO with the highest precedence will always win. The settings in the GPO with the next highest precedence will always win over the GPO with the next lowest precedence.

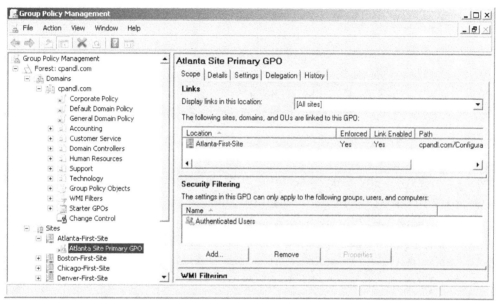

FIGURE 7-4 Review details on the Scope tab to determine whether a linked policy is enforced.

You can also determine whether policy objects linked at a specific level are enforced by completing these steps:

1. In the GPMC, select the site, domain, or OU that you want to work with in the console tree.

2. In the details pane, select the Group Policy Inheritance tab in the details pane. If a policy object linked at the selected level is enforced, you'll see an (Enforced) entry in the Precedence column, as shown in Figure 7-5.

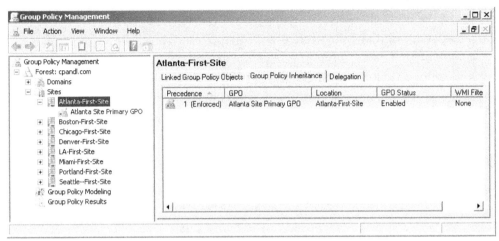

FIGURE 7-5 Check for the Enforced notation.

Controlling Group Policy Processing and Refresh

Policy processing and refresh settings control when and how policy is applied. You have many options for customizing or optimizing Group Policy processing and refreshes in your environment. Key tasks that you might want to perform include the following:

- Changing the default refresh interval
- Enabling or disabling policy object processing completely or by setting category
- Changing the processing preference for user and computer settings
- Configuring slow-link detection and subsequent processing
- Manually refreshing Group Policy

Before exploring these techniques in the sections that follow, let's first examine how policy is processed and refreshed. When you work with Group Policy processing and refresh, you might also want to know which policy objects have been applied and when the last policy refresh occurred on a particular computer. For details, see "Determining Effective Settings and Last Refresh" later in this chapter.

Policy Processing and Refresh Essentials

In Group Policy, policy preferences and settings are divided into two distinct sets: computer policies and user policies. Computer policies apply to computers and are stored under Computer Configuration in Group Policy. User policies apply to users and are stored under User Configuration in Group Policy.

After you create and link a GPO to a site, domain, or OU, the policy preferences and settings that the GPO contains do not take effect immediately. Instead, the policy preferences and settings within the GPO are applied the next time policy is processed or refreshed. The same is true when you change the policy preferences and settings within a GPO—the changes do not take effect until the next time policy is processed or refreshed.

I distinguish between initial processing of policy and refresh processing of policy because the two tasks work in very different ways. Initial processing refers to the way policies are processed the first time policy is applied. Refresh processing refers to the way policies are processed during subsequent applications of policy.

Whether we are talking about initial processing or refresh processing, it is important to note that policy is never pushed out to clients from domain controllers. Instead, the Group Policy client running on a computer is responsible for making policy requests. A domain controller responding to a request makes policies available, and the client pulls the policies it needs from the domain controller.

Initial policy processing of computer policies is triggered when a computer is started. Generally, this means that when a computer is started and the network connection is initialized, the initial computer policies are applied.

Initial processing of user policies is triggered when a user logs on to a computer. Generally, this means that when a user logs on to a computer, the initial user policies are applied.

Because user policies are applied after computer policies, user policies have precedence over computer policies by default. This means that if computer and user settings conflict, user settings have priority and take precedence.

After policy settings are applied, the settings are refreshed automatically to ensure that they are current. By default, Group Policy on domain controllers is refreshed every 5 minutes. For other types of servers and on workstations, Group Policy is refreshed every 90 minutes by default. A random offset of up to 30 minutes is added to reduce impact on domain controllers and the network during updates (making the effective refresh window 90 to 120 minutes).

During a refresh of Group Policy, the client computer contacts an available domain controller in its local site. If one or more of the policy objects defined in the domain have changed, the domain controller provides a list of all the policy objects that apply to the computer and to the user who is currently logged on, as appropriate. The domain controller does this regardless of whether the version numbers of the listed policy objects have changed. By default, the computer processes the policy objects only if the version number of at least one of the policy objects has changed. If any one of the related policies has changed, all of the policies have to be processed again to account for inheritance and the interdependencies within policies.

Security settings are a notable exception to the processing rule. By default, these settings are refreshed every 16 hours (960 minutes) regardless of whether policy objects contain changes. A random offset of up to 30 minutes is added to reduce impact on domain controllers and the network during updates (making the effective refresh window 960 to 990 minutes). Also, if the client computer detects that it is connecting over a slow network connection, it informs the domain controller, and only the Security Settings and Administrative Templates policy settings are transferred over the network, which means that by default only Security Settings and Administrative Templates policy settings are applied when a computer is connected over a slow link. The way slow-link detection works is configurable in a policy.

Real World   The major factor affecting the way that Group Policy refreshes work is link speed. If a computer detects that it is using a slow connection (the exact definition of which is configurable in Group Policy), the computer modifies the way policy changes are processed. Specifically, if a client computer detects that it is using a slow network connection, only the Security Settings and Administrative Templates are processed. Although you cannot turn off the processing of Security Settings and Administrative Templates, you can configure other areas of policy so that related settings are processed across a slow network connection.

Following this, you can summarize the core mechanics of policy processing and refreshes in this way:

- Initial processing occurs when a computer starts or when a user logs on. During initial processing, all applicable policy objects are processed.
- Refresh processing occurs every 5 minutes on domain controllers and every 90 to 120 minutes on workstations. During refresh processing, changes in applicable policy objects are processed.
- Security reprocessing occurs every 960 to 990 minutes. During security reprocessing, all security settings are reapplied regardless of whether they have changed.

That in a nutshell is how policy processing and refreshes work. Because initial processing occurs in the foreground and occurs synchronously (meaning each policy object is applied in order), the startup and logon processes cannot be completed until policy processing is completed. Because refresh processing occurs in the background, it does not force the user to wait while a refresh occurs. Instead, changes simply are applied as policy is refreshed.

Policy Processing and Refresh Exceptions

The operating system running on a computer, the computer configuration, and the configuration of Group Policy itself can alter the way policy processing and refreshes work. The default setting for Windows Server 2003, Windows Server 2008 and Windows Server 2008 R2 is to synchronously process policy objects in the foreground every time a computer starts or a user logs on. This means that each policy object is processed in order for both the computer (during startup) and the user (during logon). During startup, each policy object must be processed in turn to complete the startup process. During logon, each policy object must be processed in turn to complete the logon and make the interface available to the user. Because this type of processing forces startup or logon to wait until processing is finalized, this type of processing is referred to as *synchronous foreground processing*.

Windows desktops use this behavior only the first time a computer is started after joining the domain. After that, Windows desktops perform asynchronous foreground processing at startup and logon, a type of processing that works like background refresh processing. Because asynchronous foreground processing does not force the startup or logon processes to wait, the user gains access to the user interface more quickly during logon.

This modified behavior would work wonderfully if it weren't for the fact that some policy settings can be applied only during foreground processing. Areas of policy that can be applied only during synchronous foreground processing include policy settings for:

- Deployed printer connections
- Folder redirection
- Offline files
- Scripts
- Software installation

In addition, areas of policy preferences affected this way include drive maps and printers. These and other policy preferences and settings that require synchronous foreground processing will not be applied during asynchronous foreground processing or during background refresh processing.

To guarantee the application of these types of preferences and settings, I recommend creating a GPO called Force Synchronous Processing. In this GPO, enable the Always Wait For The Network At Computer Startup And Logon Policy setting. Once you create the GPO, you can:

- Link the GPO to the appropriate containers for which forced synchronous processing is required. This ensures that Windows waits for Group Policy to be applied in the foreground synchronously during startup and logon.
- Unlink the GPO when you no longer want to force synchronous processing. This allows desktop versions of Windows to default to background refresh only.

Because the Always Wait For The Network At Computer Startup And Logon Policy setting is under Computer Configuration, the setting is processed by computer (not user) objects. Finally, it is important to note that while most security-related policy settings can be applied to a computer during background refresh, some security-related policy settings require a restart of the computer.

Refreshing Group Policy Manually

As an administrator, you might need to refresh Group Policy manually. For example, you might not want to wait for Group Policy to be refreshed at the automatic interval, or you might be trying to resolve a problem with refreshing policy and want to force Group Policy to be refreshed.

On computers running Windows, you can refresh Group Policy manually by using the Gpupdate command-line utility. Gpupdate performs a background refresh of Group Policy on the computer to which you are currently logged on or connected. Table 7-1 provides a summary of the options you can use with Gpupdate.

TABLE 7-1 Options for Gpupdate

OPTION	DESCRIPTION	REQUIRES ELEVATED COMMAND PROMPT
/Target:Computer	Refreshes only the computer policies.	No
/Target:User	Refreshes only the user policies.	No
/Force	Forces the Group Policy client to refresh all policies. By default only policies that have changed are refreshed.	No
/Wait:WaitTime	Sets the number of seconds to wait for processing to finish before returning the command prompt. The default wait time is 600 seconds. Use a value of 0 to return the command prompt immediately. A value of -1 means to wait infinitely.	No
/Logoff	Forces a logoff after policy is refreshed, which may be required for policies that can be processed only during logon.	Yes
/Boot	Forces a restart after policy is refreshed, which may be required for policies that can be processed only during startup.	Yes
/Sync	Sets the next application of foreground policy to be performed synchronously at startup and at logon.	Yes

You can initiate a background refresh in several ways. If you enter **gpupdate** at a command prompt, both computer policies and user policies are refreshed on the local computer. You can also refresh user and computer policies separately. To refresh only computer policies, enter **gpupdate /target:computer** at the command prompt. To refresh only user policies, enter **gpupdate /target:user** at the command prompt.

Keep in mind that only policy settings that have changed are processed and applied when you run Gpupdate. You can change this behavior using the /Force parameter. The /Force parameter forces a refresh of all policy settings.

With a forced refresh, if some user policies require synchronous foreground processing, you'll be prompted to log off. Press Y to log off so that the policies can be applied, or press N to cancel the logoff. You'll see a reboot prompt for computer policies that require synchronous foreground processing.

You can use Gpupdate to log off a user or restart a computer after Group Policy is refreshed. This is useful because some group policies are applied only when a user logs on or when a computer starts up. To log off a user after a refresh, add the /Logoff parameter. To restart a computer after a refresh, add the /Boot parameter.

Using the /Sync option, you set a flag that changes the way Gpupdate works. Instead of causing a refresh to occur, including the /Sync option tells the computer to perform synchronous foreground processing during the next startup and logon. Any additional options you include can be used to further control the forced synchronous foreground processing. For example, if you add /Target:Computer, only computer policies are targeted and then applied during the next boot cycle. If you add /Target:User, only user policies are targeted and then applied during the next logon cycle. If you want to force the user to log off, the computer to restart, or both, you can add the /Logoff option, the /Boot option, or both.

Real World   When you've installed Windows PowerShell 2.0 and WinRm 2.0 on computers in your organization, you can easily execute commands on those computers from your management computer. Consider the following sample Windows PowerShell script:

```
$names = @("corpc85","corpc86","corpc87")
$sb = {Get-WmiObject Win32_OperatingSystem | '
Invoke-WmiMethod Reboot}
Invoke-Command -scriptblock $sb -computer '
$names -asjob
```

Invoke-Command uses WinRM to run Windows PowerShell remotely. Here, you create an array of computer names, define a script block, and then invoke the script block on the remote computers as background

---

jobs. This actually pushes the Get-WmiObject and Invoke-WmiMethod commands out to each specified computer where they then execute locally.

In addition to executing its own cmdlets, Windows PowerShell also can execute external commands that have their own executable files (as long as the executables are in the command path). Knowing this, you can easily execute other types of commands on remote computers as well. The following example runs Gpupdate on a group of remote computers:

```
$names = @("corpc85","corpc86","corpc87")
$sb = {Gpupdate}
Invoke-Command -scriptblock $sb -computer '
$names -asjob
```

This actually pushes the Gpupdate command out to each specified computer, where it then executes locally. Keep in mind that WinRM uses TCP port 80 for HTTP and TCP port 443 for HTTPS by default, and these ports must be open between your management computer and the target computers.

Changing the Refresh Interval

After Group Policy is initially applied, it is periodically refreshed to ensure that it is current. The default refresh interval for domain controllers is 5 minutes. For all other computers, the default refresh interval is 90 minutes, with up to a 30-minute variation to avoid overloading the domain controller with numerous concurrent client requests. This means an effective refresh window for non–domain controller computers of 90 to 120 minutes.

You can change the refresh rate. A faster refresh rate reduces the possibility that a computer won't have the most current policy configuration. A slower refresh rate reduces the frequency of policy refreshes (which can also reduce overhead with regard to resource usage), but it also increases the possibility that a computer won't have the most current policy configuration.

In a large organization with many computers, you might want to reduce policy-related resource usage on your domain controllers, or you might want to reduce policy-related traffic on your network. To do this, you can change the default refresh interval. Here are some examples:

- If policy is changed infrequently and you want to relax the processing rules, you can increase the refresh window to reduce resource usage. For example, you could use a refresh interval of 15 minutes on domain controllers and 120 minutes on other computers.
- If policy is changed frequently and you want to ensure faster application, you can reduce the refresh window (while increasing resource usage). For example, you could use a refresh interval of 5 minutes on domain controllers and 45 minutes on other computers.

You can change the Group Policy refresh interval on a per-policy-object basis. To set the refresh interval for domain controllers, complete the following steps:

1. In the GPMC, right-click the Group Policy object you want to modify, and then click Edit. This GPO should be linked to a container that contains domain controller computer objects.
2. Under Computer Configuration, navigate to Policies\Administrative Templates\System\Group Policy folder.
3. Double-click the Group Policy Refresh Interval For Domain Controllers policy. This displays a Properties dialog box for the policy, as shown in Figure 7-6.
4. Define the policy by selecting Enabled.

   Use the first Minutes combo box to set the base refresh interval. You will usually want this value to be between 5 and 59 minutes.
5. Use the other Minutes combo box to set the minimum and maximum time variation for the refresh interval. The variation effectively creates a refresh window, with the goal to avoid overloading that might result from numerous simultaneous client requests for a Group Policy refresh.
6. Click OK to save your settings.

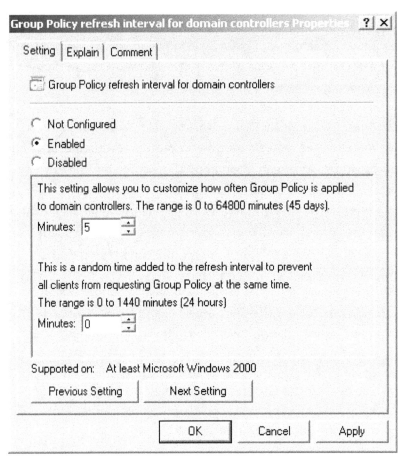

FIGURE 7-6 Change the refresh interval for domain controllers.

To set the refresh interval for non–domain controller computers (member servers and workstations), complete the following steps:

1. In the GPMC, right-click the Group Policy object you want to modify, and then click Edit. This GPO should be linked to a container that contains computer objects.

2. Under Computer Configuration, navigate to the Policies\Administrative Templates\System\Group Policy folder.

3. Double-click the Group Policy Refresh Interval For Computers policy. This displays a Properties dialog box for the policy, as shown in Figure 7-7.

4. Define the policy by selecting Enabled.

5. Use the first Minutes combo box to set the base refresh interval. You will usually want this value to be between 60 and 180 minutes.

6. Use the other Minutes combo box to set the minimum and maximum time variation for the refresh interval. The variation effectively creates a refresh window, with the goal to avoid overloading that might result from numerous simultaneous client requests for a Group Policy refresh.

7. Click OK to save your settings.

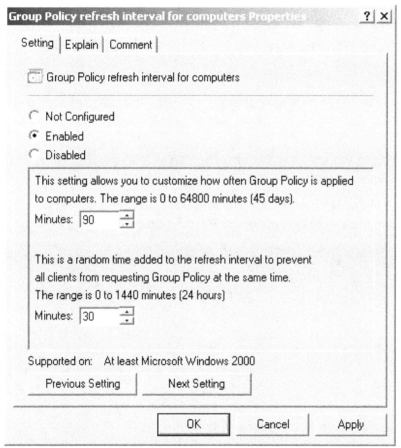

FIGURE 7-7 Change the refresh interval for member servers and workstations.

Modifying GPO Processing

You can enable or disable processing of policy objects either completely or partially. Completely disabling a policy object is useful if you no longer need a policy now but might want to use it in the future, or if you're troubleshooting policy-processing problems. Partially disabling a policy object is useful when you want the related policy settings to apply to either users or computers but not both.

By partially disabling a policy, you can then ensure that only the per-computer policy settings or only the per-user policy settings are applied. In cases in which you are trying to speed up policy processing, you might also want to disable user or computer settings. However, you should do this only when you've fully determined the impact of this change on your environment.

You can enable and disable policies partially or entirely by completing the following steps:

1. In the GPMC, select the container for the site, domain, or OU with which you want to work.

2. Select the policy object you want to work with, and then click the Details tab in the details pane, as shown in Figure 7-8.

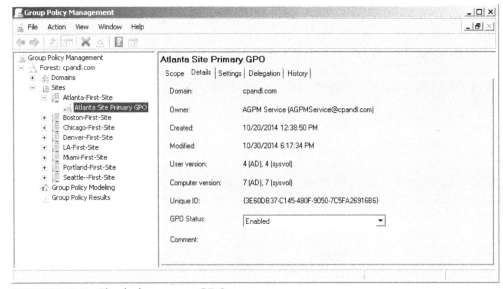

FIGURE 7-8 Check the current GPO status.

3. Use the GPO Status list to choose one of the following status settings:

- **Enabled**   Allows processing of the policy object and all its settings.
- All Settings Disabled   Disallows processing of the policy object and all its settings.
- **Computer Configuration Settings Disabled**   Disables processing of Computer Configuration settings; only User Configuration settings are processed.
- **User Configuration Settings Disabled**   Disables processing of User Configuration settings; only Computer Configuration settings are processed.

4. When prompted to confirm that you want to change the status of this GPO, click OK.

Configuring Loopback Processing

When Group Policy is applied, computer policies are applied before user policies. Because Group Policy uses a last-writer-wins methodology, this means that user policy settings override computer policy settings when a conflict occurs between settings in Computer Configuration and settings in User Configuration. It is also important to point out that computer settings are applied from the computer's GPOs, and user settings are applied from the user's GPOs.

In some special situations, you might not want this behavior. In a secure lab or kiosk environment, for example, you might want user settings to be applied from the computer's GPOs to ensure compliance with the strict security rules and guidelines for the lab. On a shared computer, you might want user settings to be applied from the computer's GPOs but also allow user settings from the user's GPOs to be applied. Using loopback processing, you can allow for these types of exceptions and obtain user settings from a computer's GPOs.

To configure loopback processing, complete the following steps:

1. In the GPMC, right-click the Group Policy object you want to modify, and then click Edit.

2. Under Computer Configuration, navigate to the Policies\Administrative Templates\System\Group Policy folder.

3. Double-click the User Group Policy Loopback Processing Mode policy. This displays a Properties dialog box for the policy, as shown in Figure 7-9.

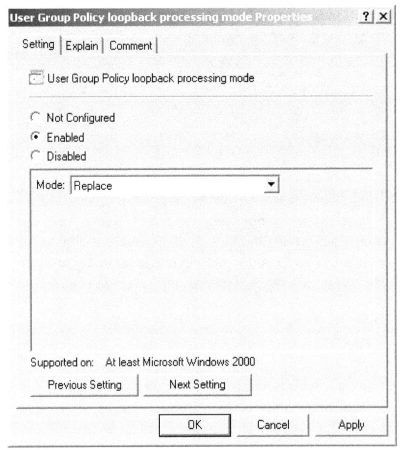

FIGURE 7-9 Set the loopback mode to either Replace or Merge.

4. Define the policy by selecting Enabled, and then use the Mode list to select one of these processing modes:

   ▪ **Replace** When you use the Replace option, user settings from the computer's GPOs are processed and the user settings in the user's

GPOs are not processed. This means the user settings from the computer's GPOs replace the user settings normally applied to the user.

- **Merge**   When you use the Merge option, user settings in the computer's GPOs are processed first, then user settings in the user's GPOs are processed, and then user settings in the computer's GPOs are processed again. This processing technique combines the user settings in both the computer and user GPOs. If there are any conflicts, the user settings in the computer's GPOs have preference and overwrite the user settings in the user's GPOs.

5. Click OK to save your settings.

Configuring Slow-Link Detection

A computer connected to a local area network (LAN) does not necessarily have a fast link, nor does a computer connected using a remote connection necessarily have a slow link. The default value for what Group Policy considers a slow link is any rate slower than 500 kilobits per second (Kbps). You can change this threshold by using Group Policy.

Slow-Link Detection Essentials

Active Directory uses slow-link detection to help reduce network traffic during periods of high latency. This feature is used by Group Policy clients to detect increased latency and reduced responsiveness on the network and then take corrective action to reduce the likelihood that processing Group Policy will further saturate the network. Once a slow link is detected, Group Policy clients reduce their network communications and requests to reduce the overall network traffic load by limiting the amount of policy processing they do.

The technique that client computers use to determine whether they are using a slow network connection depends on the operating system:

- The client computer sends a sequence of pings to the domain controller to which it is connected. The response time from the domain controller (which is an indicator of latency) determines the next step. If the response time from any of the pings is 10 milliseconds or less, the client maintains or resumes processing of Group Policy following normal (full) procedures. If the response time from the domain controller is more than 10 milliseconds, the computer pings the domain controller three times with a 2-KB message packet and uses the average response time to determine the network speed.
- With Windows Vista, Windows Server 2008, and later versions of Windows, the Group Policy client determines the link speed by using the Network Location Awareness (NLA) service to sample the current TCP traffic between the client and the logon domain controller. Prior to beginning a refresh, the Group Policy service running on the client requests the NLA service to start sampling TCP bandwidth on the network interface that hosts the domain controller. The Group Policy service continues to communicate with the domain controller as it gathers the information required to do a policy refresh. Then the Group Policy service requests the NLA service to stop sampling the TCP traffic and provide an estimated bandwidth between the computer and the domain controller based on the sampling.

By default, if the connection speed is determined to be less than 500 Kbps (which could also be interpreted as high latency/reduced responsiveness on a fast network), the client computer interprets this as a slow network connection and notifies the domain controller. As a result, only the Administrative Templates (registry-based) settings and critical security settings are requested and then applied by default. Table 7-2 provides a detailed summary of which settings are applied over a slow link by default and whether a policy area is reapplied during refresh even if it hasn't changed by default.

TABLE 7-2 Default Settings for Policy Refresh over a Slow Link

POLICY AREAS	REQUESTED OVER A SLOW LINK?	PROCESS EVEN IF NOT CHANGED?
Administrative Templates	Yes (Cannot be disabled)	No
Applications Preferences	Yes	Yes
Data Sources Preferences	Yes	Yes
Deployed Printer Connections	No	No
Devices Preferences	Yes	Yes
Disk Quotas	No	No
Drive Maps Preferences	Yes	Yes
EFS Recovery	No	No
Environment Preferences	Yes	Yes
Files Preferences	Yes	Yes
Folder Options Preferences	Yes	Yes
Folder Redirection	No	No
Folders Preferences	Yes	Yes
Internet Explorer Maintenance	Yes	No
Ini Files Preferences	Yes	Yes
Internet Settings Preferences	Yes	Yes
IP Security	Yes	No
Local Users And Groups Preferences	Yes	Yes
Network Options Preferences	Yes	Yes

Network Shares Preferences	Yes	Yes
Power Options Preferences	Yes	Yes
Printers Preferences	Yes	Yes
Regional Options Preferences	Yes	Yes
Registry Preferences	Yes	Yes
Registry security settings	No	No
Scheduled Tasks Preferences	Yes	Yes
Scripts	No	No
Security	Yes (Cannot be disabled)	Yes
Services Preferences	Yes	Yes
Shortcuts Preferences	Yes	Yes
Software Installation	No	No
Software Restriction Policies	Yes	No
Start Menu Preferences	Yes	Yes
Wired Policy	Yes	No
Wireless Policy	Yes	No

You can configure slow-link detection using the Group Policy Slow Link Detection policy. Under Computer Configuration, you'll find this policy in the Policies\Administrative Templates\System\Group Policy folder. If you disable this policy or do not configure it, clients use the default value of 500 Kbps per second to determine whether they are on a slow link. If you enable this policy, you can set a different slow-link value, such as 256 Kbps per second.

The only way to disable slow-link detection completely is to enable the Group Policy Slow Link Detection policy and then set the Connection Speed option to 0. This setting effectively tells clients not to detect slow links and to consider all links to be fast.

You can optimize processing for various areas of Group Policy individually as well. To do this, you use Computer Configuration policies found in the Policies\Administrative Templates\System\Group Policy folder. Key policies include:

- **Disk Quota Policy Processing** By default, updates to policy settings for disk quotas are not processed over slow links. This doesn't, however, change the meaning of or enforcement of any current disk quotas defined in a GPO. Previously obtained policy settings for disk quotas are still enforced.

- **EFS Recovery Policy Processing** By default, updates to policy settings for Encrypting File System (EFS) recovery are not processed over slow links. This doesn't, however, change the meaning of or enforcement of any current EFS recovery options defined in policy. If you turn off EFS recovery processing, previously obtained policy settings for EFS recovery are still valid and enforced.

- **Folder Redirection Policy Processing** By default, updates to policy settings for folder redirection are not processed over slow links. Note that folder redirection settings are only read and applied during logon. Thus, if a user connects over a slow network during logon, the folder redirection settings will not apply by default and the user's folders will not be subsequently redirected. This behavior is typically what you want, especially if users are connecting via a dial-up or another slow remote connection.

- **Internet Explorer Maintenance Policy Processing** By default, updates to policy settings for Windows Internet Explorer maintenance are processed over slow links. If always having the most current Internet Explorer maintenance settings is important to the safety and security of the network, you should allow processing across a slow network connection. This ensures that the settings are the most current possible given the current Group Policy refresh rate.

- **IP Security Policy Processing**   By default, updates to policy settings for IP Security are processed over slow links. If you turn off processing, it doesn't change the meaning of or enforcement of any current IP Security policies. Previously obtained policy settings for IP Security are still valid and enforced.

- **Scripts Policy Processing**   By default, updates to policy settings for scripts are not processed over slow links. Note that policy-defined scripts are executed only when specific events occur, such as logon, logoff, shutdown, or startup.

- **Security Policy Processing**   Updates to policy settings for security are always processed regardless of the type of link. By default, security policy is refreshed every 16 hours even if security policy has not changed. The only way to stop the forced refresh is to configure security policy processing so that it is not applied during periodic background refreshes. To do this, you select the policy setting Do Not Apply During Periodic Background Processing. Because security policy is so important, however, the Do Not Apply setting means only that security policy processing is stopped when a user is logged on and using the machine. One of the only reasons you'll want to stop security policy refresh is if applications are failing during refresh.

- **Software Installation Policy Processing**   By default, updates to policy settings for software installation are not processed over slow links. This means new deployments of or updates to software are not made available to users who connect over slow links. This is typically a good thing because deploying or updating software over a slow link can be a very long process.

- **Wireless Policy Processing**   By default, updates to policy settings for wireless networking are processed over slow links. If you turn off processing, it doesn't change the meaning of or enforcement of any current wireless policies. Previously obtained policy settings for wireless networking are still valid and enforced.

Each of these Processing settings, as well as other related Processing settings, can be enabled or disabled to modify the way processing works. If you enable a Processing setting, you'll have additional optimization options, which can include:

- **Allow Processing Across A Slow Network Connection**   Select this option to enable slow-link processing. Clear this option to disable slow-link processing.
- **Do Not Apply During Periodic Background Processing**   Select this option to disable background processing (allowing only foreground processing at startup and logon). Clear this option to enable background processing.
- **Process Even If The Group Policy Objects Have Not Changed**   Select this option to process the related area of policy even if there aren't any changes. Clear this option to process only the related area when there are changes.

Generally, policy areas related to preferences are processed even if they haven't changed. This is important to note because policy preferences are configured by default so that they are reapplied during policy refresh. If you don't want preferences in a particular policy area to be automatically reapplied during refresh, you have two choices. You can:

- Override the default setting on a per-preference basis.   To do this, select the Apply Once And Do Not Reapply option on the Common tab when you configure a related preference.
- Override the default setting for a policy area on a per-GPO basis. To do this, enable the related Processing policy setting and then clear the Process Even If The Group Policy Objects Have Not Changed check box.

Configuring Slow-Link Detection and Policy Processing

You can configure slow-link detection and related policy processing by completing the following steps:

1. In the GPMC, right-click the policy object you want to modify, and then click Edit.

2. Under Computer Configuration, navigate to the Policies\Administrative Templates\System\Group Policy folder.

3. Double-click the Group Policy Slow Link Detection policy.

4. Select Enabled to define the policy, as shown in Figure 7-10, and then use the Connection Speed combo box to specify the speed that should be used to determine whether a computer is on a slow link. For example, if you want connections of less than 256 kilobits per second to be deemed slow, enter **256**. If you want to disable slow-link detection completely for this policy object, enter **0**.

5. Click OK to save your settings.

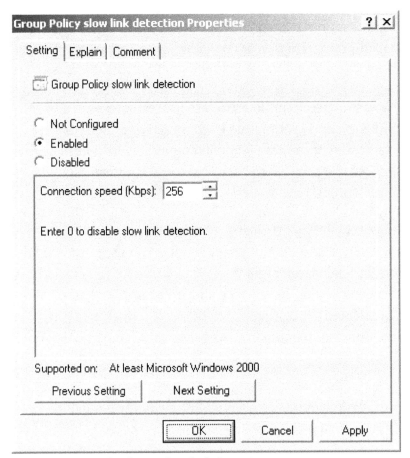

FIGURE 7-10 Configure slow-link detection.

Configuring Slow-Link and Background Policy Processing

Policy preferences are refreshed in full every 90 to 120 minutes. Security settings are refreshed in full every 16 hours. Other areas of Group Policy are not refreshed fully. For these areas, only policies that have changed are refreshed. Sometimes, however, you might want to force clients to reprocess policy settings even if they haven't changed on the server.

> **Real World**   Consider the case in which a local OU administrator has made changes to a local computer that might affect how the computer operates. If the local admin has modified the registry or another area of the operating system directly, these changes won't be reflected as changes to Group Policy. To try to overwrite and fix these types of changes, you might want to reapply Group Policy. As long as Group Policy writes to the related area of the registry or to the operating system configuration in general, the problem will be resolved.

You can optimize slow-link and background processing (refresh) of key areas of Group Policy by using the Computer Configuration policies in the Policies\Administrative Templates\System\Group Policy folder. The key configuration options available include:

- **Allow Processing Across A Slow Network Connection**   Ensures that the extension settings are processed even on a slow network
- **Do Not Apply During Periodic Background Processing**   Overrides refresh when extension settings change after startup or logon
- **Process Even If The Group Policy Objects Have Not Changed** Forces the client computer to process the extension settings during refresh even if the settings haven't changed
- **Background Priority**   Sets the relative priority for the related background process as either normal, below normal, low, or idle

> **Tip**   By default, Background Priority is set to idle, which means the related process has no priority at all. Because all prioritized processes go before no-priority processes, there is a strong possibility that no-priority processes will not get adequate processing time on a highly

active system. To prevent this from happening, you can increase the priority as appropriate.

To configure slow-link and background policy processing of key areas of Group Policy, complete these steps:

1. In the GPMC, right-click the policy object you want to modify, and then click Edit.
2. Under Computer Configuration, navigate to the Policies\Administrative Templates\System\Group Policy folder.
3. Double-click the policy you want to configure. The key policies for controlling slow-link and background policy processing include:

- Applications Policy Processing
- Data Sources Policy Processing
- Deployed Printer Connections
- Devices Policy Processing
- Disk Quotas Policy Processing
- Drive Maps Policy Processing
- EFS Recovery Policy Processing
- Environment Policy Processing
- Files Policy Processing
- Folder Options Policy Processing
- Folder Redirection Policy Processing
- Folders Policy Processing
- Internet Explorer Maintenance Policy Processing
- Ini Files Policy Processing
- Internet Settings Policy Processing
- IP Security Policy Processing
- Local Users And Groups Policy Processing
- Microsoft Offline Files Policy Processing
- Network Options Policy Processing
- Network Shares Policy Processing
- Power Options Policy Processing
- Printers Policy Processing

- Regional Options Policy Processing
- Registry Policy Processing
- Scheduled Tasks Policy Processing
- Scripts Policy Processing
- Security Policy Processing
- Services Policy Processing
- Shortcuts Policy Processing
- Software Installation Policy Processing
- Software Restriction Policies
- Start Menu Policy Processing
- Wired Policy Processing
- Wireless Policy Processing

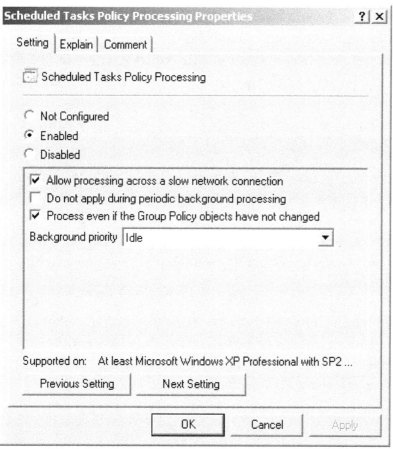

FIGURE 7-11 Optimize policy processing.

4. Select Enabled to define the policy, as shown in Figure 7-11, and then make your configuration selections. The options will differ slightly depending on the policy selected and might include the following:

- Allow Processing Across A Slow Network Connection
- Do Not Apply During Periodic Background Processing
- Process Even If The Group Policy Objects Have Not Changed
- Background Priority

5. Click OK to save your settings.

Planning Group Policy Changes

Before you change Group Policy, you should model the effects of policy changes you'd like to make and back up the current Group Policy configuration. After you implement Group Policy or perform updates to Group Policy, you should review the results. Then, when you have finished with the update and review processes, you should back up the Group Policy configuration again.

Testing Implementation and Configuration Scenarios

Modeling Group Policy for planning is useful when you want to test various implementation and configuration scenarios. For example, you might want to model the effect of a slow link or the use of loopback processing. You can also model the effect of moving users or computers to another container in Active Directory or the effect of changing security group membership for users and computers.

All domain and enterprise administrators have permission to model Group Policy for planning, as do those who have been delegated the Perform Group Policy Modeling Analyses permission. To model Group Policy and test various implementation and update scenarios, complete these steps:

1. In the GPMC, right-click the Group Policy Modeling node, and then click Group Policy Modeling Wizard.

2. When the Group Policy Modeling Wizard starts, click Next. The Domain Controller Selection page, shown in Figure 7-12, is displayed.

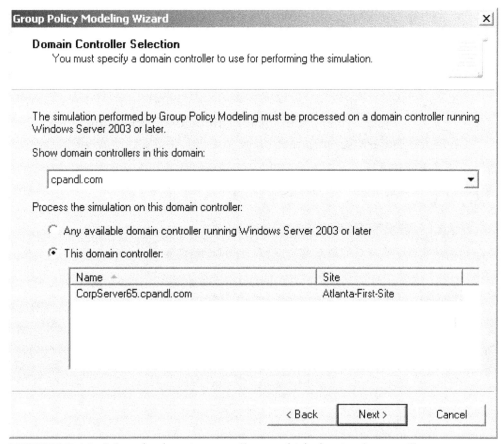

FIGURE 7-12 Select the domain controller on which the simulation will run.

3. Under Show Domain Controllers In This Domain, select the domain for which you want to model results.

4. Under Process The Simulation On This Domain Controller, the Any Available Domain Controller option is selected by default. If you want to use a specific domain controller, select This Domain Controller, and then choose a specific domain controller from the list. Click Next.

5. On the User And Computer Selection page, shown in Figure 7-13, select the modeling options for users and computers. In most cases,

you'll want to model policy for a specific container using user and computer information. In this case, do the following:

- Under User Information, select Container, and then click Browse to display the Choose User Container dialog box. Choose any of the available user containers in the selected domain. For example, you can simulate policy settings for users in the Customer Service OU.
- Under Computer Information, select Container, and then click Browse to display the Choose Computer Container dialog box. Choose any of the available computer containers in the selected domain. For example, you can simulate policy settings for computers in the same OU you selected under User Information or in a different OU, such as in the Technology OU.

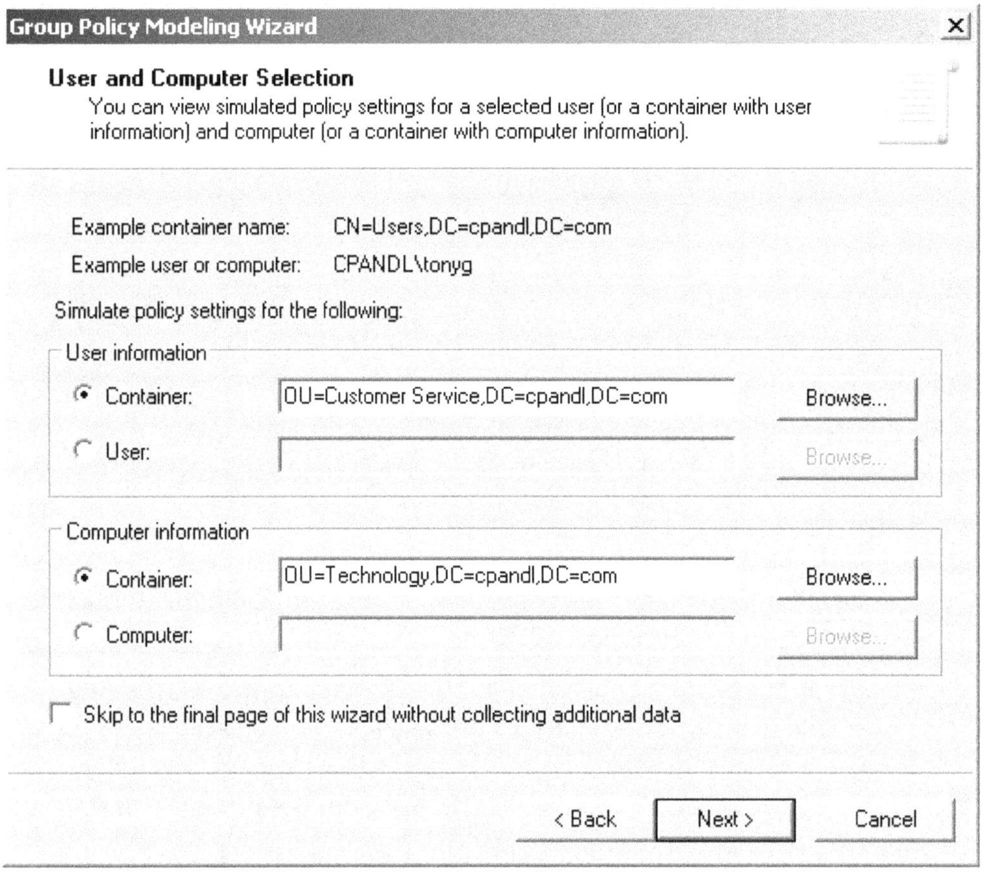

FIGURE 7-13 Define the simulation criteria for users, computers, or both.

6. Click Next. The Advanced Simulation Options page, shown in Figure 7-14, is displayed. The advanced options allow you to modify the simulation for network and subnet variations, such as slow-link detection, loopback processing, and accessing the network from a particular site. Select any advanced options as necessary.

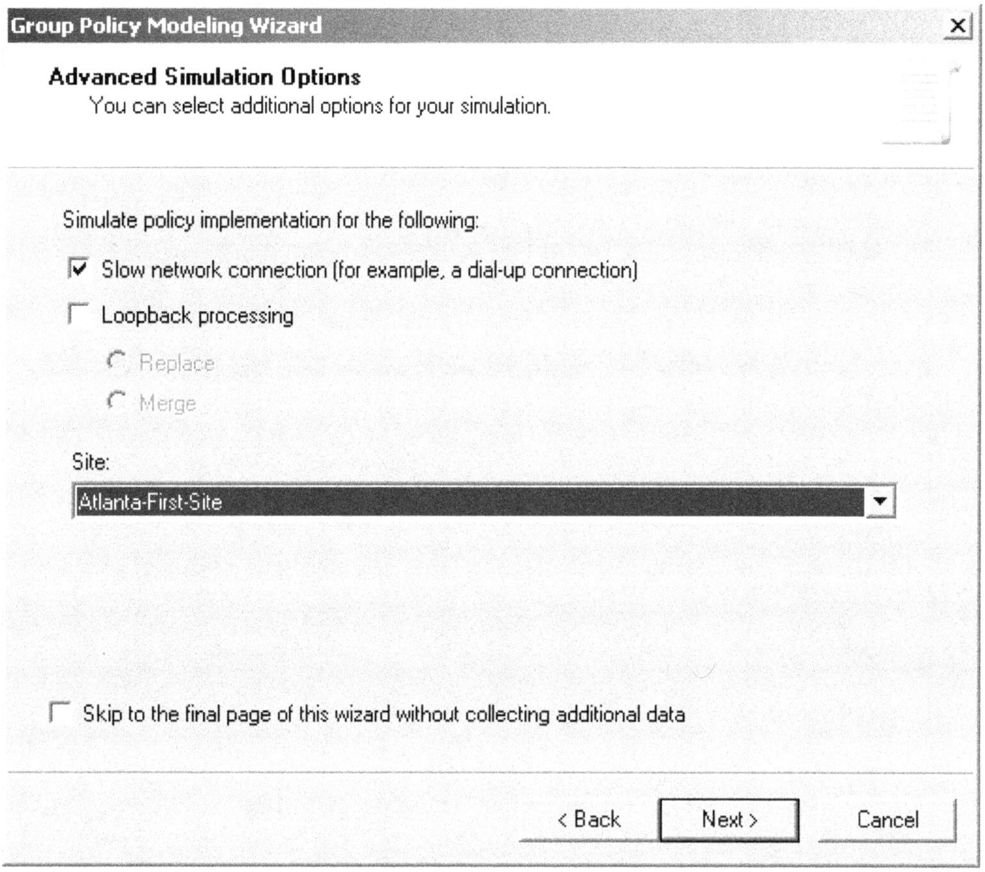

FIGURE 7-14 Specify advanced simulation criteria.

7. Click Next. If you are modeling user information, the User Security Groups page, shown in Figure 7-15, is displayed.

8. Use the options on this page to simulate what would happen if you were to add a user to a designated security group. By default, the simulation is for a user who is a member of the implicit security groups Authenticated Users and Everyone. If you want to simulate membership in additional groups, you can add the groups here. For

example, if you want to see what would happen if a user in the
designated container were a member of the Engineering security
group, you can add this group to the Security Groups list. You might
want to do this, for example, if you've configured security filtering for
some policy objects.

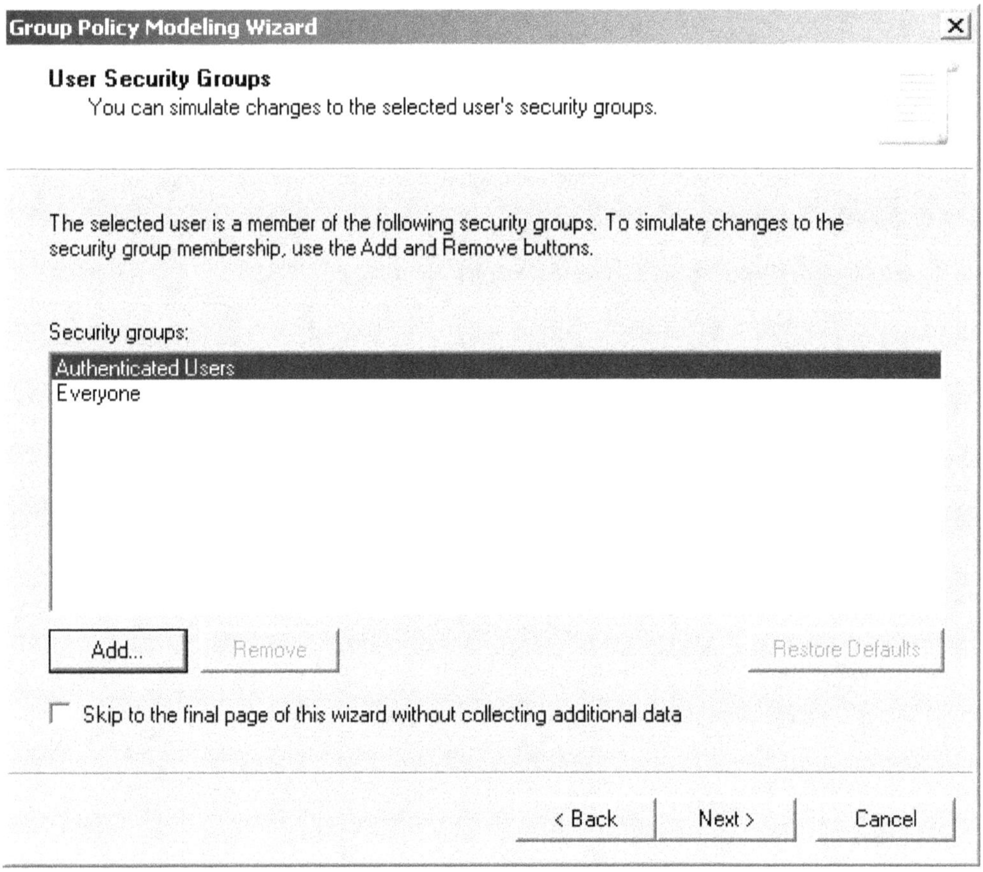

FIGURE 7-15 Simulate user membership in various security groups.

9. Click Next. If you are modeling computer information, the Computer
   Security Groups page, shown in Figure 7-16, is displayed.

10. Use the options on this page to simulate what would happen if you
    were to add a computer to a designated security group. By default, the
    simulation is for a computer that is a member of the implicit security
    groups Authenticated Users and Everyone. If you want to simulate
    membership in additional groups, you can add the groups here. For

example, if you want to see what would happen if a computer in the designated container were a member of the Domain Controllers security group, you can add this group to the Security Groups list.

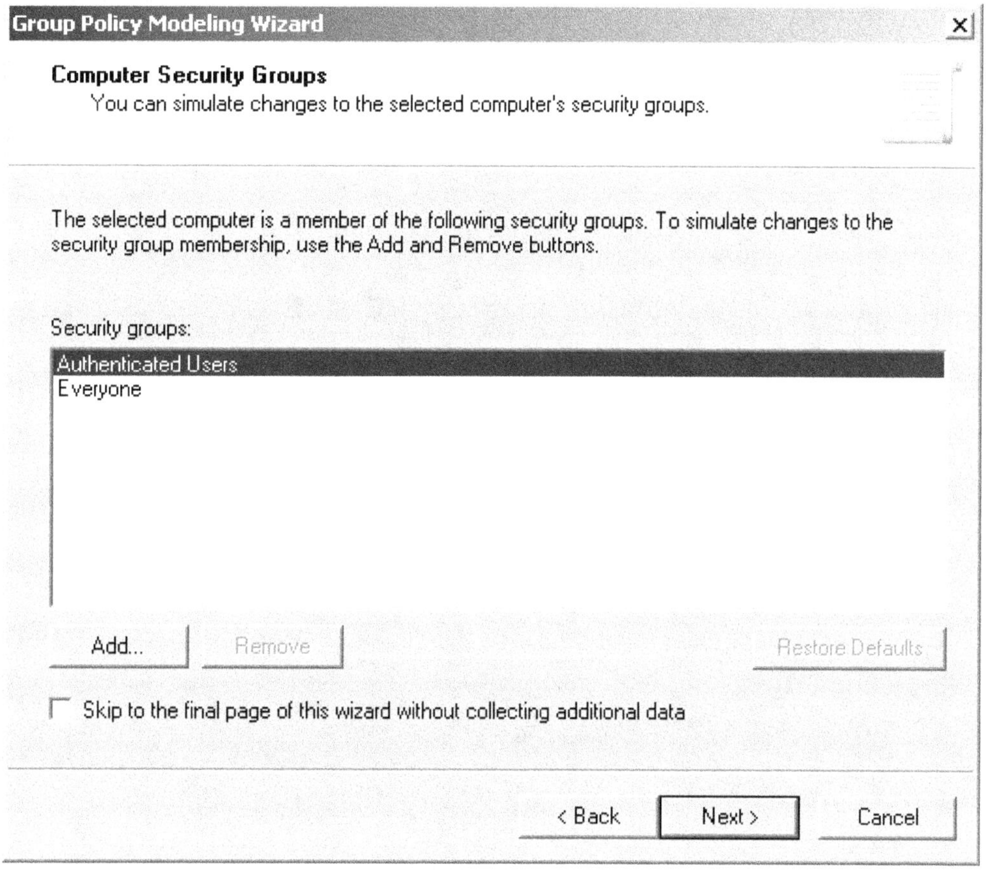

FIGURE 7-16 Simulate computer membership in various security groups.

11. Windows Management Instrumentation (WMI) filters can be linked to policy objects. By default, selected users and computers are assumed to meet all WMI filter requirements, which is what you want in most cases for modeling, so click Next twice to skip the WMI Filters For Users and WMI Filters For Computers pages.

12. If the default behavior isn't what you want, on the WMI Filters For Users page, select Only These Filters and then click List Filters. The wizard searches for and lists all applicable filters. If you don't want a filter to apply, click it and then click Remove. Click Next to continue.

Repeat the selection process on the WMI Filters For Computers page and then click Next again.

13. To complete the modeling, click Next, and then click Finish. The wizard generates a report, the results of which are displayed in the details pane. As shown in Figure 7-17, the name of the modeling report is generated based on the containers you chose.

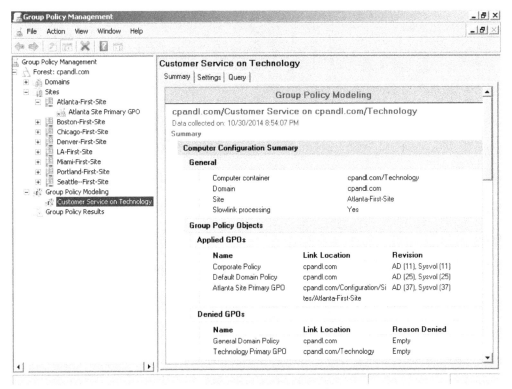

Figure 7-17 Name the report and then view the report details.

14. Click on the report's name to highlight it for editing. Type a descriptive name for the modeling report, and then press Tab. On the report, click Show All to display all the policy information that was modeled.

15. You can then work through the various nodes of the report to view the effective settings for users, computers, or both in the selected container and for the selected modeling options.

Determining Effective Settings and Last Refresh

You can also use Group Policy modeling to log Resultant Set of Policy (RSoP). RSoP allows you to review:

- All of the policy objects that apply to a computer.
- The last time the applicable policy objects were processed (refreshed).
- The user currently logged on to a computer (if any).

All domain and enterprise administrators have permission to generate RSoP, as do those who have been delegated permission to Read Group Policy Results Data. To generate RSoP, complete these steps:

1. In the GPMC, right-click the Group Policy Results node, and then click Group Policy Results Wizard.

2. When the Group Policy Results Wizard starts, click Next. On the Computer Selection page, shown in Figure 7-18, select This Computer to view information for the local computer. If you want to view information for a remote computer, select Another Computer and then click Browse. In the Select Computer dialog box, type the name of the computer, and then click Check Names. After you select the correct computer account, click OK.

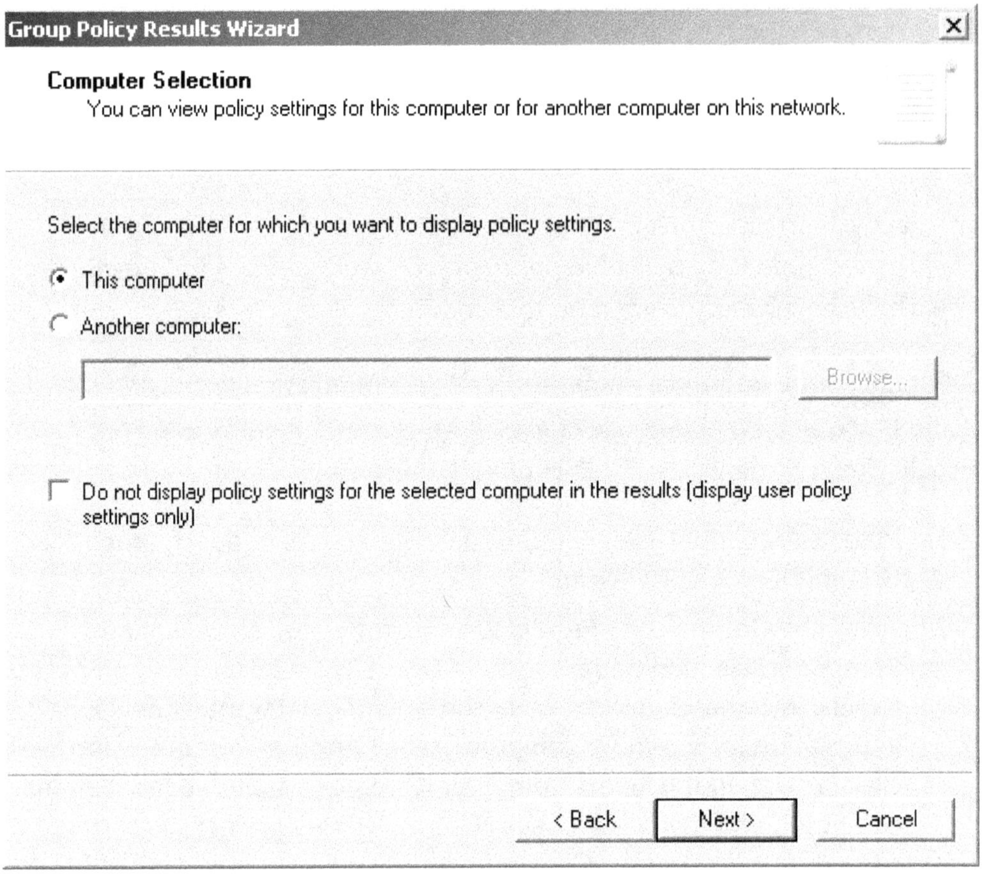

Group Policy Results Wizard

Computer Selection
You can view policy settings for this computer or for another computer on this network.

Select the computer for which you want to display policy settings.

- This computer
- Another computer:

  [   ] Browse...

- Do not display policy settings for the selected computer in the results (display user policy settings only)

< Back | Next > | Cancel

FIGURE 7-18 Select the computer for which you want to log RSoP.

3. By default, both user and computer policy settings are logged. If you want to see results only for user policy settings, select Do Not Display Policy Settings For The Selected Computer. Click Next.

4. On the User Selection page, shown in Figure 7-19, select the user whose policy information you want to view. You can view policy information for any user who has logged on to the computer. If you want to see results only for computer policy settings, select Do Not Display User Policy Settings.

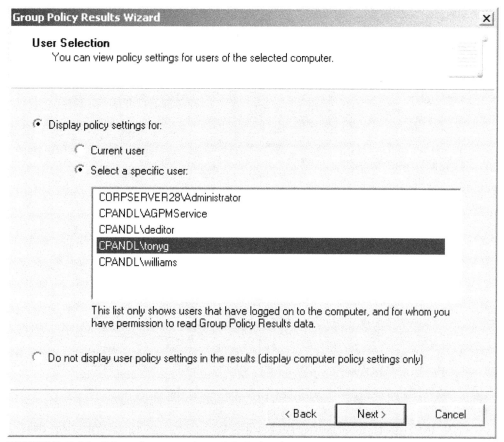

FIGURE 7-19 Select the user whose RSoP for this computer you want to view.

5. To complete the modeling, click Next twice, and then click Finish. The wizard generates a report, the results of which are displayed in the details pane.

6. As shown in Figure 7-20, the name of the modeling report is generated based on the user and computer you chose. Click on the name to highlight it for editing. Type a descriptive name for the modeling report, and then press Tab.

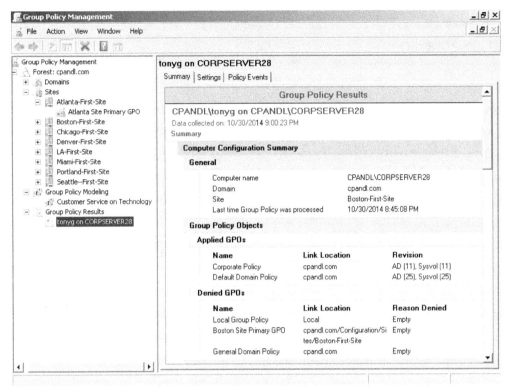

Figure 7-20 Name the report, and then view the report details.

7. On the report, click Show All to display all the policy information that was modeled. You can then work through the various nodes of the report to view the effective settings for the selected user, computer, or both.

To view the last time the computer or user policy was refreshed, look under Computer Configuration Summary, General or User Configuration Summary, General and then check Last Time Group Policy Was Processed, as appropriate.

To view applied policy objects for the computer or user, look under Computer Configuration Summary, Group Policy Objects, Applied GPOs or User Configuration Summary, Group Policy Objects, Applied GPOs, as appropriate.

To view denied policy objects for the computer or user, look under Computer Configuration Summary, Group Policy Objects, Denied GPOs or User Configuration Summary, Group Policy Objects, Denied GPOs, as appropriate.

The entries under Denied Policy objects show all policy objects that should have been applied but weren't. This typically occurs because the policy objects were empty or did not contain any computer or user policy settings. A policy object also might not have been processed because inheritance was blocked. If so, the Reason Denied is stated as Blocked SOM. Scope of Management (SOM) refers to the location to which a GPO is linked. There are three types of SOMs: sites, domains, and OUs. If inheritance was blocked, this caused the GPO to fall outside the SOM. As a result, the GPO was not applied.

Chapter 8. Maintaining and Restoring Group Policy

As an administrator, you'll perform many different tasks to maintain and recover Group Policy. In other chapters of this book, I've covered most of the key tasks. In this chapter, I cover the following additional tasks:

- Planning for new enterprise needs
- Maintaining Group Policy object (GPO) storage
- Copying, importing, and migrating GPOs
- Backing up and restoring Group Policy
- Troubleshooting Group Policy

Growing Your Enterprise Policy Configuration

Standard configurations for Group Policy work well when applications run on client computers and users log on within their home forests. In more diverse enterprise environments, however, applications don't always run on client computers and users don't always log on within their home forests. As a result, you might need to configure Group Policy to work with thin clients, terminal servers, or cloud computing. You might also need to configure Group Policy to work across forests. These concepts are discussed in this section.

Policy Processing for Thin Clients, Terminal Services, and Cloud Computing

In the enterprise, users might run applications on remote terminal servers, or they might use Internet-accessible on-demand services (referred to as cloud computing architecture). In either case, the underlying computing architecture runs on servers rather than on client computers. In these environments, you need to carefully consider how you will use Group Policy.

In many cases, you'll want everyone who logs on to your terminal servers to have the same settings, regardless of who they are. To do this, you can configure loopback processing to use Replace mode, as discussed in "Configuring Loopback Processing" in Chapter 7, "Managing Group Policy

Processing." In Replace mode, user settings from the GPOs applied to the terminal servers are processed, and the user settings in the user's GPOs are not processed. Thus, the user settings from the terminal server's GPOs replace the user settings normally applied to the user.

To ensure that Group Policy is processed as expected, you need to create an organizational unit (OU) for your terminal servers and then move the computer objects for your terminal servers to this OU. After you reboot the terminal servers to ensure that the move is processed, you can be sure that any user policy settings on GPOs linked to the terminal servers OU will apply to users who log on to your terminal servers.

Typically, administrators within your organization are responsible for managing and configuring your terminal servers, including managing the underlying hardware. In contrast, with Internet-accessible on-demand services, third-party computer-services organizations usually manage the underlying hardware, while members of your organization manage virtual server environments. Rather than logging on to a central server, users access individual applications running within the virtual server environment over the Internet. Therefore, in this configuration, you typically would not want to use loopback processing.

Policy Processing Across Forests

An Active Directory forest operating at the Windows Server 2003 or higher functional level can be joined to another forest using cross-forest trusts. When a user from one forest logs on to a computer in another forest, the Group Policy client running on the computer disables processing of cross-forest policy and enforces loopback processing in the current forest for the user. As a result, the computer processes GPOs as if it was using the loopback processing Replace mode and logs a related event in the Application log. This means that the computer:

- Ignores GPOs that would normally apply to the user in his or her home forest.

- Processes only the computer's GPOs, and applies both the computer settings and the user settings from those GPOs.
- Logs event ID 1109 in the Application log. This event states that a specified user from a different forest logged on to the local machine and that loopback processing was enforced in this forest for this user account.

> ***Real World***   As long as the computer is running the latest service pack, policy processing across forests uses Replace mode by default. Additionally, as discussed in more detail in "Working with Domain and Forest Trusts" in Chapter 8,"Managing Trusts and Authentication," in *Active Directory Administration: The Personal Trainer*, cross-forest trusts can be configured to allow forestwide authentication or to use selective authentication. The forestwide authentication configuration allows unrestricted access by users in another forest. The selective authentication configuration requires users from another forest to be specifically granted authentication permissions.

Computers process policy across forests in this way to protect themselves from settings that could potentially affect their stability and security. Generally, this is a good thing because administrators in one forest might not have any control over the policy settings in another forest. However, if you have tested various configurations and are sure that the user GPOs do not affect stability or security, you might want to configure policy so that both user and computer GPOs are always applied. To do this, you can enable the Allow Cross-Forest User Policy And Roaming User Profiles setting. Under Computer Configuration, you'll find this policy in the Administrative Templates\System\Group Policy folder.

Applying the Allow Cross-Forest User Policy And Roaming User Profiles setting to servers generally affects security in some way, so typically you want to ensure that this setting is applied only to workstation versions of Windows. To do this, you can configure the setting in GPOs that do not apply to servers or you can create a GPO called Allow Cross-Forest Policy and link it to OUs that affect only workstations.

Maintaining GPO Storage

Each Group Policy object has a related Group Policy container (GPC) and a related Group Policy template (GPT). The sections that follow discuss techniques for working with the GPC and GPT separately from the GPO itself.

Examining Group Policy Containers

The Group Policy container (GPC) for a GPO is:

- Stored in the Active Directory database.
- Replicated through normal Active Directory replication.
- Used to store properties related to the GPO.
- Identified with a globally unique identifier (GUID).

You can use Active Directory Users And Computers to view the GPC associated with every GPO you've created. In Active Directory Users And Computers, choose Advanced Features on the View menu. Expand the System and Policies nodes, and you'll see the GPC objects for the domain to which you are currently connected.

As shown in Figure 8-1, each GPC is identified by its GUID. While the GUID for each GPO you create is unique, the two default GPOs have the same GUID in every domain. If you expand the GPC folder, you'll see that each GPC has a subfolder named Machine and a subfolder named User.

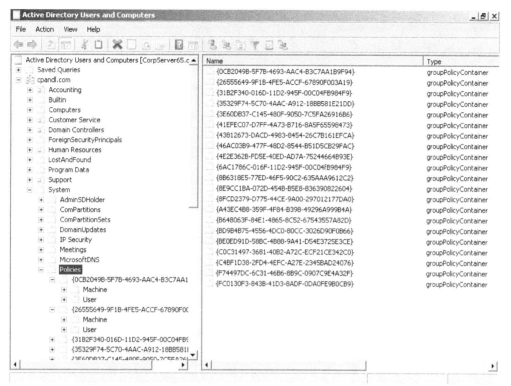

FIGURE 8-1 Locate Group Policy containers.

If you right-click a container and select Properties, you can view detailed information about the GPC. On the Object tab, shown in Figure 8-2, you'll see the following information:

- **Canonical Name Of Object**   Shows the object's place in the directory tree as a logical path from the highest container to the object itself—for example, imaginedlands.com/System/Policies/{3E60DB37-C145-480F-9050-7c5fa26916b6}.
- **Object Class**   Shows the object class, which in this case is groupPolicyContainer.
- **Created**   Shows the date the GPC was created.
- **Modified**   Shows the date the GPC was last modified.
- **Update Sequence Number (USNs)**   Shows the current and original USN for the object.

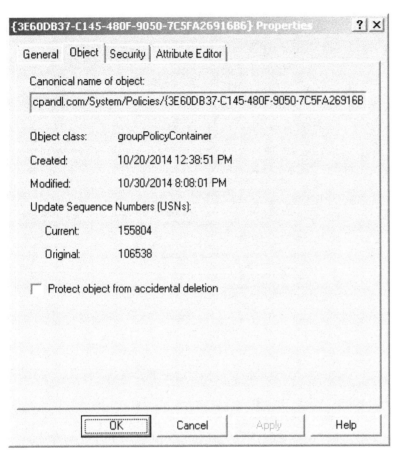

FIGURE 8-2 Review object properties for a GPC.

On the Security tab, shown in Figure 8-3, you can determine who has access to the GPC in Active Directory. Generally, these values are as set in the Group Policy Management Console (GPMC) for the related GPO and should not be modified directly.

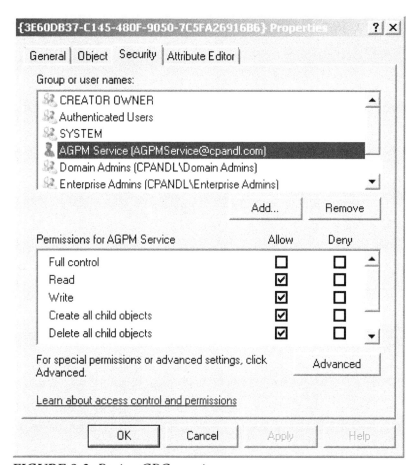

FIGURE 8-3 Review GPC security.

On the Attribute Editor tab, shown in Figure 8-4, you'll find the complete set of attributes associated with the GPC. Some of the key properties include:

- **cn** Shows the common name of the GPC, such as {3E60DB37-C145-480F-9050-7c5fa26916b6}. This is the name of the GPC relative to the parent container in which it is stored. This property is also referred to as the *relative distinguished name* (RDN).

- **displayName** Shows the friendly name of the object as assigned in the user interface, such as Atlanta Site Primary GPO.

- **distinguishedName** Shows the object's place in the directory tree as a logical series of containers, from the object itself to the highest container with which it is associated—for example, CN={3E60DB37-

C145-480F-9050-7c5fa26916b6}, CN=Policies, CN=System, DC=imaginedlands, DC=com.

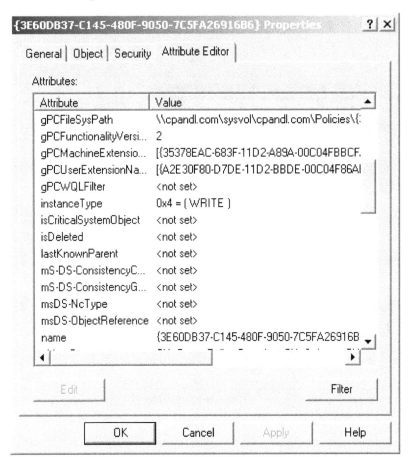

Figure 8-4 Review GPC attributes.

- **gPCFileSysPath** Shows the physical path to the associated Policies folder (the GPT) stored in the SYSVOL. The Policies folder has the same name as the GPC itself.
- **gPCFunctionalityVersion** Shows the version number of the Group Policy extension tool that created the Group Policy object.
- **gPCMachineExtensionNames** Shows the list of GUIDs that tell the client-side engine which client-side extensions (CSEs) have machine data in the GPO. CSEs are listed according to their GUIDs and the GUID of the

Microsoft Management Console (MMC) snap-in for the Administrative Templates node.

- **gPCUserExtensionNames** Shows the list of GUIDs that tell the client-side engine which CSEs have user data in the GPO. CSEs are listed according to their GUIDs and the GUID of the MMC snap-in for the Administrative Templates node.
- **objectClass** Shows the object class, which in this case is groupPolicyContainer.
- **USNChanged** Shows the current USN for the object.
- **USNCreated** Shows the original USN for the object.
- **versionNumber** Shows the version of the object.
- **whenChanged** Shows the date the GPC was last modified.
- **whenCreated** Shows the date the GPC was created.

The version number tracks changes in a GPO. When you create a new GPO, the version number is 0. As you edit a GPO, the version number increases according to the following formula:

```
Version = (Number of User Configuration changes * 65536) +
(Number of Computer Configuration changes)
```

According to the formula:

- When you configure a setting in Computer Configuration, the GPMC adds 1 to the version number. If you were to then not configure the setting, the GPMC adds 1 to the version number again.
- When you configure a setting in User Configuration, the GPMC adds 65,536 to the version number. If you were to then not configure the setting, the GPMC adds 65,536 to the version number again.

This formula makes it possible for the GPMC to track changes to Computer Configuration and User Configuration using a single value. In the GPMC, if you select a GPO in the console tree and then click the Details tab in the details pane, you see the separate version details for Computer Configuration and User Configuration, as shown in Figure 8-5.

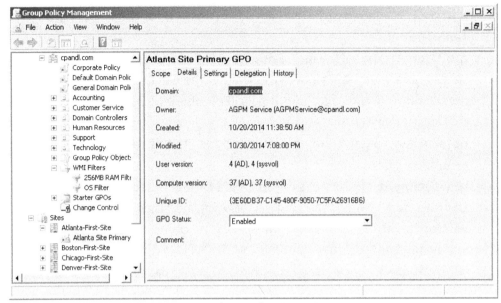

FIGURE 8-5 Check the version number in the GPMC.

Here the User Configuration was modified four times and the Computer Configuration modified 37 times: (65,536 * 4) + 37 equals 262,181. If you were to compare the version information shown in the GPMC to the versionNumber attribute, you'd find the version number was 262,181.

> **Real World**   The GPC and the GPT store the same version number for a GPO. However, in situations where replication hasn't been completed, the GPC and GPT version numbers could be different. In this case, you'd get a warning message that the GPC and GPT weren't in sync. With Windows Server 2003 and later, the GPC and GPT do not need to be in sync for Group Policy to be processed.

Examining Group Policy Templates

The Group Policy template (GPT) for a GPO is:

- Stored in the SYSVOL.
- Replicated through SYSVOL replication.
- Used to store files related to the GPO on disk.
- Identified with a globally unique identifier (GUID).

You can view the GPT associated with every GPO you've created by accessing the SYSVOL folder on a domain controller. As discussed in "Managing SYSVOL Storage" in Chapter 6, "Maintaining and Migrating the SYSVOL," the default location of the SYSVOL is either %SystemRoot%\SYSVOL or %SystemRoot%\Sysvol_dfsr, depending on whether the SYSVOL is replicated using File Replication Service (FRS) or Distributed File System (DFS) Replication. Within the domain subfolder of the SYSVOL, you'll find several subfolders:

- **Policies**   Stores the GPT files for each GPO you've created
- **Scripts**   Stores shutdown, startup, logon, and logoff scripts used in your GPOs
- **StarterGPOs**   Stores the starter GPOs you've defined for the domain

Within the Policies folder, each GPT is identified by the GUID of the GPO with which it is associated, such as {3E60DB37-C145-480F-9050-7c5fa26916b6}. (See Figure 8-6.) The GPT can contain the following:

- **Gpt.ini**   A file that stores the version number of the GPT.
- **Adm**   A folder that stores the Administrative template (.adm) files associated with a GPO. This folder is used only when you create or edit GPOs on computers running legacy versions of Windows. Otherwise, .adm files are stored locally in the %SystemRoot%\policydefinitions folder or in the central store.
- **Machine**   A folder that stores on-disk files for the Computer Configuration section of the GPO.
- **User**   A folder that stores on-disk files for the User Configuration section of the GPO.

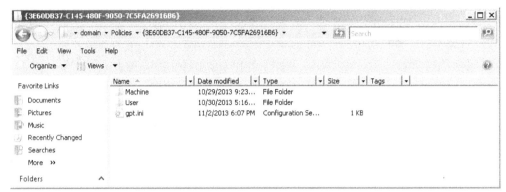

FIGURE 8-6 Examine the GPT for a GPO.

Within the Machine folder, you'll find the following:

- **Applications**   A folder that stores Application Advertisement Scripts (AAS) files associated with applications deployed with Group Policy Software Installation under Computer Configuration.
- **GptTmpl**   A file stored in the Microsoft\WindowsNT\SecEdit folder that is used to stored computer security settings defined under Computer Configuration in the Windows Settings\Security Settings area of the GPO.
- **Registry.pol**   A file that stores the configured registry settings in Computer Configuration under the Administrative Templates area, as well as settings for Software Restriction Policies configured under Computer Configuration.
- **Scripts\Shutdown**   Stores settings related to shutdown scripts in a file called Scripts.ini; can also store the actual scripts.
- **Scripts\Startup**   Stores settings related to startup scripts in a file called Scripts.ini; can also store the actual scripts.

Within the User folder, you'll find the following:

- **Applications**   A folder that stores Application Advertisement Scripts (AAS) files associated with applications deployed with Group Policy Software Installation under User Configuration.

- **Fdeploy.ini**   A file stored in the Documents And Settings folder that is used to stored folder redirection settings defined under User Configuration.
- **Microsoft\IEAK**   A folder that stores custom settings and files related to Internet Explorer Maintenance settings. Key customization settings are stored in the Install.ins file. Related bitmap images and imported settings are stored in subfolders of the Microsoft\IEAK\Branding folder.
- **Registry.pol**   A file that stores the configured registry settings in User Configuration under the Administrative Templates area, as well as settings for Software Restriction Policies configured under User Configuration.
- **Scripts\Logoff**   Stores settings related to logoff scripts in a file called Scripts.ini; can also store the actual scripts.
- **Scripts\Logon**   Stores settings related to logon scripts in a file called Scripts.ini; can also store the actual scripts.

Understanding GPC and GPT Processing

For a GPO to be processed by a Group Policy client, the GPC and GPT must be present on the domain controller that authenticated the computer in the domain. The GPC and GPT do not have to have the same version number. Regardless, if the version number of the GPC or GPT is different from the version number the client has stored in the registry from the last time Group Policy was refreshed, the client processes policy because it detects that a change has occurred.

If the version numbers of the GPC and GPT are not identical, it simply means that changes were made to one part of the GPO or the other and replication has not been completed. By default, the GPC and GPT parts of a GPO are written to the PDC emulator in the domain. The PDC emulator is responsible for replicating the GPC and GPT to other domain controllers. Because Active Directory replication and SYSVOL replication occur at different intervals, the GPC and GPT for a policy object can easily become out of sync.

In the Group Policy Management Console, you are connected to the PDC emulator in the domain by default. As a result, you see and work with Group Policy as it is reflected on the PDC emulator. You can connect to a different domain controller as discussed in "Setting Domain Controller Focus Options" in Chapter 3, "Group Policy Management."

When you change domain controllers, you view and work with Group Policy as it is reflected on that domain controller. If you edit a GPO, any changes you make are made on that domain controller, and that domain controller in turn replicates the changes. You can change the focus when you are editing a GPO. To do this, complete the following steps:

1. In the Group Policy Management Editor, select the top-level policy node.
2. On the View menu, select DC Options.
3. In the Options For Domain Controller Selection dialog box, shown in Figure 8-7, choose one of the following options and then click OK:

- **The One With The Operations Master Token For The PDC Emulator** Choose this option to view and edit the GPO as it exists on the PDC emulator.
- **The One Used By The Active Directory Snap-ins** Choose this option to view and edit the GPO as it exists on the domain controller currently in focus.
- **Use Any Available Domain Controller** Choose this option to view and edit the GPO as it exists on any available domain controller in the domain.

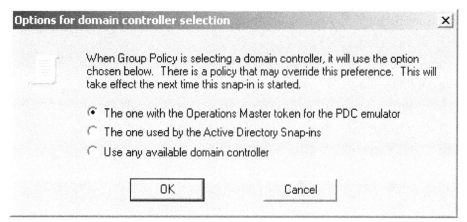

FIGURE 8-7 Change focus during editing if necessary.

When Group Policy is deployed to client computers, the Group Policy client performs initial processing and refresh processing as a normal part of its operations. The client is responsible for requesting policy; policy is never pushed to the client. The client is responsible for:

- Determining whether it is on a slow link.
- Discovering all the GPOs that apply to the computer or user.
- Discovering which client-side extensions (CSEs) are required.
- Applying GPOs and refreshing those GPOs as necessary.

To perform these tasks, the Group Policy client uses the following protocols and ports:

- Computers running legacy versions of Windows use Internet Control Message Protocol (ICMP) to detect slow links. ICMP ping must be allowed for any firewalls between the client and the authenticating domain controller.
- Computers running Windows Vista, Windows Server 2008 or later use Network Location Awareness (NLA) to sample TCP traffic between the client and the authenticating domain controller. This sampling must be enabled for any firewalls between the client and the authenticating domain controller.

- For authentication to Active Directory, clients use remote procedure call (RPC) on TCP port 135.
- For querying Active Directory, clients use Lightweight Directory Access Protocol (LDAP) on UDP and TCP port 389.
- For Domain Name System (DNS) lookups, clients use TCP port 53.
- For querying the GPT in the SYSVOL, clients use server message block (SMB) over IP on UDP and TCP port 445.

If the client cannot connect to the authenticating domain controller on any of these ports, Group Policy processing will fail. Because of this, it is important to ensure that clients have appropriate access to their authenticating domain controllers over the network.

The client-side extensions (CSEs) are contained in dynamic-link libraries (DLLs). Once the client has the CSEs, the client can process them. On computers running legacy versions of Windows, the Group Policy client runs with the privileges of the Winlogon process—a system service with the highest level of privileges on the computer. On computers running Windows Vista, Windows Server 2008 or a later version of Windows, the Group Policy client runs under the Group Policy Client Service—a system service with reduced execution privileges. Both clients process each CSE DLL in turn and store information related to each CSE process in the registry keys under HKLM\Software\Microsoft\Windows NT\CurrentVersion\Winlogon\GPExtensions (see Figure 8-8). CSEs are registered according to their GUID. The order in which the CSE GUIDs are listed represents the order in which the CSEs were processed. If you select a CSE GUID, note the following:

- **(Default)** Specifies the exact area of policy to which the CSE relates, such as Wireless Group Policy.
- **DllName** Specifies the name of the CSE DLL.
- **EnableAsynchronousProcessing** Specifies whether asynchronous processing is used. 1 indicates it must be asynchronous; 0 indicates it must be synchronous.

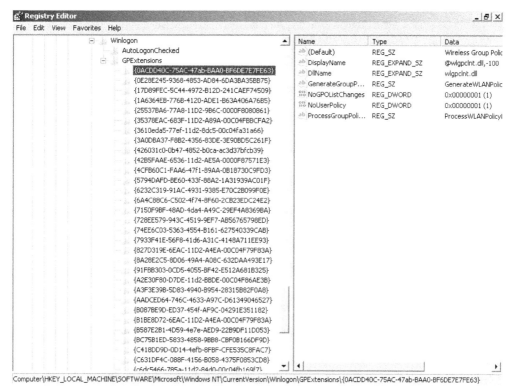

FIGURE 8-8 Review CSEs processed by a client.

- **EventSources** Specifies the event sources that can generate related events in the event logs.
- **NoBackgroundPolicy** Specifies whether the CSE supports background processing. 1 indicates it does not support background processing; 0 indicates it does.
- **NoGPOListChanges** Specifies whether the CSE is processed regardless of whether related policies have changed. 1 indicates it is not processed regardless of changes; 0 indicates it is always processed.
- **NoMachinePolicy** Specifies whether the CSE supports per-computer settings. 1 indicates it does support per-computer settings; 0 indicates it does not.
- **NoSlowLink** Specifies whether the CSE is processed over a slow link. 1 indicates it is not processed over a slow link; 0 indicates it is.
- **NoUserPolicy** Specifies whether the CSE supports per-user settings. 1 indicates it does support per-computer settings; 0 indicates it does not.

- **PerUserLocalSettings** Specifies whether the CSE caches policies for the user in the machine section of the Registry. 1 indicates it does cache policies; 0 indicates it does not.
- **RequiresSuccessfulRegistry** Specifies whether the CSE DLL must be registered with the operating system. 1 indicates it must be registered; 0 indicates it does not.

> **Note** If you want to modify settings, you should do so by editing the appropriate Group Policy objects. Chapter 7 discusses the techniques you can use to configure most of these settings.

Copying, Importing, and Migrating GPOs

The GPMC features built-in copy and import operations. The copy feature allows you to copy existing GPOs from one domain to another. The import operation allows you to create backup copies of GPOs in one domain and import them into another domain. Because no trust is necessary for the copy and import operations to work, the target domain for the copy or import operation can be a parent domain, child domain, a domain in a different tree or forest, or even an external domain for which no trust exists.

However, it is important to note that the copy and import operations work only with the policy settings within a policy object. These operations don't copy a policy object's links or any Windows Management Instrumentation (WMI) filters that might be associated with a policy object.

Additionally, if your GPOs reference security principals or contain UNC paths, you may need to map security principals or UNC paths contained in your GPOs to different values. This process is handled as a migration.

Copying GPOs

In the GPMC, you can copy a GPO and all its settings in one domain and then navigate to the domain into which you want to paste the copy of the GPO. The source and target domains can be any domains to which you can connect in the GPMC and for which you have permission to manage GPOs. The specific permissions you need are as follows:

- In the source domain, you need Read permission to create the copy of the policy object.
- In the target domain, you need Write permission to write the copied policy object. Administrators have this privilege, as do users who have been delegated permission to create GPOs.

Additionally, be sure that the destination domain is trusted by the source domain and that you have GPO Create permissions on the destination domain. You can confirm GPO Create permissions on a domain by using the GPMC. In the GPMC console tree, expand Group Policy Objects in the destination domain and then click the Delegation tab to check which users or groups can create GPOs in the domain.

You can copy a policy object from one domain to another domain to which you have a connection and permissions by completing the following steps:

1. In the GPMC, expand the entry for the forest you want to work with, expand the related Domains node, and then expand the related Group Policy Objects node.
2. Right-click the GPO you want to copy, and then click Copy.
3. Access the target domain. Expand the entry for the forest, expand the related Domains node, and then expand the related Group Policy Objects node.
4. Right-click the target domain's Group Policy Objects node, and then click Paste.
5. If the source and target domains for the copy operation are the same, you'll see a dialog box like the one shown in Figure 8-9. Otherwise, the Cross-Domain Copying Wizard starts. When you click Next, you see a wizard page with similar options.

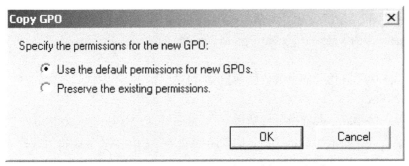

FIGURE 8-9 Specify how permissions should be applied.

6. Choose to create a copy of the policy object with the default permissions for the selected domain, or copy the existing permissions to the new policy object. In most cases, you'll want to use the default permissions for new GPOs to ensure that administrators in the target domain can access and work with the copied policy object.

7. Click OK or Next as appropriate. The rest of the wizard pages relate to migration tables, which allow you to refine the copied settings so that the proper security principals and UNC paths are used (based on the local environment). For example, you might need to specify that the permissions for the Managers group should be migrated to the ManagementTeam group in the new policy object, or you might need to specify new locations for folder redirection in the new domain.

> **Note** You'll find detailed information about migration tables in "Migrating GPOs" later in this chapter.

Importing GPOs

Copying GPOs between domains works fine when you have connectivity between domains and the appropriate permissions. If you are an administrator at a remote office or have been delegated permissions, however, you might not have access to the source domain to create a copy of a policy object. In this case, another administrator can make a backup copy of a policy object for you and then send you the related data. When you receive the data, you can import the backup copy of the policy object into your domain to create a new policy object with the same settings.

Anyone with the Edit Settings Group Policy management privilege can perform an import operation. Additionally, you need to have access to the backup GPO files.

To import a backup copy of a policy object into a domain, complete the following steps:

1. In the GPMC, expand the entry for the forest you want to work with, and then expand the related Domains node by double-clicking it.

2. Right-click Group Policy Objects, and then click New. In the New GPO dialog box, type a descriptive name for the new GPO and then click OK.

3. Right-click the new GPO, and then click Import Settings. When the Import Settings Wizard starts, click Next.

4. Because the import operation overwrites all the settings of the policy object you select, you are given the opportunity to back up the policy object before continuing, as shown in Figure 8-10. If you want to back up the GPO, do the following and then click Next. Otherwise, simply click Next.

a. Click Backup. In the Back Up Group Policy Object dialog box, click Browse.

b. Use the Browse For Folder dialog box to select a secure save location for the GPO. Optionally, type a description of the GPO.

c. Click Backup. When the backup process is complete, click OK to return to the Import Settings Wizard.

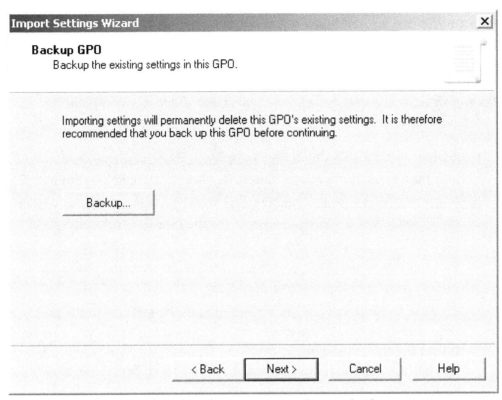

FIGURE 8-10 Back up the policy object you are working with, if necessary.

5. Use the options on the Backup Location page to type or browse for the name of the folder containing the backup copy of the policy object you want to import. This step is a bit confusing because you were just given the opportunity to back up the current policy object, but this step relates to the backup folder for the policy object you want to import. Click Next.

6. If there are multiple backups stored in the designated backup folder, you'll see a list of them on the Source GPO page, as shown in Figure 8-11. If there are multiple versions of GPOs and you want to see only the latest version, select the Show Only The Latest Version Of Each GPO check box.

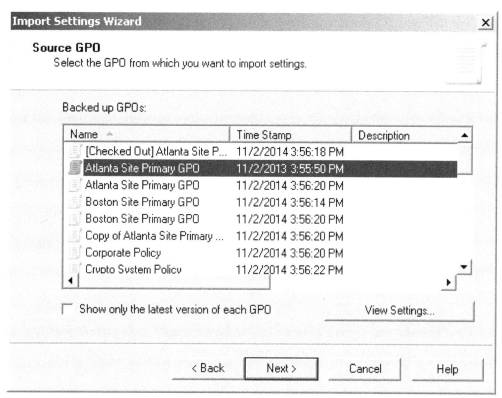

FIGURE 8-11 Select the GPO backup you want to use.

7. Select the GPO you want to use by clicking it. If you want to review the settings for the GPO, click View Settings. When you are ready to continue, click Next.

8. The Import Settings Wizard scans the GPO for references to security principals and UNC paths that might need to be migrated. If any are found, you are given the opportunity to create migration tables or use existing migration tables (as discussed in "Migrating GPOs.")

9. Continue through the wizard by clicking Next, and then click Finish. This starts the import process. When the import is complete, click OK.

Migrating GPOs

When copying or importing GPOs from one domain to another, the process is fairly straightforward, except when your GPOs reference security principals or contain UNC paths. If your GPOs reference security principals or contain

UNC paths, you are given the opportunity to create migration tables to map the values contained in the source GPO to different values in the target GPO.

Migration tables help you map:

- Permissions on a GPO in the source domain to the required permissions on a GPO in the target domain. The permissions on a GPO describe which users, computers, and computer groups will process that GPO and which users or user groups can view and edit policy settings in the GPO or delete the GPO.
- Security principals defined in the source domain to the required security principals in the target domain. Specifically, policies such as User Rights Assignment, Restricted Groups, File System, Registry, or System Services allow you to specify particular users or groups that can access or configure those resources. The security identifiers (SIDs) for those users and groups are stored in the GPO and must be modified to reflect the users and groups in the GPO's new location.
- UNC paths defined for software installation, folder redirection, or scripts in the source domain to the required UNC paths in the target domain. For example, you might have a GPO that references redirected folders stored on a server in the source domain. In the target domain, the folders may need to be redirected to a different server.

When you are working with the Cross-Domain Copying Wizard or the Import Settings Wizard, you configure migration settings on the Migration References page. You can elect to transfer references to security principals and UNC paths using the following options:

- Copy Them Identically From The Source
- Using This Migration Table To Map Them In The Destination GPO

When you select the copy option, the values are copied exactly from the source GPO to the target GPO. When you select the migration table option, you can:

- Click Browse to search for and select an existing migration table. Migration table files end with the .migtable file extension by default.
- Click Edit to edit a migration table you've selected in the Migration Table Editor.
- Click New to create a migration table in the Migration Table Editor.

In addition to creating migration tables automatically as part of the copy and import operations, you can also create migration tables in advance and use them in your copy and import operations. One advantage of creating a migration table in advance is that you can be sure that the migration settings you define are exactly what you want.

A single migration table can be used for more than one GPO, which means you can use a single migration table that covers every possible security principal and UNC path combination for a given migration of GPOs from one domain to another. In that case you can simply apply the same migration table to every GPO that you are deploying, and those principals and paths that match will be correctly mapped.

You can create migration tables using the Migration Table Editor (Mtedit.exe). To start this tool, click Start, type **mtedit.exe** in the Search box, and then press Enter. As Figure 8-12 shows, the Migration Table Editor starts with a blank migration table that you can populate manually by typing entries into the grid or populate automatically by using one of the auto-populate methods.

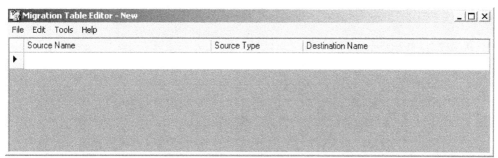

FIGURE 8-12 Start the Migration Table Editor.

The easiest way to start creating a migration table is to use an auto-populate method from either a backup GPO or a live production GPO. To populate a migration table from a live production GPO, complete the following steps:

1. On the Tools menu, click Populate From GPO.

2. In the Select GPO dialog box, shown in Figure 8-13, use the Look In This Domain list to select the source domain.

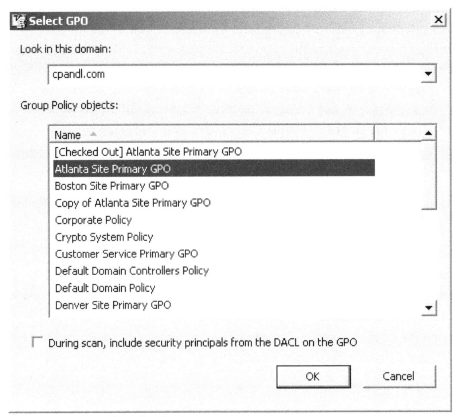

FIGURE 8-13 Select the GPO to scan.

3. Use the Group Policy Objects list to select the source GPO. If you want to include the security principals who have permission on the GPO, as well as security principals and UNC paths used within the GPO, select the During Scan, Include Security Principals check box.

> ***Tip*** You can select multiple GPOs or multiple backup GPOs when auto-populating a single migration table. This allows you to use a single migration table for all GPOs in a domain.

4. When you click OK, the Migration Table Editor scans the GPO for security principals and UNC paths and then lists the related source values, as shown in Figure 8-14.

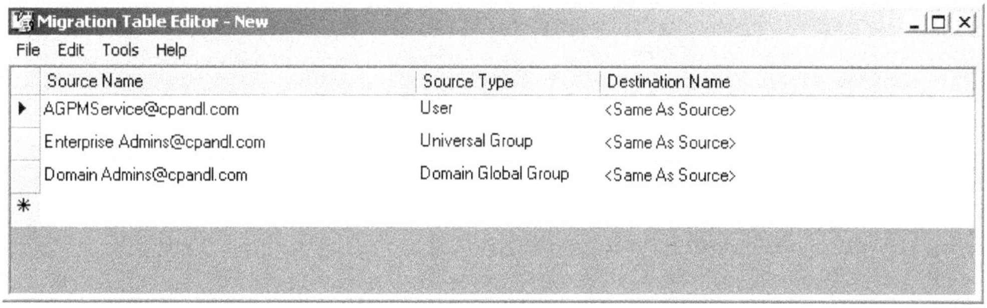
Migration Table Editor - New
File Edit Tools Help
Source Name
Source Type
Destination Name
AGPMService@cpandl.com
User
<Same As Source>
Enterprise Admins@cpandl.com
Universal Group
<Same As Source>
Domain Admins@cpandl.com
Domain Global Group
<Same As Source>

Figure 8-14 Map values from the source domain to the target domain.

To auto-populate a migration table from a backup of a GPO, complete the following steps:

1. On the Tools menu, click Populate From Backup.
2. In the Select Backup dialog box, click Browse. Use the Browse For Folder dialog box to select the folder containing the backup copy of the policy object you want to work with.
3. If there are multiple backups stored in the designated backup folder, you'll see a list of them, as shown in Figure 8-15. If there are multiple versions of GPOs and you want to see only the latest version, select the Show Only The Latest Version Of Each GPO check box.

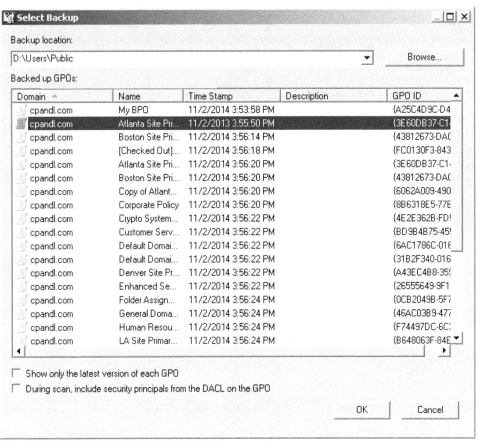

FIGURE 8-15 Select the GPO backup you want to use.

4. Use the Backed Up GPOs list to select the source GPO. If you want to include the security principals who have permission on the GPO, as well as security principals and UNC paths used within the GPO, select the During Scan, Include Security Principals check box.

5. When you click OK, the Migration Table Editor scans the GPO for security principals and UNC paths and then lists the related source values, as shown previously in Figure 8-14.

In the Migration Table Editor, the Source Name column lists the source name of the security principal or the source UNC path. The Source Type column lists the type of object. The Destination Name lists the target name of a security principal or the source UNC path in the target domain.

Table 8-1 lists the different object types that can be mapped. The Free Text or SID object type is a catch all for security principals that are referenced by name but weren't resolved to an actual SID. If you enter user, computer, or group names in the editor, you can use the Free Text or SID object type so that you don't have to resolve security principals to their SIDs. The Migration Table Editor does not support mapping to a built-in security group such as the built-in Administrators group.

TABLE 8-1 Object Types That Can Be Mapped in the Migration Table Editor

OBJECT TYPE	USED TO MAP
User	Individual user accounts
Domain global group	Domain global groups
Domain local group	Domain local groups
Universal group	Universal groups
Computer	Computer names
UNC path	UNC paths used in policies
Free Text or SID	Undetermined security principal, such as a group name that isn't resolved to an actual SID

Security principals can be specified by their Universal Principal Name (UPN), Security Accounts Manager (SAM) name, or Domain Name System (DNS) name. The syntax is:

- UPN   SecurityPrincipal@UPN suffix, such as WilliamS@imaginedlands.com
- SAM   NetBIOS domain name\user, such as IMAGINEDL\williams
- DNS   DNS domain name\user, such as imaginedlands.com\Williams

With computer names, you must include the dollar sign ($) as part of the name:

- UPN   Computer Name$@UPN suffix, such as CorpServer18$@imaginedlands.com
- SAM   NetBIOS domain name\computer name$, such as IMAGINEDL\CorpServer18$
- DNS   DNS domain name\Computer name$, such as imaginedlands.com\CorpServer18$

With UNC paths, enter the full path following the syntax:

```
\\servername\sharename
```

For example:

```
\\FileServer24\data
```

With the Free Text or SID type, enter a string or the string representation of a SID. For example, "WilliamS" or "S-1-5-21-4027440173-2312786515-3063062-1108". However, SIDs cannot be specified in the destination field.

> **Tip**   When you select Advanced Features on the View menu in Active Directory Users And Computers, you can view the SID for a security principal. Right-click the security principal, and then select Properties. In the Properties dialog box, select the Attribute Editor tab and then scroll down until you see the objectSid attribute.

Modify the Destination Name column for each security principal and UNC path as appropriate. The default Destination Name value is Same As Source, which means that the same security principal or UNC path will be used in the destination GPO as the source. In this case, the value is copied without modification and the mapping accomplishes no changes. Typically, you will need to change the destination name for one or more source entries when migrating a GPO. To change the destination field, you can type an entry or right-click the field and then choose Browse or Set Destination. Choosing Browse allows you to select a security principal in any trusted domain. If you choose Set Destination, you can choose one of three options:

- **No Destination**   If you specify No Destination, the security principal is not included in the destination GPO when it is migrated. This option is not available for UNC path entries.
- **Map By Relative Name**   If you specify Map By Relative Name, the security principal name is assumed to already be in the destination domain, and that name will be used for the mapping. For example, if the source name is Domain Admins for the tech.imaginedlands.com domain and you are migrating the GPO to the eng.imaginedlands.com domain, the name Domain Admins@tech.imaginedlands.com will be mapped to Domain Admins@eng.imaginedlands.com. The group must already exist in the destination domain for the import or copy operation to succeed. This option is not available for UNC path entries or for security principals that are designated as the Free Text or SID type.
- **Same As Source**   If you specify Same As Source, the same security principal is used in both the source and destination GPOs. Essentially, the security entry is left as is.

If you try to map from one group type to another, you will receive a warning. For example, if you have a source security principal that is a domain global group and you select a domain local group as the destination, you will be warned that the destination name is a different type from the source. If you then try to validate the file without making changes, the validation process will fail. However, you can still use the migration table to perform a migration.

Before saving a migration table, you should validate it. To do this, on the Tools menu, click Validate. The validation process:

- Determines whether the XML format of the resulting file is valid.
- Validates the existence of destination security principals and UNC paths.
- Checks that source entries with UNC paths do not have destinations of Map By Relative Name or No Destination, which are not supported.
- Checks that the type of each destination entry in the table matches the type in Active Directory.

When you enter data manually, the validation process is especially important as a way to ensure that an entry error does not prevent a successful migration. If you need to delete a row, click the gray box to the left of the row (this selects the row), right-click, and then click Delete.

> **Note** Validation can fail because you do not have the permission to resolve the security principals or UNC paths specified in the file. This does not mean that the file will not work as expected during a migration, provided that the user who performs the migration can resolve the security principal and UNC names.

Keep in mind that a GPO comprises two parts—the GPC, the portion that is stored and replicates as part of Active Directory, and the GPT, the portion that is stored and replicates as part of the SYSVOL. Because these are two separate objects that need to replicate across your network, both need to be synchronized before the new GPO is applied, and it might take an extended period of time to replicate to all locations in an extended Active Directory deployment.

In the GPMC, you can view the replication status on a given domain controller. In the console tree, expand Group Policy Objects in the domain containing the GPOs that you want to apply, click a GPO you want to check, and then click the Details tab in the details pane. If the GPO is synchronized on that domain controller for User Configuration, the Active Directory and SYSVOL version numbers will be identical under User Version. If the GPO is synchronized on that domain controller for Computer Configuration, the Active Directory and SYSVOL version numbers will be identical under Computer Version. However, the user version and computer version numbers do not need to match.

To deploy a new GPO using import and migration operations, complete the following steps:

1. In the GPMC, expand the entry for the forest you want to work with, expand the related Domains node, and then expand the Group Policy Objects node.

2. Right-click the GPO to be updated, and then click Import Settings. When the Import Settings Wizard starts, click Next.

3. On the Backup GPO page, click Backup to back up the existing production GPO before performing the import. In the Backup Group Policy Object dialog box, specify the location where the GPO backup is to be stored, type a description for the backup, and then click Backup. After the GPO backup is complete, a message states that the backup succeeded. Click OK.

4. On the Backup GPO page, click Next.

5. On the Backup Location Page, specify the folder that contains the backup of the GPO that you want to import and then click Next. You must have access to the folder where you backed up your GPOs. If your backups were completed on a server in another domain, you might need to map a drive to that folder from the computer on which you are running the import operation.

6. On the Source GPO page, click the GPO that you want to import, and then click Next.

7. On the Scanning Backup page, the wizard scans the policy settings in the backup to determine references to security principals or UNC paths that need to be transferred and then displays the results of the scan. Click Next.

8. On the Migrating References page, select Using This Migration Table To Map Them To New Values In The New GPOs, and then specify a path to the migration table you created for this migration.

9. If you want the entire migration to fail if a security principal or UNC path that exists in the source GPO is not present in the migration table, select Use Migration Table Exclusively. Use this option to import the GPO only if all security principals found in the backed-up version are accounted for in the migration table.

10. Click Next. Confirm that you specified the correct migration options, and then click Finish. After you click Finish, the migration of the GPO begins. After the wizard completes the import operation, a message will state that the import was successful. Click OK.

The import process does not import GPO links or WMI filter settings. Check the links to the GPO to ensure that it is linked to the appropriate container objects. Check the WMI Filtering settings to ensure that the GPO is either not applying filters or is applying the appropriate filters.

In the event that you have a problem with a GPO after you deploy it, the best way to roll back the deployment is to restore the original GPO by using the backup GPO that you created.

Backing Up and Restoring GPOs

Just as you back up other types of critical data, you should back up your GPOs. The GPMC provides separate procedures for backing up production GPOs, starter GPOs, and WMI filters.

> **Real World** As discussed in Chapter 4, "Advanced Group Policy Management," using change control protects your GPOs in many ways. Change control archives copies of all your controlled GPOs. If you delete a GPO, the deleted GPO is moved to a recycle bin from which it can be recovered later. When you are working with a GPO's history, you can view unique versions and restore the archived copy of a GPO to a particular version simply by right-clicking the version to restore and selecting Deploy. You can also mark unique versions of a GPO so that they cannot be deleted. To do this, right-click a particular version of a GPO and then click Do Not Allow Deletion. As extensive as these features are, however, they are still not a substitute for regular GPO backups.

Backing Up GPOs

Typically, you'll want to create two types of backups for your GPOs:

- GPO backups that are stored on a designated domain controller and then backed up as part of that computer's routine system backup

- GPO backups that are stored on removable media, such as CD-ROM or DVD, that can be stored in a lock box and rotated periodically to storage off site

As with any backup process, you should develop a specific backup strategy for GPOs. Here is an example:

1. Designate a domain controller in each domain as the policy backup computer. In most cases, you will want this computer to be the PDC emulator for the domain because this is the default domain controller to which the GPMC connects.

2. Before backing up the designated domain controller by using the normal system backup process, create a backup of your domain's GPOs. You should create a new backup periodically (weekly or monthly, in most cases). You should also create a backup before you change policy settings and again after you've finalized policy.

3. You should periodically create media backups of your GPOs. This means storing the backups on removable media, on CD-ROM or DVD, or at another location. You should have designated secure storage on site and periodically rotate backup sets off site.

It is also important to note what won't be backed up with your GPOs:

- Your backup will not contain IPSec settings; these are backed up with system state backups. Because of this, you should track any IPSec settings used so that you can restore them after you restore your GPOs.
- While the locations of domain and OU links are backed up with a GPO, restoring a backup does not restore those links. This is a safety precaution to ensure that you don't inadvertently relink a GPO to a location to which it shouldn't be linked. However, as the backup process does record where the GPO was linked within a domain or OU at the time of the backup, you can use this information to manually relink the GPO after you restore it. Site links are not listed, however.
- Your backup will not contain WMI filters, starter GPOs, or the contents of the Advanced Group Policy Management (AGPM) archive. You must back up these items separately from GPO backups.

Using the GPMC, you can back up individual GPOs in a domain or back up all GPOs in a domain by completing the following steps:

1. In the GPMC, navigate to the Group Policy Objects container for the domain with which you want to work. Do one of the following:

    - If you want to back up all GPOs in the domain, right-click the Group Policy Objects node, and then click Back Up All.
    - If you want to back up a specific GPO in the domain, right-click the GPO, and then click Back Up.

2. In the Back Up Group Policy Object dialog box, shown in Figure 8-16, click Browse, and then use the Browse For Folder dialog box to set the location in which the GPO backup should be stored.

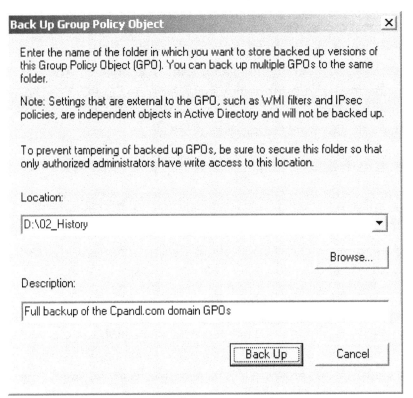

FIGURE 8-16 Specify the backup location and description.

3. In the Description field, type a description of the contents of the backup.

4. Click Back Up to start the backup process.

5. The Backup dialog box, shown in Figure 8-17, shows the progress and status of the backup. Click OK when the backup is complete.

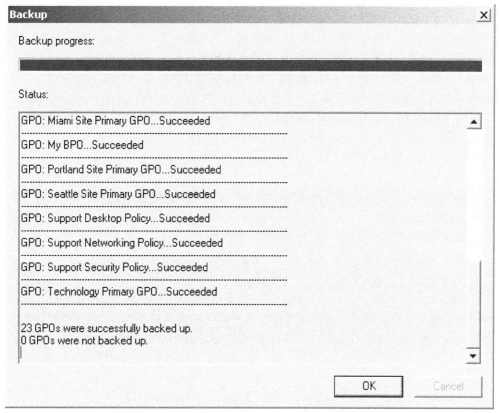

FIGURE 8-17 Review the backup progress.

When doing a full backup, you should be able to back up all GPOs successfully, including checked out GPOs. If a backup fails, check the permissions on the GPOs and the folder to which you are writing the backup. You need Read permission on a GPO and Write permission on the backup folder to create a backup. By default, members of the Domain Admins and Enterprise Admins groups should have these permissions.

Restoring GPOs

Using the GPMC, you can restore a GPO to the exact state it was in when it was backed up. The GPMC tracks the backup of each GPO separately, even if you back up all GPOs at once. Because version information is also tracked according to the backup time stamp and description, you can restore the last version of each GPO or a particular version of any GPO.

To restore a GPO, you need Edit Settings, Delete, and Modify Security permissions on the GPO and Read permission on the folder containing the backup. By default, members of the Domain Admins and Enterprise Admins groups should have these permissions.

When you restore a GPO, the following occurs:

- Except for IPSec settings, all preferences and settings inside the GPO are restored.
- The friendly (display) name and GUID are restored.
- The security and permissions on the GPO itself are restored.
- Any link to a WMI filter is restored.

When you restore a GPO, you do not need to delete the original GPO. The restore operation simply replaces the original GPO with the backed-up copy of the GPO.

You can restore a GPO by completing the following steps:

1. In the GPMC, navigate to the Group Policy Objects container for the domain with which you want to work.
2. Right-click the Group Policy Objects node, and then click Manage Backups. This displays the Manage Backups dialog box, shown in Figure 8-18.

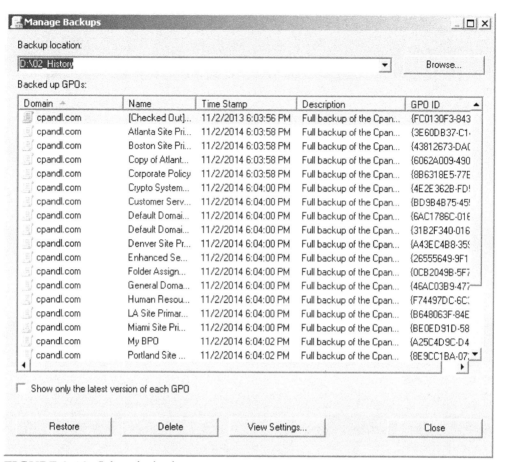

Manage Backups

Backup location:

D:\02_History

Browse...

Backed up GPOs:

Domain ▲	Name	Time Stamp	Description	GPO ID ▲
cpandl.com	[Checked Out]...	11/2/2013 6:03:56 PM	Full backup of the Cpan...	{FC0130F3-843
cpandl.com	Atlanta Site Pri...	11/2/2014 6:03:58 PM	Full backup of the Cpan...	{3E60DB37-C1.
cpandl.com	Boston Site Pri...	11/2/2014 6:03:58 PM	Full backup of the Cpan...	{43812673-DA(
cpandl.com	Copy of Atlant...	11/2/2014 6:03:58 PM	Full backup of the Cpan...	{6062A009-490
cpandl.com	Corporate Policy	11/2/2014 6:03:58 PM	Full backup of the Cpan...	{8B6318E5-77E
cpandl.com	Crypto System...	11/2/2014 6:04:00 PM	Full backup of the Cpan...	{4E2E362B-FD!
cpandl.com	Customer Serv...	11/2/2014 6:04:00 PM	Full backup of the Cpan...	{BD9B4B75-45!
cpandl.com	Default Domai...	11/2/2014 6:04:00 PM	Full backup of the Cpan...	{6AC1786C-01E
cpandl.com	Default Domai...	11/2/2014 6:04:00 PM	Full backup of the Cpan...	{31B2F340-016
cpandl.com	Denver Site Pr...	11/2/2014 6:04:00 PM	Full backup of the Cpan...	{A43EC4B8-35!
cpandl.com	Enhanced Se...	11/2/2014 6:04:00 PM	Full backup of the Cpan...	{26555649-9F1
cpandl.com	Folder Assign...	11/2/2014 6:04:00 PM	Full backup of the Cpan...	{0CB2049B-5F7
cpandl.com	General Doma...	11/2/2014 6:04:00 PM	Full backup of the Cpan...	{46AC03B9-477
cpandl.com	Human Resou...	11/2/2014 6:04:00 PM	Full backup of the Cpan...	{F74497DC-6C;
cpandl.com	LA Site Primar...	11/2/2014 6:04:00 PM	Full backup of the Cpan...	{B648063F-84E
cpandl.com	Miami Site Pri...	11/2/2014 6:04:00 PM	Full backup of the Cpan...	{BE0ED91D-58
cpandl.com	My BPO	11/2/2014 6:04:02 PM	Full backup of the Cpan...	{A25C4D9C-D4
cpandl.com	Portland Site ...	11/2/2014 6:04:02 PM	Full backup of the Cpan...	{8E9CC1BA-07;

☐ Show only the latest version of each GPO

| Restore | Delete | View Settings... | Close |

FIGURE 8-18 Select the backup to restore.

3. In the Backup Location field, enter the folder path to the backup or click Browse to use the Browse For Folder dialog box to find the folder.

4. All GPO backups in the designated folder are listed under Backup Policy objects. To show only the latest version of the GPOs according to the time stamp, select Show Only The Latest Version Of Each GPO.

5. Select the GPO you want to restore. If you want to confirm its settings, click View Settings, and then verify that the settings are as expected by using Windows Internet Explorer.

6. When you are ready to continue, click Restore. Confirm that you want to restore the selected GPO by clicking OK. The Restore dialog box, shown in Figure 8-19, shows the progress and status of the restore operation.

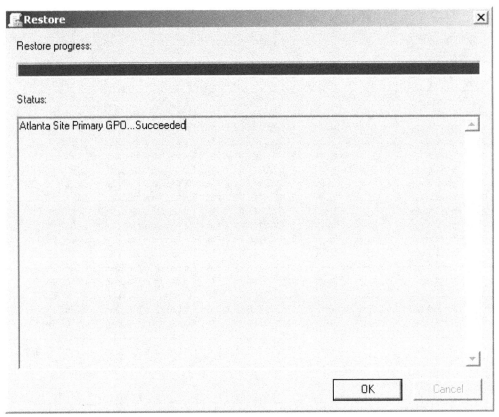

FIGURE 8-19 Track the restore status.

7. In the Restore dialog box, click OK when the restore is complete, and then restore additional policy objects as necessary or click Close to close the Manage Backups dialog box.

If a restore fails, check the permissions on the GPO and the folder from which you are reading the backup. To restore a GPO, you need Edit Settings, Delete, and Modify Security permissions on the GPO and Read permission on the folder containing the backup.

The locations of a GPO's links are backed up with the GPO. However, a restore of a backup will not restore GPO links. As a result, you must manually verify GPO links and create or remove links as appropriate. To see where a GPO had links when it was backed up, complete the following steps:

1. In the GPMC, navigate to the Group Policy Objects container for the domain with which you want to work.

2. Right-click the Group Policy Objects node, and then click Manage Backups.

3. In the Manage Backups dialog box, select the backup of the GPO you want to examine and then click View Settings.

4. A summary report of the GPO's settings is then displayed in Internet Explorer. Click the Links heading to display a list of domain and OU links the GPO had when it was backed up. Site links are not listed, however.

Backing Up and Restoring Starter GPOs

The backup and restore processes for starter GPOs are separate from the backup and restore processes for production GPOs. To back up starter GPOs, complete the following steps:

1. In the GPMC, navigate to the Starter Objects container for the domain with which you want to work. Do one of the following:

    ▪ •If you want to back up all starter GPOs in the domain, right-click the Starter GPOs node, and then click Back Up All.

    ▪ •If you want to back up a specific starter GPO in the domain, right-click the GPO, and then click Back Up.

2. In the Back Up Group Policy Object dialog box, click Browse, and then use the Browse For Folder dialog box to set the location in which the starter GPO backup should be stored. Optionally, in the Description field, enter a description of the contents of the backup.

3. Click Back Up to start the backup process. Click OK when the backup is complete.

To restore a starter GPO, complete the following steps:

1. In the GPMC, navigate to the Starter Objects container for the domain with which you want to work.

2. Right-click the Starter GPOs node, and then click Manage Backups. This displays the Manage Backups dialog box.

3. In the Backup Location field, enter the folder path to the backup or click Browse to use the Browse For Folder dialog box to find the folder.

4. All starter GPO backups in the designated folder are listed under Backed Up Starter GPOs. To show only the latest version of the starter GPOs according to the time stamp, select Show Only The Latest Version Of Each Starter GPO.

5. Select the starter GPO you want to restore. If you want to confirm its settings, click View Settings, and then verify that the settings are as expected by using Internet Explorer.

6. When you are ready to continue, click Restore. Confirm that you want to restore the selected starter GPO by clicking OK.

7. In the Restore dialog box, click OK when the restore operation is complete. Restore additional starter GPOs as necessary, or click Close to close the Manage Backups dialog box.

Backing Up and Restoring WMI Filters

The backup and restore processes for WMI filters are separate from the backup and restore processes for production GPOs. In the GPMC, you can only back up and restore WMI filters one at a time. WMI filter links are not restored when you restore a WMI filter. See "Applying or Removing a WMI Filter" in Chapter 5, "Searching and Filtering Group Policy," for details about linking WMI filters to GPOs.

> **Tip** The LDIF Directory Exchange utility (LDIFDE.exe) is available on Windows Server 2008 when you install the Remote Server Administration Tools. You can use LDIFDE.exe to back up and restore multiple WMI filters at one time. For more information, see *http://go.microsoft.com/fwlink/?linkid=109519*.

To back up a WMI filter, complete the following steps:

1. In the GPMC, navigate to the WMI Filters container for the domain with which you want to work.

2. Right-click the WMI filter you want to back up, and then select Export.

Use the Export WMI Filter dialog box to select the save location for the filter and set the backup file name. WMI filters are saved as .MOF files.

3. Click Save.

When you export a WMI filter to a .MOF file, you can import the filter to the same domain or to any other domain to which you have access. To restore a WMI filter, complete the following steps:

1. In the GPMC, navigate to the WMI Filters container for the domain with which you want to work.
2. Right-click the WMI Filter node, and then click Import.
3. Use the Import WMI Filter dialog box to select the .MOF file in which you saved the filter.
4. Click Open. In the Import WMI Filter dialog box, review the name, description, and queries associated with the filter. This dialog box is identical to the New WMI Filter and Edit WMI Filter dialog boxes discussed in "Managing WMI Filters" in Chapter 5.
5. The import can succeed only if a WMI filter with the name you set on the filter does not exist in the domain. Therefore, if a WMI filter with the current name already exists in the domain, you need to rename this filter.
6. Because the backup process might modify the queries contained in the filter, you should review the queries to ensure that no extra characters or unwanted changes have been made. After you've made any necessary changes, click Import.

Backing Up and Restoring the AGPM Archive

Each AGPM server you've deployed maintains an archive of controlled GPOs. The archive stores old versions of the GPOs as well as versions of deleted GPOs that are stored in the recycle bin. If you examine the archive folder, you'll see that it contains a number of directories and files.

As part of your backup routine, you should create a backup of the archive folder. You can do this simply by copying the entire folder to another location. If you ever need to restore the AGPM archive, whether on a new server or the original server, you can restore the archive by completing the following steps:

1. Using the Services utility, stop the AGPM Service.
2. Using Windows Explorer, copy the contents of the backup folder to the archive folder the server is using with AGPM.
3. Using the Services utility, start the AGPM Service.

> **Note** The account under which the AGPM Service runs must own the AGPM archive. If you configured a new AGPM server, ensure that the current log-on-as account has full control over the AGPM archive files.
>
> **Real World** When you restore the AGPM archive on a new server and you've configured e-mail notification for AGPM, you'll also need to reset the password for any mail-enabled user account you are using for notification. The account password is stored within the archive in an encrypted format. The encryption protecting the password causes the password to fail if the archive is moved to another computer. You can resolve this by using the GPMC. In the GPMC, select the Change Control node in the domain in which you want to manage GPOs. In the details pane, select the Domain Delegation node. Under Send Approval Requests, confirm the user information provided. Reenter and reconfirm the password for the user account, and then click Apply.

Recovering the Default GPOs

As discussed in "Using Default Policies" in Chapter 2, "Deploying Group Policy," two GPOs are created by default when you create a new domain:

- Default Domain Controllers Policy GPO
- Default Domain Policy GPO

Because the default GPOs are essential to the proper operation and processing of Group Policy, you must ensure that these GPOs are available and can be processed. Before making any changes to the default GPOs, be sure to back up the GPOs by using the GPMC. If a problem occurs with the changes to the default GPOs and you cannot restore them from backup, you can use the Dcgpofix.exe tool to re-create the default policies in their initial state. Alternatively, if you are using AGPM and are controlling the default GPOs, a record will be maintained of any changes that you've made to the default GPOs, and you can revert to a previous state or the initial state.

Dcgpofix.exe is included with Windows Server 2008 and is located in the %SystemRoot%\System32 folder. By default, Dcgpofix restores both the Default Domain Policy and Default Domain Controller Policy GPOs. This means that you will lose most changes made to these GPOs as a result of the restore process.

Note   The only exceptions are settings for Remote Installation Services (RIS), Security Settings, and Encrypting File System (EFS), which are maintained separately and not affected by the restore operation. Nondefault security settings are not maintained, however, such as security settings configured by Microsoft Exchange, security settings configured as a result of a migration from legacy Windows, and security settings configured through Systems Management Server (SMS).

Although Dcgpofix.exe restores the policy settings that are contained in the default GPOs at the time they are generated, it does not restore other GPOs that you've created. Dcgpofix.exe is only intended for disaster recovery of the default GPOs.

The syntax for Dcgpofix.exe is as follows:

```
dcgpofix [/ignoreschema] [/Target: Domain | DC | BOTH]
```

The options for Dcgpofix.exe are as follows:

- **/ignoreschema**   By default, the version of Dcgpofix.exe included with Windows Server 2008 works only with Windows Server 2008 domains.

To allow it to work on non–Windows Server 2008 domains, you must bypass the automatic schema check by using this option.

- **/target: DOMAIN**   Specifies that the Default Domain Policy should be re-created.
- **/target: DC**   Specifies that the Default Domain Controllers Policy should be re-created.
- **/target: BOTH**   Specifies that both the Default Domain Policy and the Default Domain Controllers Policy should be re-created.

Only Domain Admins or Enterprise Admins can run Dcgpofix. To restore the Default Domain Policy and Default Domain Controller Policy GPOs, log on to a domain controller in the domain in which you want to fix default Group Policy. Enter **dcgpofix** at the command prompt.

You can also restore only the Default Domain Policy or only the Default Domain Controller Policy GPO. To restore only the Default Domain Policy, enter **dcgpofix /target: domain**. To restore only the Default Domain Controller Policy, enter **dcgpofix /target: dc**.

Troubleshooting Group Policy

Throughout this book, I've discussed many different techniques you can use for diagnosing and resolving problems with Group Policy:

- Chapter 3 examines techniques you can use to manage GPOs and delegate privileges for policy management.
- Chapter 4 examines techniques you can use to manage workflow, manage previous versions of GPOs, and recover GPOs both from history and from the AGPM recycle bin.
- Chapter 5 examines techniques you can use to search GPOs, apply security group filters, and use WMI filters.
- Chapter 6 examines techniques you can use to maintain the SYSOVL, generate diagnostics reports for replication, and troubleshoot replication issues.

- Chapter 7 examines ways you can modify policy processing, test implementation scenarios, and determine effective settings.
- Appendix A, "Installing Group Policy Extensions and Tools," discusses techniques for installing Group Policy extensions and tools.

In this section, I'll provide some additional tips and techniques for troubleshooting Group Policy.

Diagnosing Group Policy: The Basics

At a very basic level, Group Policy works like this:

1. A Group Policy client discovers through an Active Directory lookup that policy objects apply to it. Active Directory tells the client where in the SYSVOL it can find the policy file associated with the object referenced in Active Directory.
2. The client uses a Server Message Block (SMB) call to read the policy file from the SYSVOL on a domain controller.
3. The client reads any necessary settings from those policy files by using client-side extensions (CSEs) that process those settings.
4. The client applies the settings.

As you can see, the Group Policy client does all the work. The domain controller doesn't do any processing.

Whenever there are changes to Active Directory or the Windows operating system, there are questions about how to get the latest features and extensions. Technically, however, Group Policy isn't bound by the Active Directory version or the operating system version. What determines changes to policy are new policy extensions and new administrative tools.

Group Policy preferences are a good example of this:

- To manage Group Policy preferences, you need administrative tools that support the related extensions. These extensions are supported in administrative tools for Windows Vista with Service Pack 1 or later,

Windows Server 2008, and later releases of Windows. These administrative tools write the extension settings for Group Policy preferences into the same policy files that Group Policy has always used.

- To use Group Policy preferences, computers need Group Policy clients that support the related extensions as well as any related client-side extensions. With Group Policy preferences, only Windows Server 2008 or later versions of Windows include an updated Group Policy client and the required client-side extensions. For more information, see "Installing the Group Policy Preference Client-Side Extensions" in Appendix A "Installing Group Policy Extensions and Tools."

Sometimes new settings within Group Policy require schema updates to enable them to work. For example, policy settings related to BitLocker Drive Encryption require schema extensions to work. More typically, to take advantage of the latest and greatest features of Group Policy, you simply need to edit your GPOs from a management computer running the latest version of Windows. Editing a GPO on the latest version of Windows with the latest version of the administrative tools ensures that new templates are applied to the GPO and that new settings are available.

> **Note** The template format has nothing to do with the policy file that's created—it's just used to create the policy by the administrative tool itself. Originally, the Group Policy editors used the ADM file format, and these ADM files were copied into every policy object on the SYSVOL. In Windows Vista, Windows Server 2008 or later, the template format changed to ADMX. This was a complete change to an XML-based format. ADMX files aren't copied into every policy object and instead rely on a central or local store.

Common Problems with Group Policy

Many problems with Group Policy result from the way policy is inherited and processed. When trying to determine why policy hasn't been processed on a computer or for a user, it is important to keep in mind how policy is processed and applied. As discussed in Chapter 7, a variety of techniques can be used to modify the way inheritance works and policy is processed, and these modifications can lead to unanticipated results when Group Policy is applied.

If a GPO isn't being processed when you think it should, ensure that the GPO is:

- **Linked**   A GPO must be linked to the appropriate site, domain, or OU to be processed. See "Creating and Linking GPOs" in Chapter 3.
- **Enabled**   A GPO must be enabled to be processed. In cases where you've disabled Computer Configuration settings, only User Configuration settings are processed and only user settings are applied. In cases where you've disabled User Configuration, only Computer Configuration settings are processed and only computer settings are applied. See "Modifying GPO Processing" in Chapter 7.
- **Applicable**   A GPO must be configured with the appropriate permissions, filters, and targeting for it to be applicable. If a GPO is filtered out because of permissions or WMI filters, it doesn't apply. See "Using Security Group Filters" and "Using WMI Filters" in Chapter 5. If a computer or user falls outside the targeting parameters, Group Policy preferences won't apply. See "Using Item-level Targeting" in Chapter 3.

If policy isn't being applied as you expect, you should examine the network configuration of the client computer and ensure that the Local Area Connection settings for Internet Protocol (IP) are configured with the correct:

- IP address configuration
- Subnet mask
- Default gateway
- DNS server addresses

At a command prompt, you can quickly check the IP configuration by entering **ipconfig /all**. In your troubleshooting, don't overlook the importance of the event logs. Your troubleshooting should start with the event logs. In the System log, you'll find general policy events logged with the source as GroupPolicy. If policy was successfully processed for the computer, you'll see event ID 1502. If policy was successfully processed for the user, you'll see event ID 1503. If there are any processing problems, you'll see related errors, such as error code 1129, stating that processing of Group Policy failed because of the lack of network connectivity to a domain controller. To get more information about an error code, you can search Microsoft TechNet (*http://technet.microsoft.com/*).

Error 1129 can tell you right away that the computer has an IP configuration problem or that the computer's network cable isn't connected properly.

On computers running Windows Vista, Windows Server 2008 or a later version of Windows, the Group Policy Operational log provides in-depth tracking of Group Policy processing events. To access this log, complete the following steps:

1. Open Event Viewer by clicking Start, All Programs, Administrative Tools, Event Viewer.

2. In Event Viewer, expand the Applications And Services Log node. Work your way to the Group Policy Operational log by expanding the Microsoft, Windows, and GroupPolicy nodes.

3. When you select Operational in the console tree, all the related events are displayed in the details pane.

4. Click the Level column heading to sort events by level. You can then quickly see all error events, as shown in Figure 8-20.

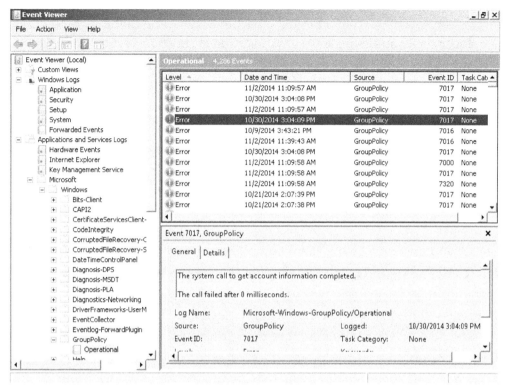

Figure 8-20 View the Group Policy Operational log.

Don't forget the foreground and background processing rules. Keep the following in mind:

- Sometimes you might need to force the computer or user profile to process policy updates, and you can use Gpupdate to do this, as discussed in "Refreshing Group Policy Manually" in Chapter 7. With forced updates, keep in mind that sometimes the first forced update of Group Policy might not work and you might need to run Gpupdate -force a second time. Why? If a computer is connected over a slow link, some client-side extensions are not processed, and it may take several forced updates to get the computer to refresh policy.
- If you move a computer to a new location in the directory or on the physical network, you might also need to restart the computer to ensure that the computer processes the correct GPOs.

- Some policies are applied only after the second logon, not after the first logon. This occurs because anything that is set to run synchronously won't run until after the second logon. As a result, sometimes a user may need to log off and log on several times to ensure that policy is fully processed. Or you may need to enable the Always Wait For The Network At Computer Startup And Logon Policy setting as discussed in "Policy Processing and Refresh Exceptions" in Chapter 7.
- Partially disabling a GPO, using loopback processing, and linking WMI filters can change the way Group Policy is processed. Always check to see how related settings are being applied.

Something as simple as the client computer not having the correct time can also cause policy processing to fail. Why? Kerberos version 5 is the default authentication mechanism for computers running Windows. Kerberos v5 checks the time stamp on authentication messages. If the time on the client and the time on the server are more than 5 minutes apart, authentication will fail. To prevent this from happening, you should configure Windows Time Service in the domain as discussed in "Configuring the Windows Time Service" in Chapter 9, "Maintaining and Recovering Active Directory," in *Active Directory Administrator's Pocket Consultant*.

Best Practice Sometimes older settings that were designed for earlier versions of Windows can have unpredictable effects when you also set related policies that apply only to newer versions of Windows. Consider the following scenario: In a GPO that applies to both users and computers, you configure firewall, IPSec, wireless networking, or auditing settings for Windows Server 2003. In the same GPO, you also configure newer policy settings for one or more of these administrative areas using policies that apply to Windows Vista and Windows Server 2008. When Group Policy is applied to computers running Windows Vista and Windows Server 2008, the overlap between the older policy settings and the newer policy settings can cause unpredictable results, making it difficult to diagnose and resolve related problems. The best practice here is to make sure that you separate older and newer policy settings that overlap. To resolve this, you could separate computers into different organizational units. Alternatively, you could use access

---

control lists with groups or WMI filters. In Chapter 5, see "Using Security Group Filters" and "Using WMI Filters" for more information on access control lists and WMI.

Diagnosing Group Policy Issues

Group Policy is refreshed automatically at a specific interval. On domain controllers, Group Policy is refreshed every 5 minutes by default. On member servers and workstations, Group Policy is refreshed every 90 to 120 minutes by default. You can refresh Group Policy manually using Gpupdate, as discussed in "Refreshing Group Policy Manually" in Chapter 7.

When you are trying to determine why policy is not being applied as expected, you should check for common problems, as discussed previously, and then examine the Resultant Set of Policy (RSoP) for the user or computer, or both, experiencing problems with Group Policy. If you run the Group Policy Results Wizard first and then run the Group Policy Modeling Wizard, you can view how settings are applied currently as well as how settings should be applied based on the container in which a user, computer, or both are located. You can compare the settings between the planning and logging modes to check for discrepancies between how you think policy is being applied and how it is actually being applied. For detailed information on using these wizards, see "Planning Group Policy Changes" in Chapter 7.

Using the Gpresult command-line utility, you can view the Resultant Set of Policy as well. Gpresult provides details on:

- The last time Group Policy was applied
- The domain controller from which policy was applied
- The complete list of applied GPOs
- The complete list of GPOs not applied because of filters
- The security group memberships for the computer and user
- Details on special settings applied for folder redirection, software installation, disk quota, IPSec, and scripts

The basic syntax for Gpresult is:

```
gpresult /s ComputerName /user Domain\UserName
```

where *ComputerName* is the name of the remote computer for which you want to log policy results, and *Domain\UserName* indicates the remote user for which you want to log policy results. For example, to view the RSoP for corp-pc28 and the user wrstanek in the ImaginedL domain, you would enter the following command:

```
gpresult /s corp-pc28 /user imaginedl\wrstanek
```

You can view more detailed output using one of the two verbose options. The /v option turns on verbose output, and results are displayed only for policy settings in effect. The /z option turns on verbose output for policy settings in effect and all other GPOs that have the policy set.

Because Gpresult output can be fairly long, you should direct the output to a file, as shown in this example:

```
gpresult /s corp-pc28 /user imaginedl\wrstanek /z > rsopsave.log
```

Under Computer Configuration, in the Administrative Templates\System\Group Policy\Logging And Tracing folder, you'll find a set of policies for configuring logging and tracing of Group Policy preferences processing (see Figure 8-21).

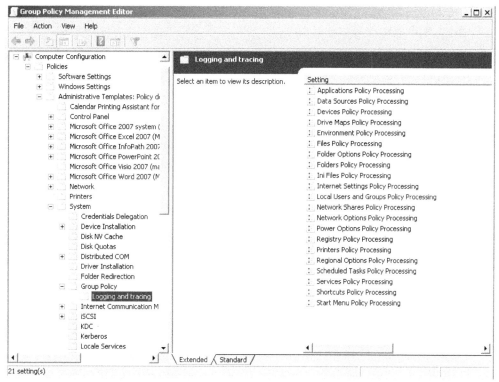

FIGURE 8-21 Configure policy to log and trace preferences.

You can configure logging and tracing separately for each major area within Group Policy preferences by completing the following steps:

1. In the Group Policy Management Editor, double-click the policy processing area to log, trace, or both.

2. In the Properties dialog box, shown in Figure 8-22, select Enabled to enable the policy.

3. Use the Event Logging list to set the type of events to log. The options include:

- Informational, Warnings, and Errors
- Warnings and Errors
- Errors Only
- None

4. On the Tracing list, select On to turn on debug tracing, or select Off to turn off debug tracing. By default, trace data is written to the %CommonAppData%\GroupPolicy\Preference\Trace folder. User trace data is written to User.log. Computer trace data is written to Computer.log. Planning trace data is written to Planning.log.

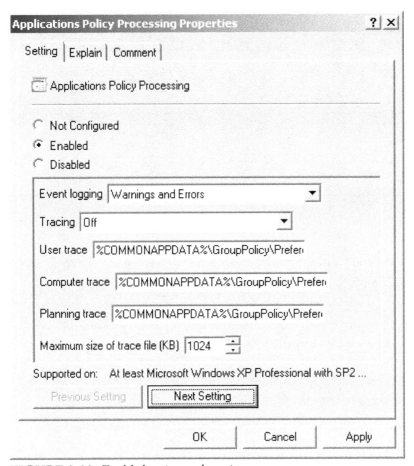

FIGURE 8-22 Enable logging and tracing.

5. If you enabled tracing, use the Maximum Size Of Trace File combo box to set the maximum size of individual trace files. The default maximum size is 1,024 kilobytes.

6. Click OK to apply the setting. Repeat this process as necessary for other preference areas.

When you are done logging and tracing, you should edit the Enabled policy settings and set them to Not Configured or Disabled to stop logging and tracing.

Restoring the Default Policy GPOs

If the Default Domain Policy or Default Domain Controller Policy GPO becomes corrupted, Group Policy will not function properly. You can resolve this problem by using Dcgpofix to restore the default GPOs to their original default state. For more information, see "Recovering the Default GPOs" earlier in the chapter.

Examining Group Policy Health

The Windows Server 2003 Resource Kit includes a Group Policy verification tool called Gpotool. You can use Gpotool to troubleshoot problems with the server-side health of Group Policy. By default, if you enter **gpotool** at a command prompt, Gpotool verifies the consistency, permissions, and version numbers of all GPOs in the current logon domain. If any problems are found, a verbose listing of the GPO in question is provided, along with the specific issues and errors. Discrepancies found may be the result of problems with replicating the SYSVOL files on domain controllers.

You can use Gpotool to check permissions on the SYSVOL by using the /checkacl option, such as:

```
gpotool /checkacl
```

Gpotool doesn't check permissions on subfolders within the SYSVOL. Gpotool only checks the permissions on the SYSVOL folder itself.

You can use Gpotool to check the state of a GPO on specified domain controllers. This is useful for determining the status of a GPO stored on particular domain controllers.

The syntax for checking the state of a GPO on specified domain controllers is:

```
gpotool /gpo:"GPOName" /domain:DomainName /dc:DomainControllers
/verbose
```

where *GPOName* is the name of the GPO to check, *DomainName* is the name of the domain, and *DomainControllers* is a comma-separated lists of domain controllers to check. Here is an example:

```
gpotool /gpo:"Default Domain Policy" /domain:imaginedlands.com
/dc:corpsvr01,corpsvr02 /verbose
```

If the GPOs are found to have no problems, an OK status is returned. If there are problems, the results show the errors or discrepancies.

> **Tip** You can download Gpotool.exe from
> http://www.microsoft.com/en-us/download/details.aspx?id=17657.

Appendix A. Installing Group Policy Extensions and Tools

Group Policy is one of the most rapidly changing areas of Windows administration. To help you keep pace with the changes, I've included in this appendix details for installing important Group Policy extensions and tools. By reading this appendix, you'll learn how to:

- Install the Remote Server Administration Tools.
- Install the client and server components for Advanced Group Policy Management (AGPM).
- Install Group Policy templates and add-ins for Microsoft Office.

Installing the Remote Server Administration Tools

The Microsoft Remote Server Administration Tools (RSAT) are a collection of tools for remotely managing the roles and features in Windows Server from a computer running a compatible operating system. RSAT supports remote management of Windows Server regardless of whether the server is running a Server Core installation or a Full Server installation.

RSAT is available in a 32-bit edition and a 64-bit edition for specific versions of Windows, such as for Windows 7 or for Windows 8.1. If your computer is running a 32-bit edition of Windows, you must install the 32-bit edition of RSAT. If your computer is running a 64-bit edition of Windows, you must install the 64-bit edition of RSAT. You can use the tools designed for either architecture to remotely manage both 32-bit and 64-bit editions of Windows Server.

The installer package for the remote administration tools is provided as an update. Microsoft assigns the installer package an identification number in the Microsoft Knowledge Base. Be sure to write down this number. If you need to uninstall or reinstall the installer package, this number will help you locate the update you need to uninstall or reinstall.

You can obtain and register the installer package for use by completing the following steps:

1. Obtain the version of the Microsoft Remote Server Administration Tools that is compatible with the operating system, architecture and service pack used on your computer. You can obtain the latest version of the tools by visiting the Microsoft Download Center (*http://download.microsoft.com/*) and searching for all downloads containing the keywords *Microsoft Remote Server Administration Tools*. After you download the executable, double-click the executable to start the installation.

> **Note**   Be sure you use the Downloads search and the All Downloads selection rather than the general search. If you use the general search, you likely will not find the correct page link.

2. If you've saved this file to a location on your computer or a network share, you can begin the installation process by accessing the file location in -Windows Explorer and double-clicking the installer file.

3. When prompted to confirm the installation, click OK. When you are prompted, read the license terms. If you accept the terms, click I Accept to continue. The installer will then install the tools as an update.

4. When the installer completes the installation of the tools, click Close. Although the installer may not state so explicitly, you may need to restart your computer to finalize the installation. You can confirm whether you need to restart by clicking Start and looking at the power button. If the power button is red and you see a small Windows Update icon within it, you need to restart your computer.

Installing the package ensures that the remote administration tools are available for selection. After RSAT has been installed, you can configure and select the remote server administration tools that you want to use by completing the following steps:

1. Click Start, click Control Panel, and then click Programs. Under Programs And Features, click Turn Windows Features On Or Off.

2. In the Windows Features dialog box, expand Remote Server Administration Tools.

3. Using the options under the Feature Administration Tools and Role Administration Tools nodes, select the remote administration tools that you want to install and then click OK. For example, to install the Group Policy Management Console and related features, select Group Policy Management.

Windows automatically configures the selected tools for use. At the command line, you'll be able to use any command-line tool that Windows has made available. The graphical versions of the tools are available on the Administrative Tools menu.

Removing the Remote Server Administration Tools

You can remove remote server administration tools that you no longer want to use by completing the following steps:

1. Click Start, click Control Panel, and then click Programs. Under Programs And Features, click Turn Windows Features On Or Off.

2. In the Windows Features dialog box, expand Remote Server Administration Tools.

3. Using the options under the Feature Administration Tools and Role Administration Tools nodes, clear the check boxes for any remote server administration tool that you want to remove, and then click OK.

If you no longer use a computer for remote administration and want to remove the remote administration tools completely, you can remove the entire installer package by completing the following steps:

1. Click Start, click Control Panel, and then click Programs. Under Programs And Features, click View Installed Updates.

2. Click the update you used to install the remote administration tools, and then click Uninstall.

3. When prompted to confirm, click Yes.

Installing Advanced Group Policy Management

Advanced Group Policy Management (AGPM) is a set of extensions for the Group Policy Management Console that includes advanced features that allow you to:

- Archive and edit GPOs offline.
- Delegate different levels of permissions for Group Policy administrators.
- Perform change management of GPOs by using check-in and check-out capabilities.
- Track workflow and perform reporting on GPOs.
- Roll back and roll forward changes to archived GPOs.
- Maintain a recycle bin of deleted GPOs and recover GPOs and GPO links from this recycle bin.

> **Note** At the time of this writing, AGPM is only available through the Microsoft Desktop Optimization Pack (MDOP) for Software Assurance, which also includes Microsoft Application Virtualization, Diagnostics, and Recovery Toolset; Asset Inventory Service; and System Center Desktop Error Monitoring. Because the Microsoft Desktop Optimization Pack for Software Assurance is available only to organizations that have an enterprise license with Microsoft that includes Software Assurance, your organization would need to have this type of enterprise license agreement. Generally, this type of license applies to organizations with at least 50 desktop computers.

AGPM uses a client/server architecture. The server component is used to archive GPOs for offline use, to control GPOs for change management, and to store related history data. The client component extends the GPMC so that it includes the additional features provided in AGPM. When AGPM is added, the only immediate difference you'll notice in the GPMC's user interface is a Change Control node under each domain node.

If you plan to deploy AGPM, keep in mind that Microsoft has released several versions of the Microsoft Desktop Optimization Pack for Software Assurance. You'll want to use at least the 2013 R2 version. Microsoft Desktop Optimization Pack for Software Assurance 2013 R2 allows you to use:

- **AGPM 3.0**   AGPM 3.0 runs on Windows Vista Service Pack 1 and Windows Server 2008. Both 32-bit and 64-bit installations are available.
- **AGPM 4.0**   AGPM 4.0 runs on Windows Vista Service Pack 1, Windows 7, Windows Server 2008 and Windows Server 2008 R2. Both 32-bit and 64-bit installations are available.
- **AGPM 4.0 SP1**   Adds support for Windows 8 and Windows Server 2012.
- **AGPM 4.0 SP2**   Adds support for Windows 8.1 and Windows Server 2012 R2.

Tip   Windows on Windows 64 (WoW64) is an x86 emulation layer. The WoW64 subsystem isolates 32-bit applications from 64-bit applications. AGPM 3.0 does not support Wow64. This means that you must install the 64-bit version of AGPM on a 64-bit version of the Windows operating system and a 32-bit version of AGPM on a 32-bit version of the Windows operating system. Communication between client and server releases with different bitness is fully supported. This means that a 32-bit AGPM client can communicate with a 64-bit AGPM server, and a 64-bit AGPM client can -communicate with a 32-bit AGPM server.

AGPM 3.0 and later have the following enhancements over early AGPM releases:

- **Customizable permissions**   Allow you to configure custom permissions for each domain. The permissions you configure for a GPO on the Production Delegation tab replace any permissions already on the GPO when it is controlled or deployed from the AGPM server. Once a GPO is under AGPM control, changes to permissions from outside AGPM are prevented.

- **More robust change tracking**   Change tracking has been enhanced to track additional types of changes made to GPOs, such as when a request was made and who made it, when a request was approved or rejected and who approved or rejected the request, when changes to AGPM delegation were made and who made them, and so on.
- **Purging of historical data**   Allows you to purge old data by specifying how many historical versions of GPOs to retain. Purging old data deletes the data from the archive, so this data is no longer accessible. As part of enhanced change tracking, the information about the change to the purge time is retained in the history and an entry is recorded in the history that data was purged.
- **Support extensions**   Adds support for Group Policy preferences, an enhanced user interface (UI) with clearer descriptions and localization in -additional languages.

A key feature added with AGPM 4.0 is the ability to export and import GPOs to different forests. AGPM 4.0 SP1 is updated to support the additional client-side extensions in Windows 8 and Windows Server 2012 and also adds support for: Central Access Policy, DNS security, DirectAccess on DNS client computers, Internet Explorer 10, default connection URLs for remote connections, Windows To Go Startup options and Windows To Go Hibernate options.

AGPM 4.0 SP2 is updated to support the additional client-side extensions in Windows 8.1 and Windows Server 2012 R2 and also adds support for: specifying Work Folder settings, auto provision synchronization, and forcing automatic setup for all users.

Because AGPM 3.0 has feature enhancements, I recommend that you use this version or a later version. If you are already using AGPM 3.0, you can upgrade to AGPM 4.0 and then upgrade AGPM 4.0 to AGPM SP1 or AGPM SP2.

Features in AGPM 3.0 and later versions are what I discuss in this book. AGPM 3.0 is designed to be used with GPMC 3.0. As described previously in

"Installing the Remote Server Administration Tools," GPMC 3.0 or later must be installed as part of the Remote Server Administration Tools.

The sections that follow detail how you can install client and server components for AGPM.

Performing a Server Installation of AGPM

Performing a server installation of AGPM installs the AGPM Service on the server and establishes the GPO archive. The AGPM Service enables offline editing by copying GPOs from a domain controller in the current domain and storing them in the AGPM archive. The AGPM Service allows you to apply updates to GPOs by copying updated GPOs back to a domain controller in the current domain.

During installation, you need to select a folder to be used for archive storage. The AGPM server stores GPO archives, deleted GPOs, and related history information in this folder. Although the permissions on this folder are used to control the tasks individual administrators can perform with respect to AGPM-managed GPOs, you shouldn't edit the permissions directly. Instead, use the extensions provided by AGPM in the GPMC to delegate permissions.

Before you install an AGPM server in a domain, you'll want to:

- Select a computer to act as the AGPM server. Generally, this computer should be a member of the domain and should not be a domain controller.
- Create a domain user account for the AGPM Service. The account should not be the Administrator account. This account should be a member of the Group Policy Creator Owners group or be delegated permission to create GPOs in the domain.
- When you create a new controlled GPO by using the AGPM extensions, the AGPM Service account is delegated permission to manage the GPO (specifically, the account is granted the edit settings, delete, and modify security permissions). To be sure that you can work with GPOs created

prior to installing AGPM, check that the AGPM Service account is either a member of a group with similar permissions or that you delegate these permissions manually as discussed in "Delegating Control for Working with GPOs" in Chapter 3, "Group Policy Management."

- Create a group account that will be the initial owner of the AGPM archive. Members of this group will be used to set up AGPM delegation and will have full control over all AGPM functions.

> **Note** Whether you are working with AGPM 3.0, 4.0, 4.0 SP1 or 4.0 SP2, the AGPM server component requires the Microsoft .NET Framework 3.5. If this version of the framework isn't installed already, you'll need to install it. Visit the Microsoft Download Center (*http://download.microsoft.com/*) and search for ".NET Framework 3.5."

You'll want to be sure that the server has adequate free space on the disk used for archive storage. When determining the size requirements, keep the following in mind: GPOs that store Administrative templates can grow to be several megabytes (MB) in size; GPOs that do not store Administrative templates typically are only a few kilobytes in size. Additionally, when you use change tracking, multiple versions of GPOs may be stored in the archive.

> **Real World** As discussed in "Keeping Group Policy Up to Date" in Chapter 2, some settings for Group Policy objects are defined in a set of files called Administrative templates. Administrative templates can use the original ADM format or the newer ADMX format. With ADM, the description of settings and the values for settings are stored in the template files, and these files are in turn stored in each GPO you create.

When ADMX is used with a central store, the description of settings and the values for settings are stored separately. Setting descriptions are defined using language-neutral files ending with the .admx file extension and language-specific files ending with the .adml extension. These files are not stored in individual GPOs. Instead, they are stored in the SYSVOL, and only the actual settings in use are stored in GPOs. Because only in-use settings are stored, these GPOs are significantly smaller than their counterparts that use ADM.

Therefore, if a domain has 100 GPOs that are 4 MB each, you'll need 400 MB of storage initially and several gigabytes of storage to store multiple versions of each GPO. On the other hand, if a domain has 100 GPOs that are 4 kilobytes (KB) each, you'll need 400 KB of storage initially and only several megabytes of storage to store multiple versions of each GPO.

The general steps to install the AGPM server vary slightly depending on the version you are installing. To install the AGPM server on the computer that will host the AGPM Service, follow these general steps:

1. Access the computer with an account that is a member of the Domain Admins group.
2. Insert the Microsoft Desktop Optimization Pack for Software Assurance CD/DVD. If Autorun is enabled, the splash screen is displayed. Otherwise, double-click Launcher.exe in the Launcher folder on the CD/DVD.
3. On the splash screen, click the Advanced Group Policy Management option.
4. On the Advanced Group Policy Management page, you'll see installation options for the available versions of AGPM. On Windows Vista SP1 or later and Windows Server 2008, you'll want to install AGPM 3.0 or later. Click Install Server (32-bit) or Install Server (64-bit) as appropriate for the bitness of the operating system.

> **Best Practice** Although you can install the AGPM server on a computer running a Windows desktop operating system, you should be sure that you understand the limitations involved when you do so. Client versions of Windows are not designed to act as servers and can handle only a limited number of network connections. Therefore, you should install the AGPM server on a client version of Windows only in small network environments, such as those used for testing and development. To ensure good performance in an enterprise

production environment, install the AGPM server on a computer running Windows Server 2008 or a later server version of Windows.

5. When the Microsoft Advanced Group Policy Management—Server Setup Wizard starts, click Next.

6. On the Microsoft Software License Terms page, review the license terms. Select I Accept The License Terms check box, and then click Next.

7. On the Application Path page, shown in Figure A-1, select a location in which to install application components for the AGPM server. The default path is %SystemRoot%\Program Files\Microsoft\AGPM\Server. Click Next.

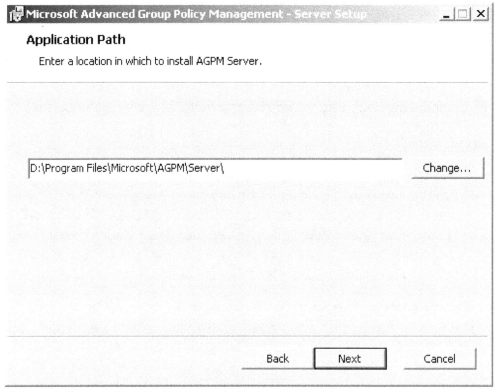

Figure A-1 Specify an application path for the server components.

8. On the Archive Path page, shown in Figure A-2, select a location for the AGPM archive. The default location is %SystemRoot%\ProgramData\-Microsoft\AGPM. Although the archive folder can be on the AGPM server or a network share, you should select a location with sufficient space to store all GPOs and history data managed by this AGPM server. Click Next.

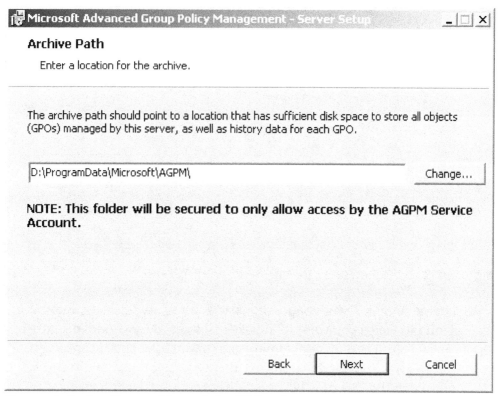

Figure A-2 Specify an archive path for GPO archives.

9. On the AGPM Service Account page, shown in Figure A-3, click Browse. Use the Select User Or Group dialog box to select the domain account under which the AGPM Service will run. After you enter and then confirm the password for this account, click Next.

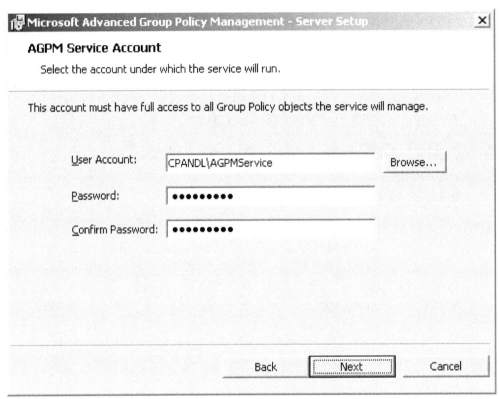

Figure A-3 Select the domain account for the AGPM Service.

10. On the Archive Owner page, shown in Figure A-4, select an account or group to which you want to initially assign the AGPM Administrator (Full Control) role. AGPM administrators with full control can assign AGPM roles and -permissions to other Group Policy administrators (including the role of AGPM Administrator). Click Next.

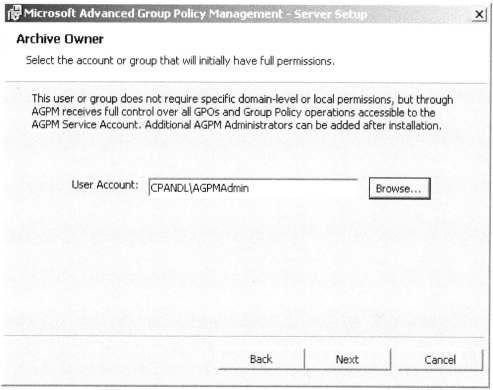

Figure A-4 Select the account or group that will control the GPO archive.

11. On the Port Configuration page, shown in Figure A-5, specify the port the AGPM Service will use to communicate with clients. The default port is 4600. By default, the wizard adds a port exception to the Windows Firewall if it is running. Click Next.

12. On the Languages page, specify the UI languages to install. By default, all supported languages are selected. If you don't want to install the UI components for a language, clear the related check box. Click Next.

13. The AGPM server components require the following additional components: Windows Communications Foundation (WCF) Activation, Non-HTTP Activation, and the Windows Process Activation Service. If these or other required components aren't already installed, they will be installed during the AGPM server installation. Click Details to see a complete list of the components that will be installed if they are not already present. When you are ready to continue, click Install.

14. When the installation is complete, click Finish to exit the wizard.

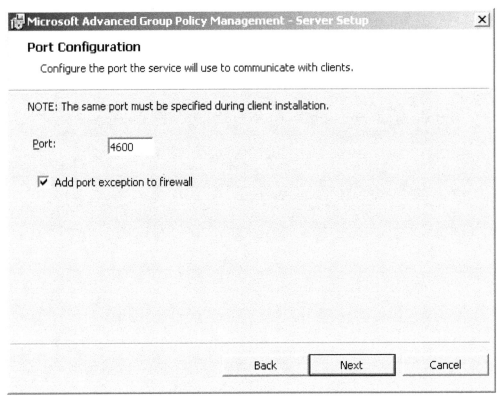

Figure A-5 Set the communications port for the AGPM Service.

You can check the server installation by:

- Verifying that the AGPM Service is installed and running. To do this, start the Services utility from the Administrative Tools menu. In the Services -utility, check that the AGPM Service is listed as Started with a Startup Type of -Automatic and that the service logs on as the service account you designated. See Figure A-6.

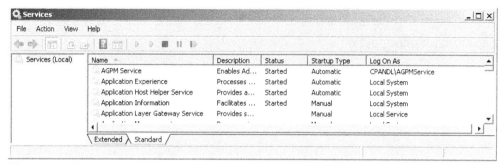

Figure A-6 Confirm that the AGPM Service is installed and running under the correct account.

- Confirming that the AGPM archive has been created. To do this, start Windows Explorer and then navigate to the archive location, as shown in Figure A-7. The default location is %SystemRoot%\ProgramData\Microsoft\AGPM. Initially the archive folder will be empty.

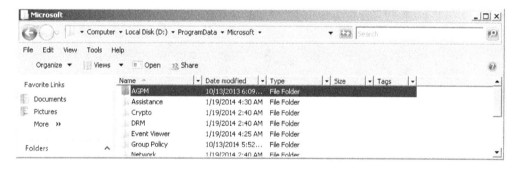

Figure A-7 Confirm that the GPO archive folder was created.

If the AGPM Service or the AGPM archive folder isn't established, you'll need to repeat the AGPM server installation. The primary reason the installation will fail is because you are logged on with a local computer account rather than a domain user account.

Performing a Client Installation of AGPM

Once you've established an AGPM server for a domain, you can install the AGPM client on computers that you use to manage GPOs. Installing the

AGPM client installs extensions for the GPMC. These extensions provide the additional functionality.

Each Group Policy administrator must have the AGPM client installed on the computers that he or she uses to manage GPOs. You do not need to install the AGPM client on computers of users who will not manage Group Policy.

For AGPM 3.0 or later, the computer on which you are installing the AGPM client must be running Windows Vista SP1, Windows Server 2008 or later and have GPMC 3.0 or later installed as part of the Remote Administration Server Tools.

The general steps to install the AGPM server vary slightly depending on the version you are installing. To install the AGPM client on a management computer, follow these general steps:

1. Access the computer with an account that is a member of the Domain Admins group.

2. Insert the Microsoft Desktop Optimization Pack for Software Assurance CD/DVD. If Autorun is enabled, the splash screen is displayed. Otherwise, double-click Launcher.exe in the Launcher folder on the CD/DVD.

3. On the splash screen, click the Advanced Group Policy Management option.

4. On the Advanced Group Policy Management page, you'll see installation -options for the available versions of AGPM. On Windows Vista SP1 or later and Windows Server 2008, you'll want to install AGPM 3.0 or later. Click Install Client (32-bit) or Install Client (64-bit) as appropriate for the bitness of the operating system.

5. When the Microsoft Advanced Group Policy Management—Client Setup Wizard starts, click Next.

6. On the Microsoft Software License Terms page, review the license terms. Select I Accept The License Terms check box, and then click Next.

7. On the Application Path page, shown in Figure A-8, select a location in which to install application components for the AGPM client. The default path is %SystemRoot%\Program Files\Microsoft\AGPM\Client. Click Next.

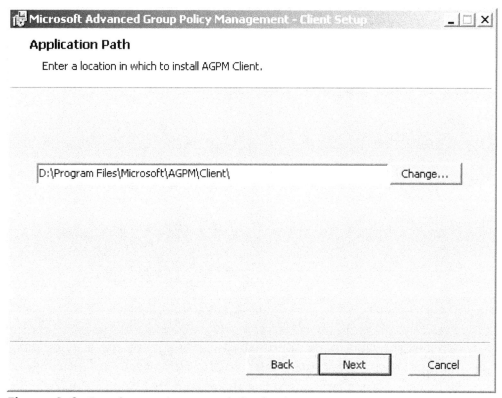

Figure A-8 Specify an application path for the client components.

8. On the AGPM Server page, shown in Figure A-9, specify the AGPM server to which the client should connect. Enter the fully qualified domain name of the server, such as corpserver23.imaginedlands.com. Next, enter the port number on which the client can connect to the AGPM Service running on the server. The default port is 4600. By default, the wizard adds a port exception to Windows Firewall if it is running. Click Next.

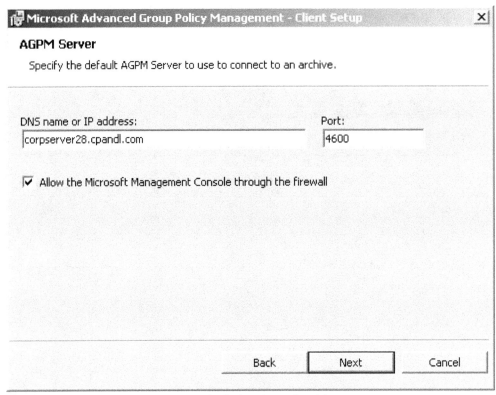

Figure A-9 Specify the server to which the client should connect.

9. On the Languages page, specify the UI languages to install. By default, all supported languages are selected. If you don't want to install the UI components for a language, clear the related check box. Click Next.

10. Click Install to install the client components. When the installation is complete, click Finish to exit the wizard.

11. Repeat the client installation on each computer that will be used for Group Policy management.

After you install the client, you can start the GPMC and verify that the client extensions are available on your management computer by following these steps:

1. Start the GPMC by clicking Group Policy Management on the Administrative Tools menu.

2. Click the node for the domain in which you've installed AGPM to expand it.

3. Under the domain node, you should see a Change Control node. When you select the Change Control node, the GPMC will try to make a connection to the GPO archive on the AGPM server. Note the following:

- If the GPMC can connect to the AGPM server, the client is configured correctly. You'll find a list of available uncontrolled GPOs on the Contents\Uncontrolled tab, as shown in Figure A-10. Later, when GPOs are under AGPM control, you'll see controlled GPOs on the Contents\Controlled tab.

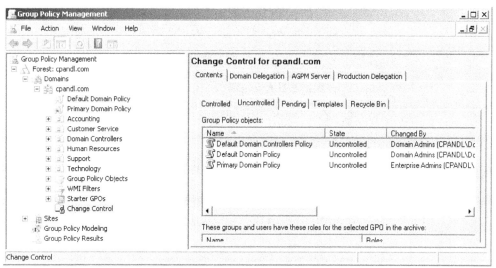

Figure A-10 Verify that you can connect to the AGPM server.

- If GPMC cannot connect to the server, you may not have correctly set the DNS name or port information for the server. As long as AGPM policy is not yet configured, you can change this information on the AGPM Server tab.
- If you don't have permission to work with the GPO archive, the GPMC can connect to the AGPM server but cannot access the archive. You'll receive an "insufficient permissions" error as shown in Figure A-11.

You'll need to add your account to the AGPM Administrator group. Then you'll need to log off and then log back on.

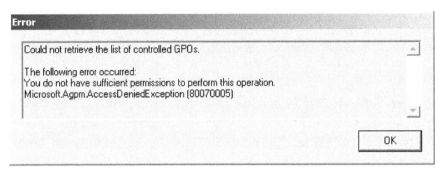

Figure A-11 Resolve a permissions error by making your account an AGPM administrator.

Next, you can make the client extensions for AGPM available to other administrators. This requires a two-step procedure:

1. In the first step, you make the Agpm.admx template available.
2. In the second step, you configure Group Policy to support AGPM.

Making the Agpm.admx Template Available

The Agpm.admx template should be available on your management computer after you install the AGPM client. If you have not established a central store, you should be able to use this template when you edit GPOs while logged on to your management computer. You can verify that the appropriate files are available by following these steps:

1. On the computer on which you have installed the AGPM client, log on with a user account that has appropriate permissions.
2. In Windows Explorer, check that the Agpm.admx file is in the %SystemRoot%\Windows\PolicyDefinitions folder and that the Agpm.adml files are in the appropriate language-specific subdirectories, such as %SystemRoot%\-Windows\PolicyDefinitions\en-us.

If you have established a central store, you'll need to copy the related ADMX and ADML files to the central store. The required ADMX file is Agpm.admx.

You'll find this file in the %SystemRoot%\Windows\PolicyDefinitions folder. For each language you installed, you'll find a related Agpm.adml in a language-specific subdirectory of the %SystemRoot%\Windows\PolicyDefinitions folder. Copy each language-specific Agpm.adml file to the appropriate subdirectory in the central store.

At an elevated, administrator command prompt, enter the following commands:

```
xcopy %SystemRoot%\PolicyDefinitions\agpm.admx
\\DC\Sysvol\DomainName\policies\PolicyDefinitions\
```

where *DC* is the host name of the target domain controller and *DomainName* is the fully qualified DNS name of the domain in which the domain controller is -located. In the following example, you copy the Agpm.admx file from your -computer to CorpServer56 in the Imaginedlands.com domain:

```
xcopy %SystemRoot%\PolicyDefinitions\agpm.admx
\\CorpServer56\Sysvol\Imaginedlands.com\policies\PolicyDefinitions\
```

Next at an elevated, administrator command prompt, enter the following commands:

```
xcopy %SystemRoot%\PolicyDefinitions\LanguageCulture\agpm.adml
\\DC\Sysvol\DomainName\policies\PolicyDefinitions\LanguageCulture\
```

where *DC* is the host name of the target domain controller, *DomainName* is the fully qualified DNS name of the domain in which the domain controller is located, and *LanguageCulture* identifies the language-specific folder, such as EN-US. In the following example, you copy the Agpm.adml file from your computer to
CorpServer56 in the Imaginedlands.com domain:

```
xcopy %SystemRoot%\PolicyDefinitions\en-us\agpm.adml
\\CorpServer56\Sysvol\Imaginedlands.com\policies
\PolicyDefinitions\en-us\
```

Configuring Group Policy to Support AGPM

Once you've ensured that the Agpm.admx template is available, you can configure Group Policy to support AGPM in one of two ways. You can:

- Use the AGPM: Specify Default AGPM Server (All Domains) policy to specify a default AGPM server for all domains. Once you configure a default AGPM server for all domains, administrators are unable to connect to any other AGPM server. You can override this policy for specific domains by enabling and then configuring the AGPM: Specify AGPM Servers policy.
- Disable the AGPM: Specify Default AGPM Server (All Domains) policy and then identify a specific AGPM server for each domain by enabling and then configuring the AGPM: Specify AGPM Servers policy. Once you identify a specific AGPM server for a domain through Group Policy, administrators are unable to connect to any other AGPM server in that domain.

You can configure Group Policy to support AGPM by following these steps:

1. On the computer on which you have installed the AGPM client, log on with a user account that is a member of the group that you selected as the Archive Owner. This group has the role of AGPM Administrator (Full Control).

2. Start the GPMC by clicking Group Policy Management on the Administrative Tools menu.

3. In the console tree, select and then right-click a GPO that is applied to all Group Policy administrators. On the shortcut menu, click Edit.

> **Note** If no single GPO is applied to all Group Policy administrators, you will need to repeat this procedure for applicable GPOs to ensure that Group Policy administrators can connect to your AGPM servers.

4. In the Group Policy Management Editor, expand User Configuration, Policies, Administrative Templates, and then select the Windows Components node.

5. Under Windows Components, select the AGPM node. In the details pane, double-click AGPM: Specify Default AGPM Server (All Domains).

6. In the AGPM: Specify Default AGPM Server (All Domains) Properties dialog box, shown in Figure A-12, do one of the following:

- If you want to configure a default AGPM server for all domains, select Enabled and then enter the fully qualified domain name, a colon, and the port number for the AGPM server, such as **corpserver28.imaginedlands.com:4600**. Port 4600 is the default port used by the AGPM Service. Click OK.

- If you want to specify AGPM servers on a per-domain basis, select Disabled and then click OK. You will then need to enable and configure the AGPM: Specify AGPM Servers policy in each domain.

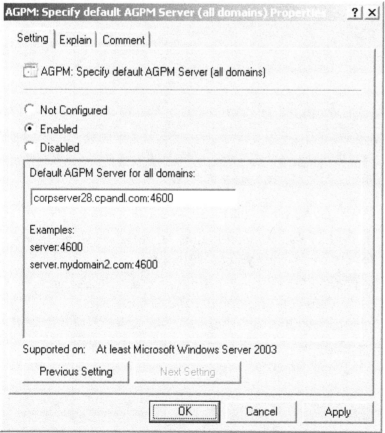

Figure A-12 Enable AGPM in Group Policy.

7. The AGPM: Specify AGPM Servers policy overrides the AGPM: Specify Default AGPM Server (All Domains) policy. If you want to identify AGPM servers on a per-domain basis, do the following:

   a. Double-click AGPM: Specify AGPM Servers.

   b. Select Enabled, and then click Show.

   c. In the Show Contents dialog box, click Add.

   d. In the Add Item dialog box, shown in Figure A-13, enter the domain for which you are identifying the AGPM server in the first text box, such as imaginedlands.com.

   e. In the second text box, enter the fully qualified domain name, a colon, and the port number for the AGPM server, such as corpserver28.imaginedlands.com:4600. Port 4600 is the default port used by the AGPM Service.

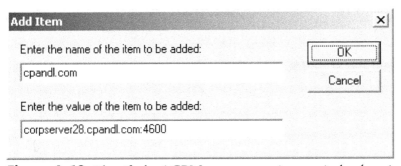

Figure A-13 Identify the AGPM server to use in a particular domain.

   f. Click OK to close the Add Item dialog box.

   g. Repeat steps c to f as necessary to identify AGPM servers for other domains. Click OK twice when you have finished.

8. Click OK. When Group Policy is next refreshed, the AGPM Server connection is configured as appropriate, and Group Policy administrators for which this GPO applies will be able to connect to the AGPM server (providing the AGPM client is installed on their management computers).

Installing Group Policy Templates and Add-ins for Microsoft Office

You can obtain Group Policy templates and add-ins for Microsoft Office at the Microsoft Download Center (*http://download.microsoft.com*). You can find and install these additions by following these steps:

1. Go to *http://download.microsoft.com* in Windows Internet Explorer. At the Download Center, click Home & Office under Download Categories. Search for "office customization tool."

2. After you perform a Home & Office search for "office customization tool," click the link for the most recent release.

3. Download and run the self-extracting executable for the version or versions of Office your organization uses.

4. When prompted, review the license terms. Select I Accept The License Terms check box, and then click Continue.

5. Select a destination folder for the folders and files in the download, and then review the folders and files you just extracted.

To use the Administrative templates in the GPMC on your management computer, copy the ADMX files to the %SystemRoot%\Windows\PolicyDefinitions folder, and copy the ADML files to the appropriate language-specific subfolder within the PolicyDefinitions folder. If you are using a central store and want to make the templates available throughout the domain, copy the ADMX and ADML files to the appropriate folders by following these steps:

1. Access a domain controller running Windows Server 2008 in the target domain by using an account that is a member of Domain Admins. Verify that a PolicyDefinitions folder has been created under %SystemRoot%\Sysvol*DomainName*\Policies, where *DomainName* is the name of the domain in which the domain controller is located and for which you are checking that a central store has been established.

2. Copy the ADMX and ADML files from the extraction location on your computer to the appropriate SYSVOL folders on the domain controller.

For example, if you extracted the download to your Documents folder in your user profile, you could copy all the required policy files from your computer to the target domain controller in a single step. Simply run the following commands at an elevated, administrator command prompt:

```
xcopy /s %UserProfile%\ADMX
\\DC\Sysvol\DomainName\policies\PolicyDefinitions\
```

where *DC* is the host name of the target domain controller and *DomainName* is the fully qualified DNS name of the domain in which the domain controller is located. In the following example, you copy the ADMX and ADML files from your computer to CorpServer43 in the Imaginedlands.com domain:

```
xcopy /s %UserProfile%\ADMX
\\CorpServer43\Sysvol\imaginedlands.com\policies\PolicyDefinitions\
```

> **Note**   See "SYSVOL Changes" in Chapter 2 for more information on working with a central store.

About the Author

William R. Stanek (http://www.williamstanek.com/) has more than 20 years of hands-on experience with advanced programming and development. He is a leading technology expert, an award-winning author, and a pretty-darn-good instructional trainer. Over the years, his practical advice has helped millions of programmers, developers, and network engineers all over the world. His current and books include *Windows 8.1 Administration Pocket Consultant*, *Windows Server 2012 R2 Pocket Consultant* and *Windows Server 2012 R2 Inside Out*.

William has been involved in the commercial Internet community since 1991. His core business and technology experience comes from more than 11 years of military service. He has substantial experience in developing server technology, encryption, and Internet solutions. He has written many technical white papers and training courses on a wide variety of topics. He frequently serves as a subject matter expert and consultant.

William has an MS with distinction in information systems and a BS in computer science, magna cum laude. He is proud to have served in the Persian Gulf War as a combat crewmember on an electronic warfare aircraft. He flew on numerous combat missions into Iraq and was awarded nine medals for his wartime service, including one of the United States of America's highest flying honors, the Air Force Distinguished Flying Cross. Currently, he resides in the Pacific Northwest with his wife and children.

William recently rediscovered his love of the great outdoors. When he's not writing, he can be found hiking, biking, backpacking, traveling, or trekking in search of adventure with his family!

Find William on Twitter at www.twitter.com/WilliamStanek and on Facebook at www.facebook.com/William.Stanek.Author.

www.ingramcontent.com/pod-product-compliance
Lightning Source LLC
LaVergne TN
LVHW081511050326
832903LV00025B/1447